Service Orchestration as Organization

Service Orchestration as Organization

Building Multi-Tenant Service Applications in the Cloud

Malinda Kapuruge
Jun Han
Alan Colman

ELSEVIER

AMSTERDAM • BOSTON • HEIDELBERG • LONDON
NEW YORK • OXFORD • PARIS • SAN DIEGO
SAN FRANCISCO • SINGAPORE • SYDNEY • TOKYO

Morgan Kaufmann is an imprint of Elsevier

Morgan Kaufmann is an imprint of Elsevier
225 Wyman Street, Waltham, MA 02451, USA

Library of Congress Cataloging-in-Publication Data
A catalogue record for this book is available from the Library of Congress

British Library Cataloguing-in-Publication Data
A catalogue record for this book is available from the British Library

ISBN: 978-0-12-800938-3

For information on all MK publications
visit our website at www.mkp.com

This book has been manufactured using Print On Demand technology. Each copy is produced to order
and is limited to black ink. The online version of this book will show color figures where appropriate.

Working together
to grow libraries in
developing countries

www.elsevier.com • www.bookaid.org

Contents

The flexibility for change is achieved on the basis of the adaptability and loose coupling among the organisational entities and the event-driven nature of process models. The structure and processes (behaviour) of the organisation can be changed during system runtime. The controllability of changes is achieved by explicitly capturing and checking the achievement and maintenance of the goals (requirements and constraints) of the aggregator and collaborating service providers. Secondly, Serendip has a novel process enactment runtime infrastructure (engine) and a supporting framework. The runtime engine and supporting framework manage the orchestration of services in a flexible manner in a distributed environment, addressing such issues as multi-process execution on shared resources, management of control and message flows, and coordination of third-party services. Thirdly, Serendip's adaptation management mechanism has been designed by clearly separating the functional and management concerns of an adaptive service orchestration. It supports runtime changes to process definitions and process instances, enabling evolutionary and *ad hoc* business change requirements. The complete Serendip framework has been implemented by extending the Apache Axis2 Web services engine.

The Serendip meta-model, language and framework have been evaluated against the common change patterns and change support features for business processes. An example case study has been carried out to demonstrate the applicability of this research in highly dynamic service orchestration environments. Furthermore, a performance evaluation test has been conducted to analyse the performance penalty of the runtime adaptation support in this work as compared to Apache ODE (a popular WS-BPEL−based process orchestration engine).

Overall, this book presents an approach to orchestrating services in a flexible but controlled manner. It facilitates changes to business processes on-the-fly while considering the business goals and constraints of all stakeholders.

About the Authors

Malinda Kapuruge received his PhD degree in Computer Science and Software Engineering from Swinburne University of Technology (Melbourne, Australia) in 2012. Currently working as an Adjunct Research Fellow in Software Engineering at Swinburne University of Technology, he is investigating how business process management practices could be used to build multi-tenanted, adaptable service-based software systems. His research interest includes business process management, service-oriented architecture, Cloud computing and adaptive software systems.

Jun Han received his PhD degree in Computer Science from the University of Queensland (Brisbane, Australia) in 1992. Since 2003, he has been Professor of Software Engineering at Swinburne University of Technology (Melbourne, Australia). His primary research focus has been the architecture and qualities of software systems. His current research interests include dynamic software architectures, context-aware software systems, Cloud and service-oriented software systems, software architecture design, and software performance and security. He has published over 200 peer-reviewed articles in international journals and conferences.

Alan Colman received his PhD degree in Computer Science and Software Engineering from Swinburne University of Technology (Melbourne, Australia) in 2006. Since 2006, he has been a researcher and senior lecturer of software engineering at Swinburne University of Technology. His primary research focus has been adaptive service-oriented software systems, context-aware software systems, software and Cloud performance prediction and control. He has published over 70 peer-reviewed articles in international journals and conferences.

Part One

a set of principles and architectural methodologies to integrate loosely coupled, distributed and autonomous software services.

The *services* in SOA can be described as well-defined, self-contained and autonomous computing modules that provide standard business functionality and are independent of the state or context of other services [2]. A business organisation may integrate a group of such services together to provide a combined business offering. The entity that aggregates these services is known as the *service aggregator*. Such an aggregation of services is known as a *service composition*. In a service ecosystem, such a composition also can be used as a service for further composition. In service composition, it is required to specify the logical coordination in which these services are invoked. The logical coordination of service invocations is known as a *service orchestration*, which is defined by the service aggregator.

Service orchestration differs from *service choreography* [24]. Service orchestration provides a participant's or a service's point of view of how it interacts with other services in collaboration, and a service orchestration is executable; in contrast, service choreography provides a global view among a set of participants or services and is not executable. A choreographic description is usually considered as a global contract or agreement that all participants commit [25–27]. Such a choreographic description is required to be mapped to a service orchestration description for execution purposes [28].

At the beginning, general-purpose programming languages such as Java and C++ were used for orchestrating services. However, such general-purpose programming languages lack the ease of redesign and the comprehensibility for business users. Such properties are essential to understand, analyse and iteratively refine the service orchestration. Consequently, a need developed for more specific service orchestration languages.

To fill this gap, workflow modelling and enactment concepts were used [29–31]. One of the influential factors to use workflows for service orchestration is the fact that workflows are being extensively used in describing assembly lines and office procedures [31]. For example, each step of processing in an assembly line is described as an activity of a workflow. Correspondingly, in a service orchestration, each service call is described as an activity of a flow. Following this trend of utilising workflows, a number of process language standards have been proposed.

One of the key objectives of these process languages is to achieve machine readability. Basically, the languages are to be understood by machines to automate the service calls or service invocations. Furthermore, the development of XML-related technologies also facilitated this trend [32]. XML has been widely used for structuring data and providing information due to its inherent advantages such as openness, extensibility and portability. Subsequently, XML became the norm for describing processes in emerging standards [33]. A typical early example is BPML [34], which is an initiative of BPMI. Another example is XPDL [35], which is based on XML serialisation, replacing its predecessor WSFL [36].

As of now, the de facto standard for automated enactment of service orchestrations is WS-BPEL [37], formally known as BPEL4WS [22]. WS-BPEL is built on top of WSDL [38], which is the standard for describing service signatures [22, 39].

However, WSDL cannot be used to describe the service interaction model and WS-BPEL filled this gap.

1.2 Service orchestration and its adaptation

In order to align service orchestration to the business needs of an organisation, the service orchestration needs to be continuously managed. Service orchestration management can be seen as a progressive extension of traditional workflow management [7, 31, 40]. The concepts of workflow management fit with service orchestration management in most cases. However, service orchestration needs to tackle a few additional requirements as it is grounded on service-based systems in a distributed and autonomous environment. This includes managing the service endpoints, service—service interactions, message transformations and exceptional situations such as network failures. The service orchestration logic needs to be managed with respect to the autonomy of the services that are composed. In a nutshell, the owner has less control compared to traditional in-house workflow management systems, where the owner can manage the workflow with relatively greater discretion and control.

New business models have emerged, changing the way the service orchestration is used in the enterprises. Consequently, there is a demand for an increased flexibility as well as improvements in the ways service orchestration systems are designed, enacted and managed. The following two sections introduce these new business models and the importance of runtime adaptability of a service orchestration.

1.2.1 Novel requirements for service orchestration

In classical *service orchestration*, a number of services are invoked in an orderly fashion to get some work done. This classical model has evolved. New business models to create online market places have emerged in the enterprise. Among them, service brokering and software-as-a-service (SaaS) can be seen as influential models for defining online market places [2, 5, 41−45]. Both service brokering and SaaS heavily depend on *service orchestration* as the underlying realisation technique, because service orchestration combines many advantages offered by both BPM and SOA. Consequently, service orchestration methodologies and best practices need to be *modernised* to support the inherent properties of these influential developments. Service brokers and SaaS vendors can be seen as service aggregators, but with varied business models.

Service brokers play a significant role in the Web services ecosystem [5]. Service brokers position themselves between the traditional *service consumers* and *service providers* and generate value by bringing the service providers closer to service consumers. Service brokers may repurpose the provided services and may add additional functionalities such as payment and monitoring mechanisms to existing service offerings. A fundamental requirement for service brokers is to aggregate a number of services to achieve a value addition. Therefore, improved service orchestration capabilities are paramount to ensure the efficient and more agile coordination of these services.

SaaS is gaining popularity as a way of on-demand delivery of software over the Internet [44]. SaaS has become popular due to advantages such as *quick return on investment* and *economies of scale* [46]. SaaS vendors can benefit from the advantages provided by service orchestration. SaaS and SOA complement each other — SaaS is a software delivery model, whereas SOA is a software construction model [45]. In order to build SaaS applications using SOA and deliver service offerings using service orchestration techniques, it is necessary to provide the support for *agility* and the support for *multi-tenancy* [42, 47] in service orchestration management systems.

In a nutshell, these new developments call for improvements in the way we design, enact and manage the service orchestration systems. This includes improvements to the existing service orchestration practices, service composition techniques, available middleware and tool support [33]. One of the fundamental requirements supporting continuous improvement is *adaptability* [48–50]. The *level* of adaptability as well as the *manner* in which the adaptability is provided need improvement due to the emergence of the service brokering and SaaS business models.

1.2.2   Runtime adaptability in service orchestration

A service orchestration system that is optimally designed for a current given business environment might not be optimal enough in the future. Firstly, the *internal factors* such as business goal changes, strategy and technology changes, continuous performance optimisations and exception handling can call for changes to the defined service orchestration. Secondly, the *external factors* such as service/network failures, new government/business regulations, unsatisfactory quality of service delivered by partner services and change in service consumer requirements can also stimulate changes in the defined service orchestration.

Irrespective of whether they are internally or externally induced, these changes may occur in an *unpredictable* manner [51]. The practices such as specifying all the execution paths or having a set of predefined adaptations for the service orchestration might not be possible. Such challenges are evident in service orchestrations used in service brokering and SaaS applications, where the consumer/tenant demands as well as the service offerings can be subject to frequent changes. Therefore, the service orchestration needs to be *continuously adapted at runtime* to ensure the '*continuing fit*' between the IT support and the real-world business process requirements.

According to Taylor et al., '*Runtime software adaptability is the ability to change an application's behaviour during runtime*' [50]. Business organisations require not only the adaptability but also the ability to continuously function while the adaptations are taking place [49]. That means, the system behaviour needs to be changed but without requiring a system stoppage and restart. A service composition is designed and deployed to achieve a business requirement. Accordingly, a single stop/start of the service orchestration engine can have significant effects on the business as well as on its customers [52, 53]. The service-level agreements [54] may get violated and the reputation of the business can be degraded. Therefore, it is necessary that the changes are carried out on the service orchestration while the service composition is functioning with minimal or no impact on its operations. In order to achieve this, the service orchestration language as well as the enactment middleware both need to be *flexible* to accommodate runtime changes.

Two main categories of changes in business processes are defined by van der Aalst et al., known as *ad hoc* and *evolutionary* [55, 56]. *Ad hoc changes* are carried out on a particular business case or a process instance [57, 58] at runtime. Usually, this type of change is carried out in order to handle exceptions or to optimise a particular process instance. Ad hoc changes do not affect the system as a whole, but only a single process instance. In contrast, the *evolutionary changes* are carried out on the process definition affecting the system as a whole. Allowing both these categories of change during runtime is important for a business organisation.

Two similar categories are also highlighted by Heinl et al. [59] as *type adaptation* and *instance adaptation*. Heinl et al. further differentiate between the terms *version* and *variant* of a process definition: a new version replaces the old version, where multiple variants can coexist. Mapping this to the business domain, business organi-sations might need to reengineer/replace existing process definitions with newer versions. Alternatively, a new variant can be created so that both the original and variant process definitions can coexist. More recent classifications while following these two categories have further extended them to broaden our understanding of business process flexibility [51, 60−64].

Many approaches were proposed to achieve increased flexibility in business processes. Some approaches attempted to improve the flexibility of existing standards [57, 65−68], while others have attempted to provide alternative paradigms [61, 69−73]. These approaches have contributed to immensely improving the flexibility of business process support by borrowing and adopting the techniques from other fields of software engineering such as *aspect-orientation* [74] and *generative-programming* [75].

Nevertheless, the increased flexibility of the system can also lead to undesirable situations [76]. In service orchestrations, safeguarding the business partnerships among the collaborating services is important. There can be numerous change requests arising during the runtime within the aggregator organisation itself (*internal*) or from the collaborating service providers and consumers (*external*). Therefore, it is necessary that the changes are carried out in a systematic and tractable manner without violating the business goals of the aggregator organisation and the collaborators [77].

The amount of flexibility required in a business process is a function of both *business domain* and *time*. The amount of flexibility varies from one business domain to another. For example, a service orchestration used in handling emergency situations might require more flexibility to adapt to unpredictable situations compared to service orchestration used in traditional billing systems, where set stan-dards and predictable protocols are followed. In addition, the same business domain may expect varying levels of flexibility as time goes on, e.g. the constraints that strictly enforce a specific ordering of business activities may become invalid due to changes in business policies and procedures.

For simplicity, if we imagine a spectrum of flexibility, as shown in Figure 1.1, with two extremes, from *nothing is changeable* (left) to *everything is changeable*

Due to the potentially numerous runtime modifications, the service composition can become complex and consequently difficult to maintain [79]. Under such circumstances, the adaptations in service orchestration are naturally discouraged as it leads to increased complexity and possible violations of system integrity. As such, the ability to achieve adaptation to process definitions or enacted process instances can be limited. Therefore, in designing a service orchestration language, it is paramount to support a proper separation of concerns, which ultimately allows the application of changes without increasing the complexity of the overall system. This includes the separation of control flow and data flow, the separation of functional structure from the management structure and the separation of internal and external data exchange of a service composite. Furthermore, the modularity in service orchestration logic is also important to ensure that the adaptations do not lead to increased complexity.

As mentioned earlier, while a service orchestration language should provide better flexibility, it also needs to have the necessary measures to *control* the flexibility to protect the business goals [76]. Complete reliance on manual verification techniques such as peer reviewing (upon a proposed modification) can be tedious and inefficient [80]. They may potentially leave many errors in the service orchestration due to human error. Such errors can be harmful in two different ways. Firstly, a wrongful modification itself can lead to loss of businesses, causing *immediate damage* to the organisation. Secondly, the confidence level of applying modifications to service orchestrations can decline, causing *implicit and gradual damage*. This leads to a frequent bypass of business process support systems, making the business process support more a liability than an asset [56]. On the one hand, it is necessary to have flexibility to deal with and survive upon unexpected change requirements. On the other hand, unrestrained flexibility can be counterproductive, as it leads to wrongful modifications that threaten the integrity of the composition. In this sense, the adaptability of a service orchestration should neither be so rigid to prevent possible changes nor be uncontrollably changeable, compromising the integrity of the composition.

It should be noted that the amount of flexibility required in service orchestration is not determined by the service aggregator alone. The aggregator has to operate in a service ecosystem as shown in Figure 1.3. The other stakeholders (collaborators) such as service consumers and service providers play a major role. The service consumers and the service providers are also businesses that have their own goals to achieve. Hindering those goals can be counterproductive in the long run. While still providing the required flexibility for the service aggregator to optimise the service offerings and maximise the profit, the service orchestration mechanism needs to provide methodologies and techniques to correctly reflect such goals and constraints in the service orchestration. The way in which such goals and constraints are specified in service orchestration should not unnecessarily restrict the possible modifications. For example, a *global* or *system-wide* specification of *all* the constraints of *all* the service providers and consumers can be overly restrictive. Such unnecessary restriction due to the global specification of constraints will hinder the aggregator from capturing a market opportunity. Instead, better modularity needs to be provided to define the scope of the constraint in a service orchestration.

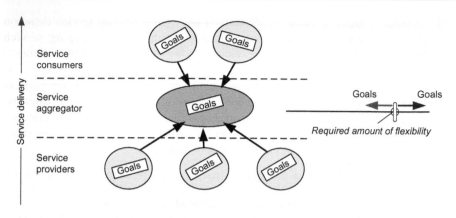

Figure 1.3 Service ecosystem and the amount of flexibility.

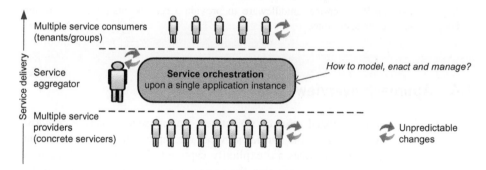

Figure 1.4 The research goal.

Therefore, it is necessary to revisit the methodologies to model, enact and manage service orchestrations. Business organisations that wish to combine and repurpose existing services require service orchestration methodologies that provide an increased but well-controlled flexibility. These service orchestration methodologies should satisfy the aforementioned novel requirements of emerging service delivery models such as SaaS and service brokering.

This research is motivated towards creating a novel service orchestration approach to comprehensively define, enact and manage adaptive service orchestrations. As shown in Figure 1.4, the service orchestration approach should be capable of serving multiple service consumers using the same application instance and service infrastructure as demanded by novel usages of service orchestrations. The same service infrastructure should be reproposed to suit the demands of service consumers along multiple service delivery channels to maximise reuse and thereby profit. The unpredictability of change requirements of both service consumers and underlying service providers needs to be handled by swiftly adapting to those changes, but in a well-controlled manner to ensure uninterrupted and well-optimised service delivery. New and varied consumer requirements need to be met. New emerging service providers need to be bound to offer services in a wider spectrum. New collaborations need to be established and existing collaborations need to be optimised.

The beneficial outcome of this research is a service orchestration approach to quickly define and deploy adaptive service orchestrations. The approach allows the service aggregator to model, enact and manage a service orchestration in an environment where unpredictability is high. In order to achieve this outcome, this research aims to achieve the following technical research objectives.

1. Provide a meta-model and a language to realise adaptable orchestrations in service compositions.
2. Design a process enactment engine to execute adaptable business processes.
3. Successfully use the enactment engine in a service-oriented environment to realise adaptive service orchestrations.
4. Design an adaptation management system to manage both ad hoc and evolutionary adaptations on service orchestrations at runtime.
5. Improve existing Web services middleware to provide a runtime platform for realising adaptive service orchestrations.

1.4   Approach overview

To address the aforementioned research objectives, we envisage *a service composition as an organisation*, where the partner services are represented and the relationships between the partner services are explicitly captured. These relationships form the basis of the *organisation* representing the service composition and providing the required abstraction and stability for defining business processes. Then, the coordination logic of the organisation (i.e. *organisational behaviour*) is defined in a flexible and reusable manner. Multiple business processes can be defined and changed to fulfil the varied and changing business requirements of many service consumers.

We call this new approach *Serendip*. The fundamental difference between the traditional approaches for service orchestration and the approach used in Serendip are shown in Figure 1.5. In traditional service orchestration approaches, a process layer is usually ground on top of a services layer. As such, services are wired according to a business process. In contrast, rather than grounding the processes directly in concrete services, the processes are grounded upon an adaptive organisational structure. Consequently, Serendip introduces a new layer (i.e. the organisation) between the process and service layers.

The organisation is made up of different organisational roles and relationships between them. Concrete services work for the organisation (i.e. are bound to the composition) by playing roles in it. The mutual obligations, interactions and constraints among the collaborators (service providers and consumers) are explicitly captured via the service relationships among these roles in the organisation. Multiple processes can be defined for such a service organisation to achieve varied business goals.

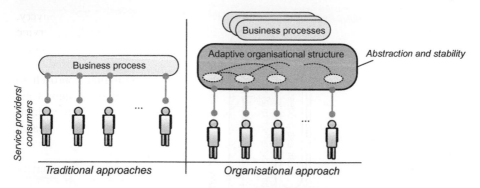

Figure 1.5 Traditional approaches vs. Serendip.

However, they share and are grounded upon the same organisational structure. The processes are defined in terms of the interactions in the organisation as captured in its service relationships between the partners. The service relationships maintain the state and interpret the runtime interactions according to its state to determine the next action among many possibilities as defined by the processes. The organisation or its service relationships provide the basis for anchoring the business processes, providing a stable basis for realising changes in the business processes and the interactions between the collaborators.

Ownership of the concrete services can be external or internal to the business organisation. The organisational structure consists of the defined service relationships between the collaborators and provides a flexible but managed platform for defining and adapting business processes at runtime. Each service relationship captures the collaboration aspects between two roles. The concrete services honour these collaboration aspects while working for the organisation by performing obligatory tasks. Many organisational behaviours are defined to specify valid ordering of task executions and to specify the constraints that should not be violated. These organisational behaviours are subjected to change according to the business requirements, however, without violating the defined constraints.

The way in which the stability for business processes has been provided in Serendip is different from the existing imperative approaches. The approaches such as WS-BPEL provide stability through the rigidity embodied in the prescriptive nature of the language. As such, the task ordering is strictly structured. However, if the stability for processes is provided by inherent rigidity, it comes with the disadvantage of lacking business agility upon due changes. In contrast, Serendip provides the stability for processes via an adaptable organisation. The amount of flexibility that can be leveraged is determined by the business domain and time. As such, a business may start with less flexibility, following a more cautious approach, and can gradually become more flexible in exploiting the available market opportunities. That is, the amount of flexibility exhibited in the IT composition modelled as an organisation truly reflects the amount of flexibility required by the business domain at a given time (Figure 1.6).

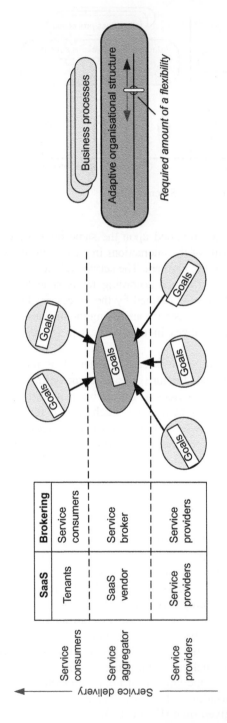

Figure 1.6 Adaptive organisational structure providing required amount of flexibility.

Motivational Scenario

2

In this chapter, we present a motivational scenario based on a business that provides roadside assistance to motorists who require assistance when their cars break down. The objective of the discussion is twofold. The first objective is to present a motivational scenario, which can be used throughout the book to explain the Serendip concepts by providing suitable examples. The second objective is to use the business example later as a *case study* to show how Serendip is applied on a concrete business scenario.

Firstly, in Section 2.1, we introduce the business model of the RoSAS[1] business organisation that provides roadside assistance as a service by integrating a number of other related services such as garages and tow trucks. Secondly, we analyse the requirement of performing controlled changes to the defined service orchestration due to unforeseen business change requirements in the given scenario. This discussion is included in Section 2.2. Thirdly, in Section 2.3, we introduce the benefits of designing a service orchestration to support *single-instance multi-tenancy* (SIMT). Finally, in Section 2.4, we list a number of requirements that should be satisfied by a service orchestration approach, summarising the overall discussion.

2.1 RoSAS business model

RoSAS is a business organisation that provides roadside assistance services to motorists. To provide roadside assistance, RoSAS expects to integrate a number of service providers that are already available and repurpose their business offerings as part of the roadside assistance business. These include garage/auto-repair services to repair the cars, tow trucks for towing damaged cars and taxi services to provide alternative transportations. Apart from these external services, RoSAS requires hiring case officers to handle the assistance requests. All these are different functional requirements that should be satisfied in order to carry out a roadside assistance business.

Consequently, as the aggregator RoSAS envisions multiple functional positions in its business model that needs to be filled. These positions will be filled by both the service consumers and providers. For example, a motorist is a service consumer whilst a garage is a provider. In common, let us call these *collaborators*, because what drives the RoSAS business is the collaboration among these service providers and consumers. These collaborators can be either internal or external to the RoSAS

[1]RoSAS = RoadSide Assistance Service.

process design can significantly increase due to the need to accommodate many such uncommon isolated requirements. However, being flexible in catering such isolated uncommon requirements would give RoSAS an advantage over its competitors in attracting and retaining customers.

On the other hand, a change such as payment protocol update due to switching from cash-based payments to more sophisticated credit-based payments needs to be applied to the whole service orchestration. Such changes are called *evolutionary* changes [55, 56]. Evolutionary changes will ensure the continuing fit between the IT service orchestration and the real-world business processes. Upon such an evolutionary change, all the future process instances behave according to the changed or new definition. Consequently, the level of persistency is higher in evolutionary changes compared with the process instance—specific changes mentioned. An incorrect evolutionary change can cause devastating damages to the business.

Being the service aggregator, supporting both process instance—specific and evolutionary changes to business processes are very important for RoSAS. Nevertheless, both the process instance—specific and evolutionary changes need to respect the business goals of the composition (RoSAS) as well as those of its bound collaborators, i.e. both service providers and consumers. RoSAS has to facilitate the demands of its service consumers but without violating the goals of service providers. For example, a delayed towing may be accommodated for a specific process instance, but only if such a change does not lead to any violations to the underlying operations such as towing and repairing. However, the changes in underlying service provisioning should not violate the goals of service consumers either. For example, the changes in underlying payment protocols should not compromise achieving the business objectives of consumers due to the added overhead. In short, the same service orchestration should be modified as needed but without compromising the business goals of consumers, service providers and the aggregator. Therefore, it is important that the service orchestration mechanism provides an appropriate mechanism to represent and safeguard such business constraints, but without unnecessarily restricting the possible changes.

Apart from changes to business processes, there can be changes to the partner services as well. RoSAS as a service aggregator may start and terminate the agreements with certain service providers depending on factors such as performance and availability. For example, if a particular garage chain constantly underperforms and delays repairs, RoSAS may opt to find another suitable garage chain. Likewise, if a tow truck service does not cover some geographical regions, then RoSAS needs to find alternative tow truck services to handle accidents in those regions.

RoSAS is also hopeful to expand its business offerings. Depending on customer demands, for example, more services such as paramedic and accommodation services may be integrated as part of the roadside assistance process. Such aggregation of a wide variety of services gives RoSAS the competitive edge over its competitors. The design of the service orchestration should allow such future extensibility without a complete reengineering of the service orchestration.

2.3 Support for SIMT

With the emergence of Cloud computing and maturity of SOA, the *software-as-a-service* (SaaS) delivery model has gained popularity due to advantages such as economies of scale, lower IT costs and reduced time to market [20, 45]. In order to exploit the benefits of the SaaS delivery model, RoSAS expects to provide roadside assistance as a service. The target business sector in this case is *small and medium businesses (SMB)*, whose core business is not roadside assistance but can leverage roadside assistance. For example, SMBs, like car sellers, travel agents and insurance companies, may want to attract customers by providing roadside assistance to complement their core business offerings to their customers, i.e. car buyers, travellers and policy holders. In this sense, RoSAS is also acting as a *SaaS vendor* by providing its software system as a service on a subscription basis. SMBs become *SaaS tenants* who use the RoSAS software service [45, 87]. In order to fulfil this business need, RoSAS needs to model the service composition and the service orchestration to take advantage of the SaaS paradigm.

Multi-tenancy [88, 89] is one of the most important characteristics in the SaaS paradigm. Multi-tenancy of SaaS applications has been provided with different maturity levels [90, 91]. In higher-maturity models, multi-tenancy is provided by a single shared application instance, which is utilised by all its tenants [89]. This is usually known as single-instance multi-tenancy (SIMT). In lower-maturity models, multi-tenancy is achieved by using techniques such as allocating a dedicated application instance for each and every tenant. However, such solutions fail to exploit the benefits associated with SIMT, such as economies of scale.

In SIMT each tenant interacts with the system as if it is the sole user [92]. Here, the term *application instance* should not be confused with *process instance*. These are two separate concepts. A single application instance may host multiple process instances. During the lifetime of an application instance, many process instances may be enacted and terminated. A tenant can request modifications to the SaaS service to suit their changed business objectives. However, these modifications are applied on a single shared application instance [90]. Subsequently, modifications could be available to other tenants who use the same application instance. In some cases, this might be a necessity, e.g. applying a patch or upgrade. However, in other cases, modifying a common application instance can challenge the integrity of the application, compromising the objectives of RoSAS and other tenants.

One naïve solution to achieve isolation of process modifications is to allocate a *separate process definition* for each and every tenant, i.e. at a lower level of the maturity model for SaaS [90]. However, it should be noted that tenants of a SaaS application have *common business interests*. Hence, there can be significant *overlapping* between those business processes. Having separate process definitions obviously leads to code duplication. For example, how the towing should be done will be duplicated among several process definitions. Such duplication deprives the SaaS vendor (i.e. RoSAS) from exploiting the benefits of SIMT. When required, the SaaS vendor has to apply modifications repeatedly to these process definitions, which is not efficient or cost-effective and could be error-prone. Therefore, the service orchestration approach should be able to capture the commonalities among processes.

Although capturing commonalities is essential and beneficial to any SaaS vendor, it is allied with two accompanying challenges. *Firstly*, while the tenants have common business requirements, these requirements may vary in practice. RoSAS cannot assume a common code or script can continue to serve all the tenants in the same manner. These variations can be major variations or minor variations. For example, a car seller may want to provide an alternative transport (taxi) for its motorists, which might not be required by an insurance company who needs only towing and repairing. This is a major variation. Even though the *towing* is common to all customers, in practice some variations may exist in how the towing should be done. For example, a tenant might request a change to the preconditions for the towing in his process definition. This is a minor variation. Therefore, the service orchestration approach should be able to allow such major and minor variations while capturing the commonalities.

Secondly, capturing commonalities might lead to invalid boundary crossings as a single service instance is shared. To elaborate, suppose that tenant car seller requests a modification, e.g. adds a new task to handle the credit check prior to a credit-based payment. However, this modified business process might violate a business requirement of another tenant, such as the insurance company, because that will expand the overall time of completion. Moreover, such changes may even lead to violations of the business models of some of its service providers such as tow trucks and garages, e.g. by further delaying the payment.

Overall, SIMT brings many benefits to RoSAS as it allows exploiting the advantages such as economies of scale. Other SMBs that need to provide roadside assistance to their customers benefit due to advantages such as quick return on investment. Most work on meeting similar challenges has occurred in providing virtual and individualised data service to tenants. However, defining processes is also a key aspect of SOA, and is one that needs addressing if service orchestrations are to be deployed as true multi-tenanted SaaS applications.

2.4   Requirements of service orchestration

The above discussions reveal that there are a number of *business-level* desires to be satisfied by a service orchestration approach. To support these business-level requirements, the service orchestration as the IT solution should address key *IT-level* requirements.

Req1. Flexible processes: As business changes, the business processes and their support need to change accordingly, including changes to individual process instances or to a process definition (i.e. all its instances). The changes may be due to the needs of the collaborators, the aggregator or the customers. These changes can include exception handling, process improvement or capturing strategic business opportunities.

Req2. Capturing commonalities: A common application instance needs to be shared and repurposed as much as possible in order to achieve the benefits of economies of scale. The common requirements need to be captured in the service orchestration. The approach should provide necessary modularisation support to facilitate this requirement.

Req3. Allowing variations: Customer requirements are similar but not the same. The ways to achieve these business requirements can show major as well as minor variations. While capturing the commonalities, it is essential to allow variations as required. Variations should be allowed in a manner that it does not lead to unnecessary redundancy.

Req4. Controlled changes: Amidst numerous changes to business processes, the business goals of collaborators, the business goals of the aggregator and the business goals of the clients, as represented by business processes, need to be safeguarded. This is not trivial when a shared application instance is used to define multiple process definitions.

Req5. Predictable change impacts: The impacts of changes to business processes and to collaborator coordination need to be easily identified, so that remedial actions or subsequent changes can be made if the change is to be fully and consistently realised. Such impacts could flow from one process to another, from a collaborator to a whole process, or from a process to its collaborators.

Req6. Managing complexity: A service orchestration is subject to numerous runtime modifications. A single instance of a service composition is customised or repurposed in a shared manner. Such requirements can easily lead to a complex service orchestration system. If necessary arrangements are not made to address the increased complexity of service orchestration system, then it eventually may become unusable. Therefore, the service orchestration mechanism should provide a well-modularised architecture to manage the complexity.

2.5 Summary

In this chapter, we have presented a business organisation that requires better IT support to define, enact and manage its business processes. Firstly, we introduced a business model for an organisation (RoSAS) that integrates a number of third-party partner services to provide roadside assistance to motorists. The nature of such a collaborative business environment was explained by giving suitable examples.

Secondly, we explained the requirement of carrying out controlled changes in such a collaborative business environment. These changes might need to be carried out to handle a specific customer case or the system as a whole. Nevertheless, the changes need to be carried out by safeguarding the business goals of the service aggregator, service consumers as well as the service providers.

Thirdly, we introduced the importance of supporting single-instance multi-tenancy (SIMT) in service orchestration. Apart from being a mere service aggregator, RoSAS can attract many customers with the support of SIMT. Roadside assistance can be leveraged as a service by other business organisations whose core competency is not roadside assistance.

Finally, we summarised the overall discussion into a set of key requirements that a service orchestration approach should support.

Literature Review

3

This chapter presents a review of existing literature to analyse the past attempts that improved the adaptability in service orchestration. As a pretext to the discussion, Section 3.1 provides an overview of BPM (business process management). Section 3.2 then describes how BPM and SOA (service-oriented architecture) complement each other in the enterprise architecture to provide a combined solution to orchestrate distributed applications or services. Section 3.3 discusses the current understanding of the *adaptability in BPM*.

On the basis of these analysis and discussions, Section 3.4 examines the different techniques proposed in the literature to improve the adaptability in service orchestration. Each technique will be clarified with a number of example approaches. These approaches are selected based on the significance and practicality. The selection is not limited to approaches explicitly proposed for service orchestration *per se*. In some cases we go beyond the scope of service orchestration to include approaches proposed in business process modelling in general. This is done with the intention of identifying and analysing the underpinning techniques that could be used to improve the adaptability in service orchestration.

There are two main aims of this discussion. The first aim is to provide the reader with a broader understanding of how different techniques have attempted to improve the adaptability of business processes, laying a firm basis for upcoming discussions in this book. The second aim is to identify the inherent advantages and limitations of the different techniques, providing input to the work of this book.

Finally, a summary and the observed outcome of the reviewed approaches were presented in Section 3.5 based on the criteria presented in Chapter 2. The summary of review is presented in Section 3.5.1. A number of observations and lessons learnt from the existing literature have been presented in Section 3.5.2. Grounded upon the observations and lessons learnt, Section 3.6 discusses the remaining challenges in improving the adaptability in service orchestration to provide flexible support for business processes.

3.1 BPM — an overview

Prior to the era of information technology, organisations used manual and paper-based business processes to coordinate the organisational activities. Usually a file (or an artefact) is passed from one person to another within the organisation, each performing a certain task. However, this method has been unproductive, as the file among discrete *activities* [110, 111]. Constraint-based approaches are used to define the goal-driven business processes where it is easier to specify '*what*' needs to be done to achieve the goal rather than '*how*.' A path of execution or a procedure is just a *single solution* (among many) that satisfies the set of specified constraints.

Artefact-based: Artefact-based approaches define processes based on the life cycle of a set of *business artefacts* and how/when those are invoked [112]. Here, a business artefact can be a document, product or data record [113]. Artefact-based approaches show a close relationship with the activity-based approaches as the artefacts are modified as a result of performing activities. However, artefact-based approaches do not use activity as the principal concept. Instead, the principal driver for progression of a process instance is how the status of the artefact is changed. Depending on how and when the status of the artefact changes, the next activities are chosen and the process progresses [61]. Case-driven process modelling or case handling [70, 114] can also be seen as an evolution of the artefact-based approach [114], where a '*case*' can be seen as a business artefact and the process progression is determined by the completion of a case. Artefact-based process modelling has been used heavily to model product lines, inventory management and case-handling systems [70, 115].

Time-based: Time-based process modelling approaches are usually used for process scheduling and estimation purposes. In time-based approaches, the activities are represented along a time-axis by using the '*time*' as the principal concept. The start and end times are marked by explicitly representing the time dimension. Two of the early examples of this are Gantt-charts [116] and PERT charts [117, 118], which are used for decades for project management and planning purposes.

Role-based: The role-based approaches use a role as the principal concept. Initially, the roles are defined. Then, the relationship among the roles is represented via objects or via interaction specifications [119]. Role-based approaches add much value to business process modelling in collaborative environments, where each participant has a role to play [120]. Role-interaction networks (RIN) [40], role-activity diagrams (RAD) [121] and OOram [122] can be shown as such popular role-based approaches. Role-based process modelling has been used to model collaborative or interorganisational business processes.

A summary of the different categories of process modelling approaches along with popular examples from the literature are given in Table 3.1.

3.2 BPM and SOA

SOA has emerged as an architectural style that provides a loosely coupled, reusable and standard-based method to integrate distributed systems [2]. The vendor-driven push to Web services-based middleware escalated this trend [5, 22]. With SOA, legacy applications are exposed as reusable services. Services are composed to create new and value-added service offerings. This leads to the requirement of orchestrating the activities of the integrated services.

Initially, the general purpose programming languages such as C and Java were used to integrate the distributed services. However, due to their lack of agility and the need to support frequently changing business requirements, more agile languages and standards were required to orchestrate services.

The advent of BPM in enterprise architecture provided a solution for this requirement. In fact, SOA and BPM complement each other and exhibit a fine *fit*. This *fit* is mainly due to the fundamental, but complementary differences between

Table 3.1 Categories of process modelling approaches

Category	Key characteristics	Main usages	Examples
Activity-based	Flow or block-structured specification of activity ordering by using the activity as the principal concept. All activity execution alternatives are explicitly specified.	Procedural task execution, scientific workflows	WSFL [36], BPMN [13], EPC [17], BPEL [104], BPML [34], XPDL [105]
Constraint-based	Implicit specification of alternative activity executions by using constraint as the principal concept. Process execution is viewed as a CSP.	Goal-driven process modelling	Condec [110], DecSerFlow [71], SEAM [121]
Artefact-based	Explicit representation of data/artefact/product state as the principal concept. Process execution is viewed as an artefact-life cycle management problem.	Product lines, case handling	Product-based [123], Artefact [113], Case Handling [70]
Time-based	Explicit representation of time dimension as the principal concept. The tasks are organised/ scheduled along a time dimension.	Project management and planning	Gantt-charts [116], PERT charts [117,118]
Role-based	Explicit representation of roles and interactions among roles as the principal concept. Process execution is viewed as task completion of roles.	Collaborative business interactions	RIN [124], RAD [121], OOram [122]

the two disciplines as illustrated in Figure 3.3. BPM is primarily business-driven and used to efficiently coordinate the organisational activities. BPM follows a top-down approach and intends to find a solution to a specific business problem, e.g. how to complete a shipment, and how to book a ticket. In contrast, SOA is primarily IT-driven and used to specify loosely coupled and reusable distributed systems, leveraging business capabilities across organisational boundaries [4]. SOA usually employs a bottom-up development [125] and addresses the problem of how to design the system infrastructure. It should be noted that both BPM and SOA can survive without each other. In fact, they did well in the past. However, collectively BPM and SOA can bring more benefits for the enterprise architecture [3, 86, 126]. The BPM practices are used to integrate and orchestrate the distributed services in the enterprise architecture [11, 127, 128]. This leads to many languages to orchestrate services, called *service orchestration languages* as we know today.

Reflection on early proposals for service orchestration languages reveals that *activity-based* process modelling (Section 3.1) is the most influential compared to the rest. Wide usage of WFM systems and the already established imperative programming principles provided a solid foundation to define business processes for service compositions [129−131]. Furthermore, it could be seen that the technology push towards XML as a textual data format has also influenced in designing the XML-based service orchestration languages [132].

One of the early examples for XML-based languages is WSFL [36] developed by IBM. The motivation was to develop a language that can define the execution order and data exchange among Web services. WSFL was influenced by Flowmark/MQ (now, WebSphere® MQ Workflow [133]), which was a workflow language developed by IBM. Thus, many characteristics of workflows were evident in WSFL. In parallel, Microsoft was developing the XLANG [19] as their own business process modelling language. XLANG followed a block-structured methodology to define the order of activity execution. Furthermore, there were many other approaches that were proposed by leading software vendors and standardisation bodies, e.g. BPML [34] by *Intalio*, WSCI [134] by *Sun, BEA* and *SAP* collectively, ebXML [135] by *OASIS*, just to name a few. This has led to a situation of having many competing languages to define service orchestrations.

Consequently, to find a *standardised* manner to orchestrate the services, Microsoft, IBM and BEA jointly proposed the BPEL4WS 1.0 specification. The

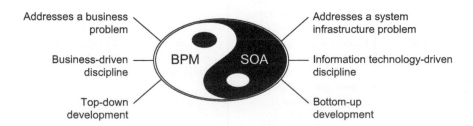

Figure 3.3 Complementary existence of BPM and SOA.

BPEL4WS specification was influenced by its predecessors WSFL and XLANG. Hence, BPEL4WS can be seen as a compromised specification of the duo [136]. This was a significant step towards the standardisation process. Then, SAP and Siebel joined hands to produce the BPEL4WS 1.1 [104], which received wide acceptance from the industry. Later, OASIS[1] officially made the WS-BPEL 2.0 [137] as an OASIS standard with the participation of many software vendors. Due to this wide acceptance and standardisation process, as of now WS-BPEL is the de facto standard for defining business processes in service compositions [136, 138]. WS-BPEL marked an important milestone in the history of service orchestration, and even today it is the most used standard for service orchestration.

Although WS-BPEL has become the de facto standard and is widely accepted by the community, mainly from the industry, it has been often criticised for the *lack of adaptability* [53, 66, 67, 139, 140]. WS-BPEL provides many fault-handling mechanisms in its specifications, but such provisions are not enough for adequately handling many runtime errors, including partner service failures [140] and *ad hoc* deviations in execution paths [63, 84, 141]. Therefore, there is increased attention from both industry and academia to improve the adaptability of BPM in service compositions.

3.3 Adaptability in BPM

The requirement for adaptability in BPM is well-understood [60, 142−144]. The primary goal of introducing adaptability to a system in general is to facilitate its survival upon the changes to the environment under which the system operates. In order to facilitate adaptability, the BPM approach needs to be flexible. Meaning, the BPM systems should provide flexible modelling approaches to model the adaptable service compositions. Much work has been done to identify the types of flexibility that should be present in BPM [59, 62, 63, 145−148].

Heinl et al. [59] identify *flexibility* as an objective of a workflow system and provide a classification schema in terms of *concepts* and *methods* to achieve the objective as shown in Figure 3.4. According to the classification by Heinl et al., flexibility can be achieved either '*by selection*' or '*by adaption*'. Flexibility by selection is usually achieved by modelling various possible execution paths. The

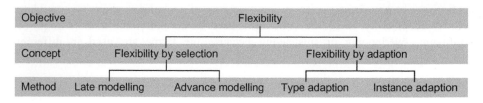

Figure 3.4 The classification scheme for flexibility, cf. [59].

---

[1]http://www.oasis-open.org/.

authors further specify two methods, i.e. late modelling and advanced modelling, to achieve flexibility by selection. In contrast, flexibility by adaption is achieved by changing the processes to reflect the new business requirements. Meaning, the execution path is 'altered' to adapt to the changing requirements. They further divides flexibility by adaption into '*type*' and '*instance*' adaptations, where the former refers to adapting a process definition and the latter adapting a process instance.

By further extending this classification, Schonenberg et al. [63] propose an extensive *taxonomy of process flexibility*. Their taxonomy defines four flexibility types, i.e. *flexibility by design*, *flexibility by deviation*, *flexibility by underspecification* and *flexibility by change*. This provides a terminology and a foundation to analyse various flexibilities presented in the proposed approaches. This classification has a significant overlapping with the classification of Heinl et al. but provides a concrete taxonomy to identify the techniques to achieve flexibility in business process support. Furthermore, many other classifications can be found in the literature [60, 62, 145−148]. However, this book uses the aforementioned taxonomy developed by Schonenberg et al. due to its widespread recognition and applicability for this work.

3.4   Techniques to improve adaptability in BPM

Over the past decade, several approaches have been proposed to improve the adaptability of the business processes support. Inevitably, a large number of approaches have targeted common standards such as WS-BPEL and BPMN due to their wide use [53, 65−67, 123, 139, 140, 149]. These approaches tried to find solutions to the adaptability concerns of these popular standards. However, another set of approaches [61, 70, 71, 150] have attempted to find alternative languages that can provide better business process support. A close inspection of these approaches taken as a whole reveals that these improvements to the adaptability have been achieved on the basis of some underpinning techniques used.

In this section, we introduce the dominant underpinning adaptation techniques as shown in Figure 3.5. These techniques are analysed, citing suitable example approaches from the literature. Note that the example approaches mentioned in this section might have some overlapping in terms of techniques they have used to achieve adaptability. In addition, the terms used by the individual authors might be confusing, overlapping or misleading because the terms are used in different

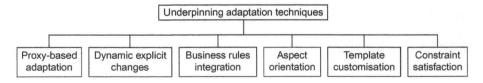

Figure 3.5 Dominant underpinning adaptation techniques.

contexts. However, this categorisation is based on the *most dominant underlying techniques* that had been employed to improve the adaptability. Due to a large number of approaches proposed in the past, this section obviously cannot provide a comprehensive analysis of *all* the available approaches. Therefore, only a sufficient number of approaches were selected based on their significant contribution, practicality and originality. These approaches will be presented with details highlighting their inherent advantages and limitations.

3.4.1 Proxy-based adaptation

One of the issues that service orchestration has to deal with is service unavailability. A service composition depends on its partner services. However, these partner services are autonomic [151]; hence, the management of partner services is beyond the control of the service aggregator. When a partner service fails, the whole process tends to fail. As a solution to this problem the technique of *proxy services* has been employed.

In the Robust-BPEL approach, an adapt-ready or more robust version of a BPEL process is generated to add the self-healing behaviours using *static proxy* [152]. This solution enhances the fault-handling capabilities of BPEL-based service orchestration upon service failures. The approach detects the requirement for adaptation by including the *service invocation monitoring* code that monitors the individual services. Upon an invocation failure, a statically generated proxy service replaces the failed service [152]. Although previously proposed approaches such as BPELJ [153] handle faults in a similar fashion by allowing Java code snippets to be used along with the core process, they require a special engine to enact the processes. In contrast, Robust-BPEL achieves the same without any modification to the BPEL orchestration engine. Furthermore, as the more robust version of a BPEL process is automatically generated, the engineering effort is also reduced. However, in terms of adaptability there are some limitations with this approach. First, it is not possible to dynamically discover and invoke an alternative service upon failures. Only the statically bound alternative proxy services are used. This limitation has been addressed in Robust-BPEL2 [65], which replaces the static proxy with a *dynamic proxy* service to locate equivalent services dynamically at runtime. Second, even if it is possible to dynamically discover alternative services, there is no means to prevent invoking the failed service again. Third, service invocation is changed only upon a monitored failure. It is not possible to provide a 'choice' based on several candidate services.

These limitations of Robust-BPEL2 are later addressed by TRAP/BPEL [140]. With the enhanced generic proxy technique, instead of mere fault-handling, the best service out of a set of candidate services can be dynamically selected. In order to achieve this, TRAP/BPEL uses *transparent shaping* [154, 155] to augment the BPEL processes to achieve adaptive behaviour. *Transparent shaping* is a technique in which an existing application is augmented with *hooks* that intercept the control when an adaptation is necessary and then redirect the control to a special code segment that handles the adaptation. This is a better technique because it is not required to change the existing behaviour of the WS-BPEL code. As such, the adaptation code is transparent to the existing WS-BPEL code. The generic proxy represents the adaptation code, where it keeps all the recovery policies to provide the self-healing behaviour. The generic proxy, developed once, can be used to provide the adaptive behaviour to many WS-BPEL processes. If there is no fault, then the specified WS-BPEL process follows the originally specified behaviour. If there is a fault, then the generic proxy will take a remedial action based on the specified recovery policies.

The eFlow [156] approach allows changes to service endpoints. It introduces such concepts as *dynamic service discovery*, *multiservice nodes* and *generic nodes* to achieve runtime adaptability. *Dynamic service discovery* avoids having static and rigid endpoints. Instead, services are dynamically selected based on service selection rules. These rules take decisions based on organisational policies and customer preferences mapped as parameters. *Multiservice nodes* allow the activation of the same service node a number of times as dynamically determined, whilst the *generic nodes* allow the dynamical selection of service nodes. In a sense, these multiservice nodes and generic nodes act as proxies allowing late binding. Another important characteristic of the approach is the ability to insert consistency and authorisation rules that verify whether the adaptation is authorised and preserve the consistency of the composition. This is a vital requirement when the approach allows process instance-specific changes. While eFlow improves the adaptability in service orchestration and most importantly even at the process instance level, the adaptations are again limited to selecting and associating eServices with a pre-defined flow or process.

A similar approach is taken by Canfora et al. [157] to achieve QoS-aware service composition. A service composition is specified as an orchestration of services. However, in contrast to TRAP/BPEL, the usage of proxy is somewhat different. Here, a proxy service acts as a midpoint to forward service requests to one of the services out of a set of candidate services. This is different from the generic proxy, where self-healing capabilities are provided to many processes as per the transparent shaping technique. Here, a proxy acts on behalf of a single abstract service of a BPEL process. The proxy maintains a list of candidates and periodically refreshes the list by adding new ones and discarding the unavailable ones. When the service invocation is necessary, the proxy will be bound according to the best concrete set of services that are selected from the most up-to-date QoS parameters [158]. The proxy provides the ability to dynamically adapt the BPEL process according to the changed QoS values without redefining the process.

Overall, proxy-based approaches are mostly used to provide self-healing capabilities upon service failures or runtime optimisations through service discovery and selection. Most importantly, the proxies de-couple the concrete services and the core orchestration, allowing late binding. However, the adaptations in the service orchestration should not be limited to late or rebinding of services. Instead, adaptability needs to be addressed in a broader context, i.e. the core orchestration also needs to change in order to *optimise the activity dependencies* to suit the ever-changing runtime environment. Efforts to change the core service orchestration are analysed in the following sections.

3.4.2   Dynamic explicit changes

Dynamically applying changes to processes is a technique used to change the core service orchestration. In such cases, the processes are modelled using a standard process modelling language and are enacted by a standard process engine (that usually lacks in-built support for adaptability). Then, a special module monitors the enactment environment and performs adaptations on the enacted process instances to adjust the running processes to the changed business requirements. Such an approach is suitable when a business already employs a process modelling approach and later attempts to improve its adaptability, usually transparently to the existing enactment environment. In other words, the adaptability is *built on top* rather than *built within*.

One of the earliest example approaches supporting such dynamic changes in processes is proposed by Weske et al. [159] based on the WASA framework [160]. In the WASA framework, workflows stored in a database are enacted via a *workflow server* (enactment engine) [161, 162]. This work provides the adaptation capabilities by performing several operations on those enacted workflow instances or, more precisely, on the *activity models*. The *activity models* are either atomic or more complex models of activities with their own internal activity structures. Operations such as *addActivity, delActivity, addEdge* and *delEdge* are used to dynamically adapt these activity models. Similar efforts in adapting the running processes can be found in other approaches such as Chautauqua [163] and WIDE [164, 165]. WIDE allows cancelling tasks and jumping back and forth in a workflow instance upon triggered exceptions or events [164]. Chautauqua [163] allows dynamic structural changes on the enacted processes or more precisely on information control networks (ICN) [166] via the special operation called *edit*. Here, the fundamental characteristic is 'monitor and adapt.' Nonetheless, one of the limitations of these approaches is that they do not provide enough control over changes. As such, these *ad hoc* changes can lead to erroneous situations, thus raising the need for better control when performing adaptations.

While adhering to a similar principle, ADEPTflex [167] gives special attention to controlling the changes. ADEPTflex supports dynamic changes to the workflows or ADEPT models [168]. The tasks can be added or deleted from a workflow instance. Certain tasks may be skipped to speed up the execution of a workflow instance. Tasks that were modelled to be executed in parallel can be serialised (or vice versa) via another set of operations. A set of these operations is included in a change process. These changes can be applied on a *permanent* or *temporary* basis. A temporary change may be undone during the change process, whereas permanent change cannot. Later, the adaptation capabilities were improved by employing engineering techniques such as *plug and play* of process segments in ADEPT2 [169], a successor of ADEPTflex. A software engineer can select the application functions from a repository and insert them into the process template via drag and drop. One of the important features of the ADEPTflex approach is its ability to carry out a *minimal* but *complete* set of changes ensuring the *correctness* and *consistency* of running processes. The approach introduces several rules or properties to ensure the correctness and consistency upon changes to process instances. The ADEPTflex framework rejects the changes if the correctness and consistency properties are violated. Note that these correctness and consistency rules are defined in terms of states of the tasks and processes. The properties ensure that the changes do not lead a process to an incorrect or inconsistent state. For example, the framework does not allow *delete* operation on tasks that are RUNNING, COMPLETED, FAILED or SKIPPED. However, in business environments, such general state-based control to ensure consistency and correctness may not be sufficient. There are domain-specific constraints on modifications. For example, '*A payment must be carried out after a confirmation of a car repair*' is such a domain-specific constraint. It is possible that a modification that ends up in another consistent state of the process instance might violate a specific business requirement as the framework lacks support for such domain-specific consistency checks.

A similar but more service orchestration—specific approach is proposed by Fang et al. [57] to adapt enacted BPEL processes. Similar to ADEPTflex [167], activity states are considered to realise adaptation decisions in this approach. However, one improvement in this approach is that the approach proposes a set of *change patterns* to perform these adaptations or navigation changes, which is its main focus. This is in contrast to operation-based adaptations proposed earlier. These change patterns, i.e. Skip, Activate, Repeat, Retry and Stop, determine how an activity should be adapted or navigated. Each pattern is described in terms of change to produce, action to carry out, preconditions and consequences of adaptation aspects. Such aspects are grounded upon '*activity and link-based*' state transition diagrams that specify whether an activity is RUNNING, INACTIVE, FINISHED, SKIPPED, FAILED, TERMINATED or EXPIRED and a link is UNDETERMINED or DETERMINED (i.e. TRUE or FALSE). These statuses are transited according to the adaptation patterns. Furthermore, these statuses help to identify the suitable statuses to perform the adaptations as specified by the patterns. For example, an activity X may be skipped if the activity is in the INACTIVE state. The consequence of the Skip action is that the activity is now in the SKIPPED state.

Automating dynamic modifications is essential in business environments where changes are frequent. SML4BPEL (schema modification language for BPEL) [170] is a language proposed to aid dynamically modifying the BPEL process definitions. The approach allows writing down the process modification policies as rules. The SML4BPEL engine dynamically modifies the schemas according to the parsed rules. This allows automating the process modifications and instance migrations according to pre-planned modification policies. However, this approach has two main limitations. First, the adaptations need to be known at design time, which is not always the case. Second, it does not support adaptations specific to a particular process instance.

The limitations in this approach were addressed by the approach proposed by Yonglin et al. [141]. The approach gives special attention to representing the process context as part of adaptation decision-making. The rules reason about the current context represented by facts. Then, adaptations are carried out on running process instances. The context is represented at two main levels, i.e. business and computing (IT). The business context captures the current business environment, whereas the computing context captures versions of schema, status of process instance and resources allocated.

Overall, these approaches supporting dynamic explicit changes are used as a remedy for the inherent limitations of the process modelling and enactment standards and environments. The ability to continuously optimise the running processes to suit the changing business environments has made a major impact on improving BPMS. Furthermore, the separation of the *execution* concerns from the *adaptation* concerns is advantageous from the architectural point of view. Nonetheless, the process definitions were modelled with little apprehension for adaptability, and therefore the adaptability allowed is limited. The adaptability is seen as something that could be introduced later via improvements to the BPMS. The corresponding systems to perform the adaptations were proposed as an additional or a special layer on top of the existing process models. This has some similarity to a *recovery-based solution* to improving the adaptability of existing standards. Yet, the limitations were inherent in the way the processes are modelled or the lack of flexibility in process modelling concepts in the available standards. Consequently, it is needed to find more radical and flexible orchestration solutions that provide better conceptual support for adaptability, rather than completely handing the adaptability concerns to the design of BPMS.

3.4.3 Business rules integration

One of the issues with the popular orchestration standards is the imperative or procedural nature of process modelling. The businesses operating in more dynamic environments challenge the imperative and procedural process modelling paradigm as it fails to successfully capture the unpredictability and complexity of businesses. Intrinsically, the business policies (rules) that are subject to frequent changes are intermingled with the process logic, leading to an unmanageable process/rule spaghetti [106].

This consideration leads to more descriptive approaches such as the use of *business rules* [171] in modelling business processes. The business rule engines work hand-in-glove with process enactment engines to provide the required flexibility for runtime modifications. The business policies for achieving business goals are specified as business rules [172]. A widely accepted definition for a business rule is provided by the GUIDE group [173]. According to them '*a business rule is a statement that defines or constrains some aspects of the business. It is intended to assert business structure and to control or influence the behaviour of the business.*' Rather than defining these business assertions as part of business processes, they were defined as separate artefacts using more expressive rule languages. The required agility of dynamic changes to the business logic is achieved through dynamic changes to these rules as enabled by the advancements of rule engines and languages such as Jess [174], JRules [175] and Drools [176].

Traditionally, these rule engines are used to reason about the software behaviour based on the knowledge supplied as declarative rules. The policies were specified

main concepts *pointcut definition, advices* and *join-points* [74, 195]. The *advices* are an additional or separate behaviour for the core program; *join-points* specify where in the core program the advices are applied; and *pointcut definition* detects whether a given *join-point* matches. Accordingly, in service orchestration approaches, additional behaviours as advices are woven into a core process to alter its behaviour without damaging the modularity and understandability [193].

The aspect-viewing technique to integrate the business rules with business processes is used in AO4BPEL [68]. In this approach, the complete service composition is broken into two main parts, core process and rules. First, a core process that defines the flow represents the fixed part. Second, a set of well-modularised business rules that can exist and evolve independently represent the dynamic parts. A service composition is formed by weaving the business rules into the core business process (BPEL) via *pointcuts* as per AOP principles. In AO4BPEL, each BPEL activity is considered as a potential pointcut. This approach is motivated by the argument that the knowledge represented by rules tend to change more often than the core process [68]. This argument may be valid for businesses that can predict the core process and the pointcuts in advance. However, in certain situations, the core process may also need to be changed in an unpredictable manner and there can also be changes to the pointcuts. Furthermore, the way in which the aspects are woven into BPEL code can cause problems to a business user who might not be familiar with the low-level BPEL code.

This limitation has been resolved by MoDAR [149] using aspects along with model-driven development. The MoDAR approach distinguishes between a volatile part (variable model) and a fixed part (base model) of a business process. Again, the volatile part is represented as rules while the fixed part is represented by a business process. At the composition level, the rules are woven into the core process via a weave model that defines the location (*before, around* and *after*) of an activity in which the rules should be woven. The key advantage of this approach, compared to AO4BPEL, is its *model-driven* approach to generate the lower-level executable code, i.e. Drools rules and BPEL scripts. It follows that the use of aspect viewing is done at a higher level without limiting to a single execution platform. Such a higher-level aspect-viewing benefits the business users, who are not familiar with the lower-level (XML-based executable) languages such as BPEL. However, a major drawback is that if there is a change requirement of the pointcuts, the process needs to be remodelled; code needs to be generated and then deployed. Therefore, similar to AO4BPEL, this approach provides adaptability only for application scenarios in which it is possible to identify a base model and a variable model in advance.

VxBPEL [67] uses aspect viewing at the modelling language level by introducing a few extensions to BPEL language constructs. The approach facilitates different variations or configurations of a BPEL process. Variation points that have been introduced [196] are a key concept used to express the variability in software product lines. One of the key differences in VxBPEL compared to the rest is that the variability information is located right inside the business process. The advantages are clear visibility of variation points and efficient parsing. Although this requires modifying the BPEL language and the enactment engines, it is a helpful capability in capturing the variations and commonalities in service orchestrations. However, the points of the variation are still needed to be pre-defined. A configuration file will determine the current or most suitable configurations for given pointcuts. Furthermore, there is no attention given to analysing the impacts of making choices over different configurations or variations, and to protecting the integrity of the composition.

Padus [193] also uses AOP concepts to dynamically adapt the service orchestration. One improvement they have made in their approach is that the pointcuts are less fragile to changes in the core business process. The reason behind this is the use of higher-level pointcuts in contrast to lower-level pointcuts such as XPath, used previously [68, 191]. Karastoyanova et al. [66] also use AOP concepts. One of the key advantages of their approach is that it is not limited to BPEL, and hence does not require any modification to the BPEL language nor the BPEL engine, compared to the work of Michiel et al. [67]. However, again, the requirement of pre-identifying the core and volatile parts limits the amount of adaptability catered by the runtime environment.

In addition to the *process definition level*, aspect orientation has been used at the *service orchestration engine level* as well [191]. Advices are written in Java and woven into processes via XPath pointcuts. Aspects can be plugged-in or unplugged during runtime. However, the aspects do not dynamically evolve as in AO4BPEL and MoDAR. In addition, the engine is required to check the aspect-registry constantly during execution.

VieDAME [192], which is an adaptation extension to the ActiveBPEL engine [197], also uses AOP concepts in its adaptation layer. The intention of using AOP principles in VieDAME is in fact to achieve a clear separation of the engine (ActiveBPEL) and the adaptation extension (VieDAME). Therefore, they successfully avoid having a tighter coupling between the adaptation layer and the engine. Nonetheless, the adaptation in the approach is limited to service replacement, i.e. the adaptations on partner services. The approach cannot support adaptations in the control flow. Similarly, AdaptiveBPEL [194] uses aspect-weaving at the middleware level to enforce the negotiated collaboration policies [198, 199]. In both approaches, the objective is to modularise the cross-cutting concerns at the middleware (system) level rather than at the process definition (language) level.

Overall, aspect orientation has brought many advantages for business process modelling. It avoids code-scattering and tangling [200, 201], which can lead to increased complexity of service orchestration, due to cross-cutting concerns. This is especially true when aspect orientation is carried out at the process definition or the schema level as done previously [67, 68]. However, the flexibility is still limited to the points where the pointcuts are defined. Irrespective of the level at which the aspects are woven, this is still a major limitation in achieving adaptability for service orchestration at runtime. The requirement of identifying the fixed and volatile parts of a business process especially may not be feasible in environments where the collaborators play a major role. In reflecting tenants' unpredictable business requirements, for example, it may be impractical to distinguish between the fixed and volatile parts of the business process.

Nevertheless, from the point of capturing commonalities and allowing variations, aspect-orientation technique has a major advantage. The commonalities are captured in a core process and the variations are captured via the advices. For example, the variation points in VxBPEL [67] and the rules in AO4BPEL [68] capture variations while the core BPEL process captures the commonality. The same goes for MoDAR [149], where the *volatile* part captures the variations while the *fixed* part captures the commonality. However, again, the commonalities and variations captured via AOP are limited to the way in which the pointcuts are specified. There is always a requirement of foreseeing these pointcuts during the design time. This is a limitation common to the aspect-orientation technique in general.

For the requirement of achieving controlled changes, the aspect orientation achieves the control by pre-specifying the points where adaptation can happen. The JPM determines what can be changed and what cannot.

In addition, the inherent capability of AOP for achieving separation of concerns has contributed to better management of the complexity that could be introduced during runtime process change. The complexity of cross-cutting concerns is handled in advices, e.g. business rules in AO4BPEL [68] and MoDAR [149]. This helps maintain the core process without increasing its complexity amidst modifications at runtime.

3.4.5   Template customisation

Template customisation is another technique used to address the adaptability concerns of service orchestration. In template customisation, a master process is customised using available templates to dynamically create a business process. This category of adaptation approaches has its roots in *generative programming* [75, 202]. A template library or a database is used by a controller to select the templates to generate a process definition that is optimised for the business requirement. In this section we look at how the template customisation technique has been used to achieve adaptability in service orchestration.

A typical approach for template customisation is proposed by Geebelen et al. [203]. They use the concepts from dynamic Web pages [204] in Web services orchestration. The authors use the model-view-controller (MVC) pattern to achieve adaptable BPEL processes. Templates that consist of modules, i.e. clusters of BPEL activities, were dynamically integrated to generate a process according to a predefined master process. This selection of modules for the generation of a new process is carried out based on several parameters such as response time of services. The use of such techniques as meta-level master process construction and interpreted language (*Ruby*) has made the approach more adaptive. The modules and master process capture the commonalities. How the modules are used in the master process can be used to define variations. Nonetheless, it has two major limitations. First, the packaging and deployment are required each time a change is realised. Second, the approach cannot be used to achieve runtime process instance level adaptation.

These limitations are evident in the use of *reference processes* [205]. The reference processes approach has been used as an extension to the *Websphere Integration Developer* [206] to allow high-level business process design in Web service compositions. Here, a reference process is basically a designed process that captures and maintains a set of best practices specific to the business domain. In other words, the reference process acts as a template. Such a reference process is subjected to a series of customisations until the customer requirements are satisfied. The customisations involve adding, removing and modifying process elements, including activities, control- and data-flow connectors. The approach defines a formal model for customisation with detailed rules that are independent of the underlying process modelling language or notation. In addition, the approach proposes an annotation language that can describe what the possible customisations and constraints are. The reference process is annotated with these constraints. In this way, the approach also captures the commonalities via the reference process. In addition, newly generated processes can be seen as variations. However, this way of capturing commonalities and allowing variations leads to code duplication. When a new upgrade needs to be done, all the newly created customisations require separate upgrading. This possibly can lead to inconsistencies. The approach also provides limited support for controlling the adaptations. The constraints annotated prevent invalid adaptations to a certain extent. Nonetheless, there is no direct support for analysing change impacts and behavioural correctness.

Mietzner et al. [42] propose to customise a process template into a customer-specific deployable SaaS [45] application solution. The SaaS application domain requires highly customer/tenant-specific solutions. Different variations in customer requirements need to be supported. To do so, the approach uses *variability points* or points of an abstract process template that are customisable. These variability points are filled with concrete values during the customisation process. At the end of the customisation process, a highly optimised and customer-specific solution, e.g. a WS-BPEL process model, is generated. Note that the approach is actually independent of WS-BPEL and can be applied to other process languages. In another work, the same authors extend the SCA [207] architecture using variability descriptors to package and deploy multi-tenant-aware configurable composite SaaS applications [92]. In general, the core principle used is that the process template captures the commonalities while the variability descriptors and the customisation process identify and capture the required variations. As such, the potential alternatives or changes are treated as first-class entities. A collection of such variations to address a particular business need forms a *configuration*. From the business process adaptability point of view, such a configuration can lead to an adapted process [208]. However, the approach assumes that such variations and customisations can be predicted at the design time. But this can be problematic as it is not possible to predict all the points in a process template where the variations are required for future tenants.

PAWS [209] is a framework developed to improve the adaptability in Web service processes in terms of service retrieval, optimisation and supervision. The framework allows a process designer to first design the main business process as a

BPEL process that describes the activity dependencies. This process captures the main business requirements without considering the actual services that perform the tasks. This initial design can thus be seen as a process template. Then, the tasks of the designed process definition are annotated with constraints that define domain-dependent non-functional properties for each task. For example, the given *time* or *cost* of performing each task is annotated. Then, the annotated business process is enacted leaving the problem of service selection to runtime. The framework has its own *advanced service retrieval module* that selects the services based on the annotated constraints. As such, the service selection becomes an optimisation problem that considers several parameters such as user preferences and runtime context. While PAWS provides better runtime adaptability via exception handling and several self-healing features upon failures of task execution and service selection, it provides only limited support for adapting the core process. The core process always needs to be designed and annotated at the design time.

This limitation can also be seen in Discorso [210], which can be seen as a successor to PAWS [209]. Discorso is also a framework for designing and enacting dynamic and flexible business processes. In contrast to PAWS, Discorso provides richer support and user experience in service retrieval, optimisation and supervision. Discorso couples the QoS-based service selection with the automated generation of user interfaces and runtime supervision, which was not available in PAWS. Discorso also supports both human and automated activities in service orchestration. However, Discorso follows the footsteps of PAWS. It annotates process template and uses late binding techniques to facilitate runtime process optimisation and healing. Hence, runtime adaptations are still limited to service selection and error recovery. The core process represented by the annotated template cannot be changed at runtime.

Another template-based approach has recently been proposed by Zan et al. [211]. In this approach, the placeholders of a process template are replaced by process fragments. Here, a process fragment is a small process that can be integrated into a larger process by filling the placeholders of a process template. Multiple fragments of the same fragment type can be developed as possible candidates to replace a placeholder. Fragments are kept in a fragment library. Declarative fragment constraints [212] preserve the relationships among fragments, i.e. how the fragments should be used in the placeholders. Adaptation policies, which are extensions to WS policy [22], define how the fragments should be selected. Depending on the business-specific requirements, fragments are selected based on adaptation policies and used as allowed by fragment constraints. Compared to the previously presented approaches, this approach [211] provides greater flexibility as the execution order of fragments is not pre-defined. The adaptations are carried out by adding/removing fragments and modifying the relationships among these fragments. Another significant characteristic is the clear separation of adaptation logic from the business logic. Along with the modularity provided with fragments, such separation of concerns assists managing the complexity. Furthermore, there is support for capturing commonalities and allowing variations. The fragments can capture the commonalities. In addition, multiple variants of the same fragment can coexist. However, even a slight variation can lead to duplication. The reason behind this problem is that a completely new fragment needs to be designed to model the variation. In addition to this limitation, this approach has the following limitations in terms of adaptation as well. First, the placeholders are pre-defined and cannot be changed. Only the fragments that fill the placeholders can be changed. In fact, this is a common weakness of any template-based approach. Second, the approach does not support process instance adaptation. Once the process is enacted, there is no support to change the process instance.

Overall, the template customisation approaches commonly facilitate adaptability by delaying the formation of the eventual processes to runtime. For example, to generate a *fitting* process to customer needs, the MVC-based approach proposed by Geebelen et al. [203] integrates BPEL clusters according to a master process, and Mietzner et al. [42] use a customisation procedure to address different variation requirements. This allows delivering a highly customised process to a particular business environment. The templates provide agility by allowing the specification of '*half-done*' processes.

The requirement of capturing commonalities and allowing variations is also supported to a certain extent. The *templates* captured the commonalities across the potential business environments in advance, whilst the variations are captured during the *customisation process* to produce a final customised process. However, if a new variation is required the process needs to be completely regenerated. Hence, the ability of allowing variations is limited only during the process of template customisation.

Similar to the approaches adopting aspect orientation, these template-based approaches also use the rigidity provided via the template to govern the controllability of the adaptations. The customisation process is controlled by the amount of flexibility allowed in the templates. These approaches do not explicitly consider change impact analysis as only the allowed templates can be used to generate the final process and these processes are not shared among multiple users/tenants.

In comparison to aspect orientation, template-based customisation does not specifically support either separation of concerns or handling runtime complexity, in general. One reason for this is that the purpose of these approaches is different and there is less attention given to the process enactment aspect. Consequently, these approaches do not intend to perform runtime modifications but rather concentrate on generating a customised solution. For example, once the customised solution (e.g. a WS-BPEL process) is generated, an enactment environment (e.g. a BPEL engine) may execute this process in a way similar to executing any other (WS-BPEL) processes without specific support for adapting the running process.

3.4.6 Constraint satisfaction

As mentioned in Section 3.1, *constraint satisfaction* is a technique where *a solution* is chosen based on assignment of *variables* over a *variable domain* such that all *constraints* are satisfied [107]. This technique has been applied to service orchestration and to business process modelling in general to improve the adaptability. The adaptability is achieved by *not explicitly specifying* the flow of activities. Instead, the exact flow of activities, i.e. the solution, is determined by satisfying a number of explicitly specified constraints.

Mangan et al. [213] propose an approach that uses constraint satisfaction to define customisable business processes. Although this approach does not directly relate to service orchestration, many basic principles presented in business process modelling in general can be used to improve the flexibility in service orchestration. The approach targets how to build a customised process definition successfully out of many available process fragments and tasks in a pool. The success of a customised process definition is the satisfaction of domain-specific constraints that reflect business goals.

The constraints are defined at three different specification levels, i.e. selection, build and termination [214]. *Selection constraints* define how the process fragments are selected and the *build constraints* define what needs to be respected whilst a customised instance is gradually built. The *termination constraints* are the constraints that need to be satisfied by the completely built process definition or workflow. The approach supports adaptability by allowing a full process definition to be built at runtime. As such, this approach is similar to generative programming, which we have seen in *template customisation approaches* presented previously. However, the overall problem of building a valid workflow schema through a customisation process that satisfies the defined constraints is treated as a CSP. The most influential underpinning technique used here is constraint satisfaction to achieve a customisable process.

The approach successfully tackles the problem of defining business processes in environments where the execution paths are unpredictable or the number of alternative execution paths is extremely high. This is a clear improvement compared to template customisation where the execution paths are pre-defined in the templates. However, the flexibility is again limited to the design or customisation phase. There is no special flexibility provided once the process is enacted. Instead, the enacted process instance needs to follow the exact schema that was built in the design/customisation phase. The underlying problem for this limitation is that the constraints are used in the customisation phase to build a workflow, which is procedural in nature. Such procedural specifications afford little support for runtime adaptation due to the strict ordering of activities once enacted.

This limitation is also evident in the approach proposed by Rychkova et al. [215]. The approach has a declarative specification that captures the business invariants [76] to model an imperative process design or a domain-specific customisation. By formalising the concepts of the SEAM modelling language [216] with the support from the Alloy specification language [217], the approach attempts to ensure the system integrity when business processes are redesigned or customised. The business goals and strategies are captured in a SEAM specification, which is declarative. SEAM supports a hierarchical composition of objects that represents the system. SEAM properties represent the states of the *working objects* whilst *actions* change these properties of working objects [216]. The approach specifies these properties in first-order logic to allow mapping into Alloy [217], which provides formal verification support. The actions may modify the states of working objects as long as the actions lead to states where invariants are protected. The *formalism and verification* support from the Alloy Analyser tool [217] helps the engineering effort to confidently redesign business processes that suit the changing high-level strategic goals [108] of the business. Yet, the final result (i.e. the built process) is again an imperative process that is constructed by mapping the declarative SEAM specification to an imperative BPMN design. As such, the adaptability of the approach is limited to the customisation or process redesign phase as the resulting process is imperative and cannot be changed at runtime.

To avoid such limitations, more declarative specifications and, perhaps most importantly, enactment environments that support such declarative specifications are needed. The Declarative Service Flow Language (DecSerFlow) [71] is a language proposed to declaratively specify, enact and monitor service flows. The DecSerFlow language, similar to its sister language Condec [73], envisions that both process modelling and enactment are CSPs. This is a clear difference and an advantage over the approaches [73] that use constraints satisfaction to design, redesign or customise process definitions. A DecSerFlow model consists of activities that need to be executed and a set of constraints that describe the temporal properties among them. These (graphical) representations of the execution constraints among activities are translated to linear-temporal-logic (LTL) expressions [150]. A process instance is executed in a way that constraints are not violated. A process is considered to be complete when all the constraints are satisfied.

The constraints in DecSerFlow are specified in terms of existence, relation and negation formulas. For example, *existence* formula may specify that an activity must be executed. A *relation* formula may specify that an activity should precede/ succeed another. A *negation* formula may specify that an activity should not be executed (e.g. because another alternative activity has been executed). The approach provides greater benefits in terms of adaptability as it completely avoids having explicit activity execution alternatives, which is evident in the previously introduced approaches [213, 214] and also in the mainstream standards such as WS-BPEL. When the number of alternatives are very large and a procedural language is used to specify those alternatives according to *flexibility by design* [63], the process definition can be very complex. In contrast, with DecSerFlow [71], the activities do not directly relate to each other and can be executed in any order as long as the constraints are not violated. The same statement applies to the Condec [73] language. Process execution and completion are problems of satisfying all the constraints for a given model. Furthermore, the constraints can be added or removed depending on the business requirements [218].

Guenther et al. [69] propose to improve the flexibility of process modelling via case handling. In case handling, the data of a product/case are used as the principal driver of the process rather than the completion of activities [70, 115]. Although case handling is a completely different paradigm for business process modelling (Section 3.1), the underpinning technique that provides the flexibility has a lot in common with constraint satisfaction. In case handling, the next possible activities are only *constrained by the state of the case*; there is no explicit ordering of activities; and the process specification describes what needs to be done rather than how that should be done based on the case. This type of flexibility is similar to that achieved by constraint-based approaches as they all attempt to *avoid the need for explicit change* at runtime. The flexibility is given to the runtime to select the path of execution. Such flexibility is better-suited to domains where there is a strong *case metaphor* such as the medical field. A case study providing more details can be found elsewhere [219].

Overall, the flexibility provided by the constraint-based declarative approaches fundamentally relies on their ability of specifying *what* needs to be done rather than *how*. Pesic [150] calls this as the *outside-to-inside* approach, in contrast to the *inside-to-outside* way of process modelling in imperative approaches. The term *inside-to-outside* refers to that all alternatives are explicitly specified in a procedural way and new alternatives need to be explicitly added. Later, Fahland [220] attributed the reason for the improved flexibility of process modelling to the sort of information the declarative definitions deliver. According to Fahland, the declarative process definitions deliver *circumstantial information* in contrast to the *sequential information* delivered by the imperative or procedural process definitions. Consequently, such declarative process modelling approaches have made an important step in process adaptability. DecSerFlow [71] especially can extend the adaptability support to the enactment environment.

Another important contribution of the constraint-based approaches is their ability to specify the system invariants. Regev points out that 'Business processes are often the result of a *fit* between the needs and capabilities of the internal stakeholders of the business and the opportunities and threats the business identifies in its environment' [142]. Changes to the business process are required in order to ensure this *fit*. So, undoubtedly, we need to identify the properties that ensure this fit and thereby ensure the survival of the business. In service composites, the goals of the collaborators such as third-party service providers and consumers also need to be safeguarded as much as possible, in addition to those of the aggregator. While constraint-based process modelling contributes to this requirement, the monolithic representation of constraints in a service orchestration may still lead to unnecessary complexity and even restriction on possible modifications.

Nonetheless, the constraint-based approaches are criticised for their lack of support for *process comprehension* by human users. This problem is somewhat tackled by DecSerFlow [71] by providing a graphical notation to design the constraint model. Yet, the graphical notation does not provide sufficient support for understanding the possible flows of activities. For service orchestration systems, this can cause problems as multiple service invocations may have frequent tight dependencies and it is easier to say *what needs to be done* rather than *what should not be done* to define the control flow. Therefore, formulating a constraint specification is not always a practical solution. It is important that a service orchestration approach should leverage the advantages of *constraint-based approaches* (such as ensuring the system integrity amidst flexibility) but needs to provide stronger support to process comprehension.

3.5   Summary and observations

This section summarises the presented approaches and evaluates against the require-ments of a service orchestration approach described in Chapter 2. Section 3.5.1 pre-sents this summary and the evaluation. In addition, a number of observations and lessons that can be learnt are presented in Section 3.5.2.

3.5.1   Summary and evaluation

A high-level abstract view on the presented groups of approaches to improving adapt-ability in business process modelling is given in Figure 3.6. The figure illustrates how each group provides adaptability with different techniques. The figure only captures a generalised view by highlighting the distinct features among groups but should not be taken as a true representation for each approach of the group.

In proxy-based approaches, the adaptations are carried out in the proxy, which separate the error handling and optimisation from the core service orchestration. However, the proxy design and the extent of its capabilities are unique to each and every approach in the group. In the approaches that provide *dynamic changes*, the adaptations are dynamically carried out in the core service orchestration itself. In contrast, the approaches based on *rule integration* use business rules to achieve the

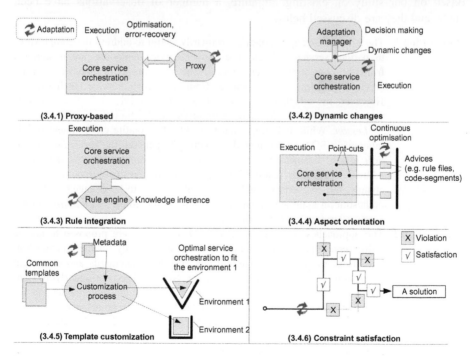

Figure 3.6 An illustration of different techniques used to improve the adaptability.

required adaptability, mainly due to the high agility provided by the business rules techniques.

Bringing the advantages of AOP [221] into the BPM domain, the *aspect-oriented approaches* use the pointcuts and advices to improve the ability of continuously optimise the service orchestration. In contrast, the *template-based approaches* use generative programming [75, 202] principles to dynamically generate the service orchestration out of templates that suit a particular business condition/environment. The approaches that use the *constraint satisfaction* technique employ *constraints* as an explicit concept in business process modelling. These approaches provide a rather different perspective to adaptability. They provide greater flexibility by only specifying the *restricting boundaries/condition* of process modelling/execution. In other words, *what cannot be done* is explicit. However, the actual path of execution is not explicitly represented and only determined by the specified constraints. Any path that does not violate the constraints is deemed valid.

A summary evaluation of the examined approaches in this chapter against the adaptation requirements for service orchestration from Chapter 2 is given in Table 3.2.

3.5.2   Observations and lessons learnt

Based on our study on existing literature, a number of observations have been made, and they are discussed below.

Observation 1. The *proxy-based* approaches are primarily useful to address the complexities in partner service failures. The partner service endpoints are de-coupled from the core service orchestration. The concerns associated with partner service selection are separated from the core service orchestration. However, the adaptability is limited to partner service selection. There is very little support to change the core service orchestration.

Lesson: While it is important to tackle the volatile environment that is inherent in SOA or distributed computing in general, the service orchestration is also business-driven. The core service orchestration is defined to address a business requirement. Hence, as the business requirements do change, the core service orchestration also needs to be changed. A service orchestration approach should be capable of providing *adaptability beyond partner service failures or changes*.

Observation 2. The approaches offering *dynamic explicit changes* are proposed to handle unforeseen requirements, and are done so as a remedy for the inherent limitations of the process modelling and enactment standards and enactment environments already in use in practice. Nevertheless, the underlying standards and supporting enactment environments lack the required support for flexibility, limiting the amount of adaptability that can be achieved.

Lesson: The adaptability cannot be built on top of rigid standards and enactment environments. Rather the standards and enactment environments should be *manufactured with adaptability in mind*.

Observation 3. Both *rules-based* and *aspect-oriented* approaches attempt to separate the concerns of adaptation. This is an important step towards improving

Table 3.2 The summary of evaluation of adaptive service orchestration approaches

Approach	Improved flexibility	Capturing commonalities	Allowing variations	Controlled changes	Predictable change impacts	Managing complexity
Proxy-based						
Robust-BPEL [222]	+	−	−	−	−	−
TRAP/BPEL [140]	+	−	?	−	−	−
Robust-BPEL2 [65]	+	−	−	−	−	−
eFLow [156]	+	−	−	+	−	−
Canfora et al. [157]	+	−	?	−	−	−
Dynamic explicit changes						
WASA [159,160]	+	−	−	−	−	−
Chautauqua [163]	+	−	−	−	−	−
WIDE [164,165]	+	−	−	−	−	−
ADAPTflex [167]	+	−	−	+	−	−
Fang et al. [57]	+	−	−	−	−	−
SML4BPEL [170]	+	−	−	−	−	−
Yonglin et al. [141]	+	−	−	−	−	−
Business rule integration						
Rosenberg [179]	+	−	−	−	−	−
Graml et al. [181]	+	?	+	−	−	−
rBPMN [184]	+	?	?	+	−	−
Aspect orientation						
AO4BPEL [68]	+	?	?	?	−	+
MoDAR [149]	+	?	?	?	−	+
Courbis [191]	+	−	−	?	−	−

(Continued)

Table 3.2 (Continued)

Approach	Improved flexibility	Capturing commonalities	Allowing variations	Controlled changes	Predictable change impacts	Managing complexity
VieDAME [192]	+	−	−	~	−	~
AdaptiveBPEL [194]	+	−	−	~	−	~
VxBPEL [67]	+	~	~	~	−	+
Karastoyanova et al. [66]	+	~	~	−	−	+
Padus [193]	+	~	~	−	−	+
Template customisation						
Geeblan 2008 [203]	+	~	~	−	−	−
Lazovic et al. [205]	+	~	~	~	~	−
Mietzner [42]	+	~	~	−	−	−
PAWS 2007 [209]	+	−	−	−	−	−
Discorso 2011 [210]	+	−	−	−	−	−
Zan et al. [211]	+	+	+	~	~	~
Constraint satisfaction						
Mangan et al. [213]	+	−	−	+	~	−
Rychkova et al. [215]	+	−	−	+	~	−
DecSerFlow [71]	+	~	~	+	−	−
Condec [73]	+	~	~	+	−	−
Guenther [69]	+	−	−	+	−	−

+, Explicitly supported; ~, supported to a certain extent; −, not supported.

adaptability in business processes. Rather than providing a monolithic representation of a business process, the core process has been separated from the
rest of the business logic that need to be adapted. The rule-based approaches
use the business rules technology to specify and realise the
adaptable business logic. In aspect-oriented approaches, the already established aspect-oriented concepts have been exploited to separate the adaptability concerns via pointcuts and advices.

Lesson: Separation of concerns is an important aspect in software engineering, which is equally valid for service orchestrations. In an adaptive service orchestration, the *separation of concerns needs to be carried out in
multiple dimensions*. This includes separation of core process from the business rules/policies, separation of control flow from data flow, separation of
adaptation concerns from management concerns.

Observation 4. Both *aspect-oriented* and *template customisation* approaches are more suited
to business domains where it is required to quickly customise a process to
suit a particular business environment. The aspects-woven base process definitions and the templates provide partially completed processes. Depending
on the factors posed by runtime environments, the remaining steps of com-
pleting the processes are carried out. The aspect-oriented approaches provide the advices woven to a process via pointcuts. Depending on the factors
posed by the runtime environment, the advices make the process adapt to
the environment in a tuneable manner.

Lesson: The amount of adaptability is limited in the templates or the
pointcuts. However, the agility offered by the already completed process
parts can help quickly address the consumer needs. In SaaS applications,
this provides a significant advantage as the tenants can be offered with such
partially completed processes as features and the final process can be assembled from them. Furthermore, the aspects can be used to provide the
required tuneability. Therefore, a service orchestration approach should *provide the ability of partial specification* for increased agility.

Observation 5. Constraint-based approaches provide flexibility without requiring an explicit
change during runtime. A large number of possible execution alternatives
are captured in the specification with a small number of constraints. These
approaches provide better flexibility and integrity protection, although there
are no explicit adaptations as such. The path of execution is implicit and
controlled by the defined constraints. However, these approaches do not provide a clear view of the path of execution. Hence, they are not applicable to
approaches where it is required to explicitly represent the path of execution.

Lesson: BPM aligns business and IT. The ability to visualise a process
from start to the end is one of the requirements of BPM to provide the
required abstraction for a business user. Therefore, while constraints are
used to ensure the integrity, there should be a way to visually represent the
path of execution. In addition, in business scenarios where it is easier to
specify what should be done, rather than what should not be done, the
constraint-driven approaches do not provide a sufficient solution. Therefore,
in such cases the process modelling can be cumbersome and possibly lead
to undetected errors. Overall, the *two fields of process modelling and constraint specification/satisfaction should be used in a complementary manner
by carefully leveraging their inherent advantage.*

behaviour without increasing redundancy. The concept of interaction membrane is explained in Section 4.6, clarifying how the data flow concerns are addressed.

Section 4.7 discusses how an organisation supports adaptable orchestrations, whereas Section 4.8 explains the concepts that help manage the complexity of an adaptable organisation. Finally, the Serendip meta-model that formally captures all the core concepts of Serendip is presented in Section 4.9.

All the sections are provided with suitable examples from the business scenario presented in Chapter 2.

4.1   The organisation

The term *organisation* has many definitions. One of the earliest definitions given by Barnard [224], who defines an organisation as '*a system of consciously coordinated activities or forces of two or more persons.*' According to Daft [225], '*organisations are social entities that are goal-directed, deliberately structured, and coordinated activity systems, linked to the environment.*' This definition is broader than Barnard's as it specifies that the purpose of organising. A similar view was taken by Rollison [226], who says '*organisations are artefacts, that are goal-directed social entities with structured activities.*' In conclusion, we can identify the following basic characteristics of an organisation.

- A goal-directed unity of multiple entities linked to its environment.
- Deliberately structured relationships among entities, interactions and their activities.

Therefore, there is always a goal that defines the purpose of the act of organising relative to the environment. In addition, the formation of structure and execution of activities are not chaotic or randomly carried out. Instead, the structure and the activities are deliberately structured to achieve its goal.

The *structure* defines how the organisation is composed, that is, what units it consist of and the relationships or the connections between these units. The activities or tasks of the organisation are organised as *processes*. For example, a hospital is a human organisation formed with the goal of treating patients. The hospital organisation consists of a well-defined structure of roles (e.g., doctor, nurse, and patient) and the relationships among these roles (e.g., doctor−nurse, nurse−patient). The roles are filled with role players such as patients who expect treatments and qualified doctors and nurses who recommend and provide treatments. The organisation defines the mutual obligations and allows interactions among these roles. In addition, processes define how the activities such as patient identification, consultation, specimen collection, issuing medicine, conducting tests and treatment are carried out. Potentially, multiple processes can be realised over the same well-defined organisational structure. In the case of a hospital, there are many ways to treat patients. Subsequently, multiple processes are defined to treat inpatients, to treat outpatients and to conduct maternity clinics.

Similarly, in a service orchestration, services collaborate with each other to attain a business goal. For example, in the RoSAS scenario introduced in Chapter 2, the service providers such as garages, tow trucks, taxis and case officers collaborate with each other to fulfil the goal of providing roadside assistance. RoSAS as the service aggregator needs to design both the structure and processes, leading to the achievement of its goal. Potentially, multiple processes need to be defined to meet the diverse requirements of the different consumers of RoSAS, building upon the same set of aggregated services to maximise reuse and to deliver organisational efficiency.

In pursuing its goals, the organisation has to ensure its survival in the presence of the changes in its environments by adapting to these changes suitably. For instance, a hospital organisation may adapt its processes and structure to changes such as high demand for treatments, advances in the techniques of treatments, unexpected epidemic conditions, industrial actions or riots. To maintain an uninterrupted and sufficient service (the goal) amidst such changing conditions, the organisation needs to *reconfigure and regulate its structure and processes* (adaptation). For example, the hospital may temporarily skip certain procedures that slow the intake of patients, allocate more staff or update the responsibilities of existing staff so that it is possible to treat more patients.

Similarly, a service orchestration also needs the adaptability to survive in its changing environment. The business requirements of RoSAS can vary over time. The service−service interactions and the performance and compliance levels are subject to continuous and unforeseen changes. New service providers such as garages with better quality of service (QoS) emerge, while existing service providers disappear [5]. The customers expect better *roadside assistance* services and perhaps have some unpredictable variations in expectations from RoSAS. Business competitors may emerge, forcing RoSAS to optimise its structure and processes continuously to provide a better service in a cost-effective manner.

Due to these similarities in the characteristics of organisations and service orchestrations, we model a service orchestration as an *adaptable organisation* that can adapt both its structure and processes to suit changing environments [81, 227]. The next two sections clarify these two aspects of an organisation, that is, the structure and the processes, in detail.

4.1.1 Structure

The current service composition methodologies are mostly process driven. Generally, a set of services are invoked according to a process. While processes are important in composing services, the structure also plays a significant role, providing the stability to define and execute the processes. A close inspection of current standards for service orchestration revealed that little attention has been given to representing the mutual relationships among services in collaboration. In terms of the roles and their relationships, the organisational structure provides an abstraction of the underlying services in collaboration. While the underlying service providers appear and disappear, from the aggregator's point of view, the goals expected by the act of composing services need to be preserved. This provides the stability and abstraction in contrast to the grounding of processes directly on concrete services. By grounding processes on a well-defined structure, which provides the stability and abstraction, the processes become more resilient to the turbulences or changes in the underlying concrete services layer.

It should be noted that the *organisation structure* should not be confused with the *process structures* as described in popular service orchestration standards. For example, XLANG [228] and WS-BPEL [104] use a block-structured [136] way of defining service orchestration. WSFL [36] and XPDL [35, 105] have a flow structure. All these structures are process-based structures that explain how the activities are ordered or structured. They do not provide sufficient detail on how the underlying services are organised and related to each other. In contrast to process structures, the organisation structure captures the aspects of how a service relates to another, what is allowed and not allowed in terms of interactions and what are the mutual obligations among the services.

Although these organisation-based service orchestrations may sound like the *service choreography*, there is a difference between the *organisational structure* and the *service choreography*. They address two completely different concerns. To elaborate, let us consider WS-CDL [229] which is a popular standard that captures the choreography among services. It allows the definition of the global view of how the collaborative processes involving multiple services such that the interactions between these services are seen from a global perspective [24]. This viewpoint is still a single projection of individual orchestrations of collaborating services. However, the purpose of the *organisational structure* in this book is *not* to project the interactions of individual services or to provide the observable behaviours of a set of services. In contrast, the organisational structure provides the stability and abstraction over the underlying services by explicitly capturing and representing the structural aspects (i.e., *roles and their relationships*) expected of the underlying services, rather than the process *or coordination* aspects. In this sense, service choreography addresses a process level concern, whereas the organisational structure addresses the structure level concerns of a service composition.

The key difference between the process structure and the organisation structure and their usage is illustrated in Figure 4.1. As shown, these structures are

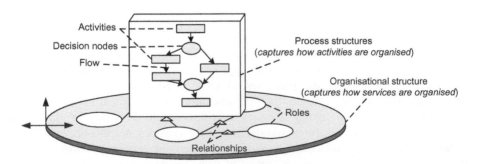

Figure 4.1 Process structure and organisational structure.

orthogonal to each other and serve different purposes. While process structures capture how the activities are organised or the activity relationships, the organisational structure captures how the roles of an organisation are organised or the role—role relationships. The fundamental purposes of the organisational structure are to provide the *abstraction* and *stability* for the organisation or service collaboration. The abstraction represents the underlying services and their relationships, and underpins the modelling of the business processes. The stability afforded by the organisational structure makes the business processes (defined on top of the organisation structure) less vulnerable to the turbulence of the underlying services.

In an organisation structure, a *role* is a position description within the organisation. For example, in a human organisation such as a hospital, the 'doctor' is a role that is obliged to treat patients on behalf of the hospital. In essence, a role represents a functional requirement of the organisation that need to be fulfilled. The actual entities that occupy or play these roles called *role players* may change during the organisation's operation. But the role that represents the requirements and the organisation that represents the goals remain unchanged irrespective of the presence/absence of a particular role player.

Similarly, within a service composition there are positions to be filled or functional requirements that need to be fulfilled. In the RoSAS service composition, for example, any user complaints/requests need to be accepted and then processed; vehicles need to be towed and then repaired; and motorists may need alternative transportations to continue their journey or perhaps some accommodation to stay overnight. For these functional requirements, the corresponding roles need to be created such as case officer, motorist, tow truck, garage, taxi providers and hotels. The players of these roles can be bound/unbound during the runtime, but the roles representing the functional requirements continue to exist. For example, the role of garage may be played by a Web service provided by a garage chain *Tom's Repair*, which accepts car repair bookings. However, if the service is unsatisfactory, this can be replaced by another Web service offered by another garage chain *BetterRepairs*.

A set of roles themselves cannot describe an *organisation structure*. In fact, a role itself cannot explain the purpose of its existence in the organisation. There are *relationships* among the roles that describe how roles connect with each other in the organisation, defining their purpose of existence. These connections capture the mutual obligations among different roles and the allowed interactions between roles. The organisation description should capture these relationships. The relationships that a role maintains with the rest of the roles in the organisation collectively define or describe the role itself. For example, the allowed interactions and obligations between the roles *doctor and patient* and between *patient and nurse* are clearly described within the hospital organisation. Most importantly, the role of *doctor* is defined by its obligations and interactions with other roles, i.e., *with nurse* and *with patient*. The role of *doctor* cannot exist alone.

Likewise, there are relationships among the roles of a service composition as well. For example, there is an obligation that a motorist informs the case officer of a breakdown, an obligation that the case officer notifies the tow truck of the towing requirement, an obligation that a garage tells the tow truck the towing destination, etc. These interactions are carried out during the runtime as defined by the service aggregator. Given the requirement of roles R_i and R_j to interact, the aggregator explicitly specifies the terms of interactions in the $R_i–R_j$ relationship, treating them as first-class entities.

Role-oriented adaptive design (ROAD) [81] introduces such an organisation structure to define self-managed software composites. In this book, we use ROAD and further extend it to provide a process definition language to define adaptable service orchestrations. ROAD defines *roles* or positions of a composite. *Players* (software entities or humans) can come and play these roles [81]. The key characteristic of ROAD relating to this work is its *contract-oriented view* of a service composite. A ROAD composite defines the *contacts* or connections between different roles played by services that form the composition. The meta-model in Figure 4.2 presents these key concepts as an organisation-based ROAD composite.

For example, the contract between the garage (GR) and tow truck (TT) is captured via the GR_TT contract as shown in Figure 4.3. The GR_TT contract defines the mutual obligations between the roles irrespective of who plays the roles of GR and TT. The players, i.e., Web services provided by *Tom's Repair* (garage chain) and *Fast-Tow* (towing provider) may play the roles GR and TT, respectively, by interacting with each other according to and through the *interactions* defined in the contracts. These interactions are evaluated according to the current state and the defined rules of the contract. The current state of the contract is captured by a

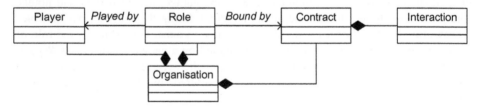

Figure 4.2 Meta-model: organisation, contracts, roles and players.

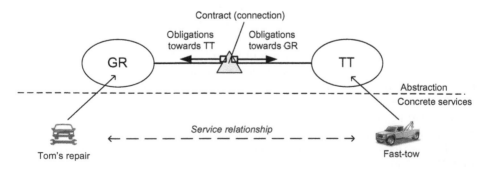

Figure 4.3 A contract captures the relationship among two roles.

number of facts (parameters) maintained by the contract. Rules may use these facts to evaluate the interactions as well as update them due to ongoing interactions. The corresponding meta-model is shown in Figure 4.4.

ROAD supports reconfiguration and regulation of the organisational composite to maintain a homeostatic relationship with its environment [48]. As such, the contracts and the roles can be added, modified and removed depending on the changing environments.

Figure 4.5 shows graphically how the RoSAS structure is modelled according to ROAD [81]. The structure consists of roles and the identified contracts between them. The identified roles are case officer (CO), tow truck (TT), garage (GR), motorist (MM) and taxi (TX). These roles will be played by the services such as Web services provided by garage chains and Web services deployed in motorists' mobiles, etc. The identified contracts are CO_MM, GR_TT, CO_GR, CO_TT and CO_TX. An existence of a contract between two roles indicates that these two roles need to interact with each other. For example, the CO_TT contract indicates that the CO and TT roles (and their role players) need to interact with each other. The corresponding description of RoSAS is given in Listing 4.1 in the form of the SerendipLang. SerendipLang (see Appendix A) is designed and used in this book to support the Serendip meta-model and present the examples. The RoSAS description lists all the roles and contracts, and specifies the specific players (service endpoints) bound to roles.

A contract specifies the terms of interactions (interaction terms) between the players concerned. These interaction terms define the mutual responsibilities of two roles bound by the contract. The players of these two roles can interact with each

Figure 4.4 Meta-model: contracts, facts and rules.

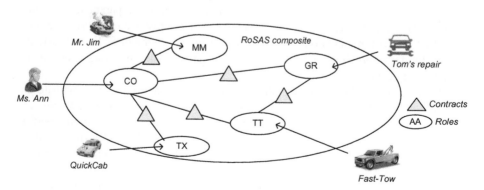

Figure 4.5 Roles and contracts of the RoSAS composite.

```
Organisation RoSAS {
    Role CO{…}
    Role MM{…}
    Role TT{…}
    Role GR{…}
    Role TX{…}

    Contract CO_TT {… }
    Contract GR_TT {… }
    Contract CO_TX {… }
    Contract CO_MM {… }
    Contract CO_GR {… }

    PlayerBinding copb "http://www.rosas.com.../CaseOfficerService" is a CO;
    PlayerBinding ttpb "http://www.fasttow.com.../TowCarService" is a TT;
    PlayerBinding grpb "http://www.tomsrepair.com.../GarageService" is a GR;
    PlayerBinding txpb "http://www.quickcab.com.../TaxiService" is a TX;
}
```

Listing 4.1 High-level RoSAS description in SerendipLang.

```
Contract CO_TT{
    A is CO, B is TT;
    ITerm orderTow (String:pickupInfo) withResponse (String:ackTowing)from AtoB;
    ITerm payTow (String:paymentInfo) from AtoB;
    RuleFile "CO_TT.drl";
}
```

Listing 4.2 A sample contract.

other, only according to these interaction terms. An interaction term captures the direction of interaction, synchronicity and the message signature.

A sample contract is shown in Listing 4.2. The contract CO_TT specifies the connection between the roles CO and TT. It specifies two interaction terms (ITerm). The direction of the interaction *orderTow* is from CO to TT (as indicated by AtoB, *where* A is CO and B is TT), meaning the CO has to initiate the interaction. It also describes the signature of messages in terms of parameters (*String: pickupInfo*) and return types (*String: ackTowing*). The presence of return type indicates that the communication is a *request−response* interaction. In contrast, the interaction term *payTow* does not specify a return type, meaning there is no response expected.

Both the roles and the contracts that capture the interactions of a composite are runtime entities. To evaluate and monitor these interactions, contractual rules are used. These rules, declarative in nature, are used to monitor and evaluate the performance of interactions and possible violations of contracts. The rules (indicated by the clause Rule File) associated with the CO_TT contract may enforce certain conditions to ensure the interactions are valid. For example, a rule to evaluate the payTow may check whether the payment exceeds a certain unusually large amount to prevent suspicious payments.

Contracts in the organisation capture an explicit connection between two services. The requirement for such explicit connections among components is highlighted in the literature [230–234]. For example, Confract [233, 235] is a framework to build hierarchical software components. The authors highlighted the importance of interface and composition contracts. In order to ensure the conformance among off-the-shelf software components, a contract-based service composition theory was proposed by Bernardi et al. [234]. This requirement also exists in service orchestration. A service orchestration solution should not be treated as a mere collection of services wired together in terms of a process structure/flow. The relationships among the services in terms of responsibilities, permissions and obligations need to be properly represented. The processes need to be grounded upon such a well-described structure that represents the service relationships. Otherwise, the runtime adaptations can be error prone, leading to noncompliant processes. Furthermore, the runtime interactions may be detrimental to meeting the goals as expected by the service aggregator. Therefore, it is important that a service orchestration approach treats these service relationships as first-class entities.

While ROAD provides a system theoretic approach to defining an adaptable organisational structure, there is a lack of process support to coordinate the activities within the organisation. Business process support is significant for an organisation to function and achieve its business goals in an efficient manner. In particular, if ROAD concepts are to be applied in a service orchestration context, support for business process modelling and enactment is crucial. Therefore, in this book we further extend ROAD to allow the definition of business processes over the adaptable organisational structure.

4.1.2 Processes

Processes represent a way to achieve a business goal. In a service composition, business goals are defined by the aggregator mainly relative to the demands of its service consumers. For example, RoSAS defines business processes to efficiently provide roadside assistance relative to the demands of its customers. Furthermore, such processes are used to coordinate the offerings of service providers. For example, towing, repairing, taxi-ing and case handling need to be coordinated using business processes.

These business processes need to be adaptable to cater for runtime error handling, optimisation and change requirements. In a service-oriented environment where a service execution is distributed and autonomous, the adaptability is a must for the survival of the aggregator's business. The adaptability needs be improved by carefully designing the service orchestration. The specific properties of service-oriented computing (SOC), such as the autonomy of collaborating services and the loose coupling between services, need to be reflected in the process support.

To make the proposed approach suitable for modern uses of service orchestration, the challenges mentioned in Chapter 2 need to be addressed in defining processes. For example, SaaS requires the support for native multi-tenancy, where a single application instance has to serve multiple tenants [45, 47, 89]. The idea of grounding processes upon an organisational structure is complementary to these requirements. The common basis provided by the organisational structure can be used to define multiple and varying business processes at runtime to meet the varied requirements of different consumer groups. Apart from the adaptability of processes, the structure of the composition is also subject to change. Therefore, the adaptability provided by the organisational structure is also equally important. In addition, the modularity provided by the explicit representation of service relationships allows the complete set of service interactions of a service orchestration to be broken down into smaller manageable units (Section 4.8.3). Such a modular specification limits the complexity that can be potentially introduced by the many runtime modifications to business processes.

This book introduces several new constructs to the ROAD meta-model [81] to provide process support. These new constructs are added with two main objectives:

1. To make the ROAD organisational structure better-suited to defining adaptable service orchestrations. Consequently, the necessary refinements to the existing ROAD meta-model have been made.
2. To provide process support and address the requirements of service orchestration. Consequently, new concepts and methodologies for service orchestration modelling and enactment have been introduced.

We identify multiple layers of a service orchestration's design, as shown in Figure 4.6. The top three layers, i.e., process, behaviour and Task, are the new additions while the bottom three layers, i.e., contracts, roles and players, already exist in the existing ROAD framework and are used with refinements in this work to make them better support the top three layers.

Starting from the bottom, the *players layer* represents a set of concrete services that are ready to participate in the business collaboration. For example, this includes

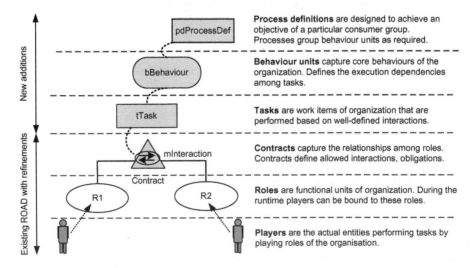

Figure 4.6 Layers of a Serendip orchestration design.

the Web services provided by garage and tow truck chains, and Web service client applications installed on motorists' mobile phones or the car's on-board emergency alert system. The *roles layer* captures the roles of the organisation that need to be filled during the runtime by the aforementioned players. On top of the roles layer, the relationships among roles are captured via the *contracts layer*. The contracts layer and roles layer together form the organisational structure as discussed. A contract between two roles defines the interactions and mutual obligations. The *task layer* is grounded upon these interactions defined in contracts. A task captures an outsourced activity that should be performed by a role player. Necessary messages/data resulting from contractual interactions are used to perform tasks. Furthermore, task executions can result in more contractual interactions. The coordination or the ordering among tasks is specified in the behaviour layer, which defines units of behaviour (i.e., *behaviour units*) in the organisation. The behaviour layer captures the common behaviours as behaviour units and defines them in a reusable manner. The *process layer* shares and reuses these behaviour units to define multiple business processes to achieve different business goals or to address the different requirements of customer groups.

In the following sections, we describe these layers in detail in terms of the underlying concepts, i.e., loosely coupled tasks, behaviour-based processes, two-tier constraints and interaction membrane. Understanding these concepts is fundamental to comprehend the Serendip service orchestration.

4.2 Loosely coupled tasks

In an organisation, tasks are defined in roles. A task is a description of an atomic activity that should be performed on behalf of the organisation. One or more tasks could be defined in a role. If bound to the organisation, a role player is obliged to perform the tasks defined in its corresponding role. Therefore, the task is defined by the organisation and yet the execution is always external to the organisation.[1] This relationship between the role, player and task is captured by the meta-model presented in Figure 4.7. Example roles and tasks of the case study are the case officer *analysing roadside service assistance requests*, the tow truck performing the task *'tow'* and the garage performing the task *'repair'* and so on. Listing 4.3 shows the task definitions of the role CO (case officer). Any player bound to the role CO

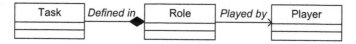

Figure 4.7 Meta-model: tasks, roles and players.

---

[1]Here the organisation refers to the composite, rather than to a *business organisation*. A *business organisation* may have internal services (players) deployed to play the roles of a composite. But from the composite (i.e., the organisation) point of view these players and their executions are external.

```
Role CO is a 'Case Officer' playedBy copb{
    Task tAnalyze{ … }//To analyse the assistance requests
    Task  tPayGR { … }//To pay the garage
    Task  tPayTT { … }//To pay the tow-truck
}
```

Listing 4.3 Task definitions of role case officer.

should be able to perform all these tasks shown.[2] The clause *playedBy* refers to an identifier of the player binding of a case officer player as shown in Listing 4.1.

4.2.1 Task dependencies

The processes in an organisation coordinate the execution of tasks. This coordination is required to enforce the *dependencies among tasks* and to determine the sequence of task executions. For example, the *tPayTT* task may not be initiated until the *tTow* task is complete. Therefore, the *tPayTT* and *tTow* tasks exhibit dependencies as required by RoSAS business.

Most of the existing orchestration approaches overspecify task dependencies, resulting in *tightly coupled* tasks in a business process [73]. For example, in WS-BPEL, the task/activity ordering is block structured. Tasks are directly related to each other and lead to static and brittle service composites [106]. Such tightly coupled rigid structures can cause unnecessary restrictions if the task dependencies are to be modified during the runtime, especially for already running process instances. Software engineers have to deal with the tight couplings among tasks to introduce new dependencies and to modify the existing dependencies. It should be noted that SOA is inherently a loosely coupled architecture [41]. The distributed software systems or services that perform these tasks are connected to each other in a loosely coupled manner. In this context, the tightly coupled task dependencies in a service orchestration prevent deliver of the true benefits of such loosely coupled architecture.

The tasks are executed by the concrete services (role players). Sufficient dependencies need to be captured among these execution steps. For example, the two tasks *tTow* and *tPayTT* should be carried out by tow truck and case officer, respectively. In this example, what prevents the task *tPayTT* from being carried out is the fact that towing has not been done. When this scenario is realised with imperative languages such as WS-BPEL, the two tasks *tPayTT* and *tTow* are placed in a sequence where *tPayTT* succeeds *tTow* as shown in Figure 4.8A. This seems to be correct as *tPayTT* should not be initiated before *tTow* is carried out. Nevertheless, such direct task linkage creates tight coupling between the two tasks during the execution. Such tight coupling can unnecessarily restrict runtime modifications that require task dependency changes. For example, an *ad hoc* deviation of a process

---

[2]A player may be another service composite that decomposes the tasks among multiple roles. See Section 4.8.1 for more information.

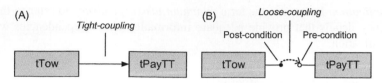

Figure 4.8 The loose coupling between tasks.

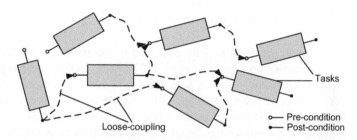

Figure 4.9 Complex dependencies among tasks.

may require that *tPayTT* is carried out due to a special order from the case officer rather than strictly after the execution of task *tTow*.

In fact, what holds back the execution of the *tPayTT* task is the nonfulfilment of its *pre-conditions*. In this case, the knowledge that the *towing has been successfully done* is the pre-condition that needs to be fulfilled in order to execute the task *tPayTT*, *not* the completion of task *tTow*. The *pre-conditions of task tPayTT* and *completion of task tTow* are two separate things and the process modelling approach should not force such misinterpretations. The practice of tight coupling among tasks as exhibited in workflows and block-structured processes can lead to such misinterpretations.

As a solution, instead of having such a direct linkage, it is important to have an indirect linkage between the tasks as shown in Figure 4.8B. In this example, the post-condition of *tTow* may act as the pre-condition of *tPayTT*. Alternatively, a post-condition of a different task may trigger the required pre-condition initiating the *tPayTT*. For example, a bonus payment could be made without requiring a *tTow* activity at all. Pre-condition of a task is a property of task itself. Consequently, *tPayTT* has the flexibility of continuously adapt its pre-conditions locally.

What's more, the task dependencies in a service orchestration are *not* always simple. There can be complex dependencies as depicted by Figure 4.9. The imperative approaches have used gateways or decision points [15, 236] to formulate these complex dependencies to support various workflow patterns [16, 29]. However, again, such *connectors* are also directly linked to the tasks. A runtime modification to those connectors can also become tedious. Obviously, orchestration modelling should *adequately* express these complex dependencies, but without *overspecification.* Let us use the term *minimum task dependency* to refer to the task dependency details that provide adequate information about dependencies without overspecification.

4.2.2   Events and event patterns

In order to capture the *minimum task dependency* to avoid the rigidity, and also to capture the complex task dependencies, we use *event patterns* to specify the pre- and post-conditions of tasks. An event here is a passive element [28], which is triggered as a result of the execution of a task. This makes the event a *soft-link* between tasks.

Usefulness of events has been heavily explored in the past, varying from database systems to enterprise application design [237–246]. Hence, the usage of the concept of *event* is well-understood. A task may be dynamically subscribed to an *event* or a *pattern of events.* Furthermore, tasks can be unsubscribed from events during the runtime. The post-conditions of a task may be dynamically modified to generate new events or to remove unwanted events. The manner in which the tasks are executed, such as quality of execution and timeliness, may decide the patterns of events that are triggered. For example, a successful completion of a towing task may lead to triggering the event *eTowSuccess*, whereas a failure may lead to triggering the event *eTowFailed.*

Tasks can be seen as both *subscribers* and *publishers* of events. Tasks are subscribers because they listen to events. Tasks are publishers because they trigger events upon the task execution. For example, the pre-event pattern of task *tTow* is (*eTowReqd * eDestinationKnown*).[3,4] This means the triggering of events *eTowReqd* and *eDestinationKnown* will lead to the execution of task *tTow* as defined in role TT. Similarly, the post-events can also be specified as an event pattern. For example, *tTow* has the post-event pattern (*eTowSuccess ^ eTowFailed*), which specifies that the execution of task *tTow* leads to triggering of either the *eTowSuccess* or the *eTowFailed* events. The dependencies of task *tTow* defined in role CO are specified according to the Serendip Language *SerendipLang* (see Appendix A) as shown in Listing 4.4.

```
TaskRef TT.tTow {
  InitOn "eTowReqd * eDestinationKnown";
  Triggers "eTowSuccess ^ eTowFailed";
}
```

Listing 4.4 Task tTow of role TT.

---

[3]As a naming convention, the prefixes *e, m, t, b* and *p* will be used for events, messages, tasks, behaviour units and process definitions, respectively.

[4]Event patterns use notations with following meanings:

  * = AND

  | = OR

  ^ = XOR

Another task such as *tPayTT* (to make a payment to Tow truck) can subscribe to event *eTowSuccess*. In other words, the initiating dependency is specified via the event *eTowSuccess*. The description for *tPayTT* is given in Listing 4.5. It shows that actual dependency for carrying out the payment is the knowledge that *towing is now successfully completed*. This knowledge is represented within the composition by *eTowSuccess* triggered by *tTow* task. Note that this knowledge can also originate from another task (if that is the business requirement). For example, the *eTowSuccess* event can be triggered due to a task execution by garage when the car is towed to the garage. Irrespective of the source, the events represent certain knowledge acquired by the organisation. It is the knowledge available to the organisation that initiates further execution of tasks. In this sense, events are independent from the *tasks that trigger* them and *tasks that refer to* them as illustrated by Figure 4.10. The events are related to tasks via the pre- and post-conditions specified in tasks as shown in the meta-model presented in Figure 4.11.

It is important to note that in this work, the concept of *the event* has been used with two important properties, i.e., events are both *publisher independent* and *subscriber independent*.

1. *Publisher independent*: An event represents knowledge or a fact irrespective of the source, e.g., the knowledge 'car towing is successful' denoted by *eTowSuccess* is independent from which task triggers that event.

```
TaskRef CO.tPayTT {
    InitOn "eTowSuccess";
    Triggers "eTTPaid";
}
```

Listing 4.5 Task tPayTT of role CO.

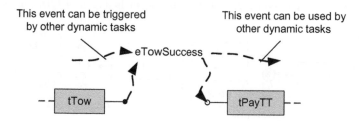

Figure 4.10 Events independent of where they originated and referenced.

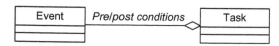

Figure 4.11 Meta-model: events and tasks.

2. *Subscriber independent*: An event is not intended for a particular subscriber. It could be subscribed by any interested entity, e.g., event *eTowSuccess* is not published for the task *tPayTT*. Any task can subscribe to this event by specifying the event as part of its pre-conditions.

4.2.3   Support for dynamic modifications

The *publisher-independent* and *subscriber-independent* usage of events improves the loose coupling nature of tasks. Such event-based loose coupling brings the following main advantages for process instance level adaptations.

1. *Dynamic task insertion/deletion*: New tasks can be dynamically inserted and subscribed to existing events as shown in Figure 4.12A. This is an advantage as there is no necessary requirement to modify the existing tasks. Only the new task needs to specify its event pattern to which it subscribes. Such agility is important for runtime modifications. For example, RoSAS might insert a new task *tNofityTowFailureToCustomer*, which will subscribe to event *eTowFailed* to handle the exception and send a notification to the member. In addition, there can be many other exception handling tasks that can simultaneously subscribe to the same event *eTowFailed*. On the other hand, when not required, task subscriptions can be removed and tasks can be deleted without much effect on the rest of the system as shown in Figure 4.12B. If *tNofityFailureToCustomer* is no longer required, for example, then the task along with its subscription can be deleted on the fly.
2. *Dynamic event insertion/deletion*: Events can be dynamically included in pre-/post-event patterns of existing tasks as shown in Figure 4.12C. New events are usually included when the existing events are *semantically insufficient* to initiate the task execution. For example, upon completion of task *tPayTT*, the event *eTTPaid* is triggered to mark the fact that the tow truck service has been paid. Suppose that if the task (*tRecordCreditPay*) needs to be initiated *only when* the payment has been made using credit, subscribing to an existing event *eTTPaid* is not *semantically enough* to initiate *tRecordCreditPay*. Thus, it is required that a new event *eTTPaidByCredit* to be inserted to the existing post-event pattern of the task *tPayTT*, which is only triggered when the payment is made using credit. Furthermore, existing and obsolete events can be deleted by modifying the pre-/post-event patterns as shown in Figure 4.12D. For instance, if

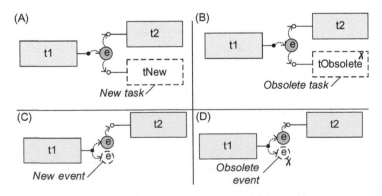

Figure 4.12 Advantages of loose coupling.

credit-based payments are no longer supported, then the event *eTTPaidByCredit* can be removed (at runtime) from the post-event pattern of the task *tPayTT*.

Naturally, there should be a proper support from the execution engine/runtime to carry out such alterations on the already running instances (see Chapter 5). However, apart from the runtime capabilities, the modelling language should provide ready support for such modifications by allowing loose coupling among tasks. The process modelling should not unnecessarily impose rigidity. As shown, the loose coupling achieved by having events as soft-links among tasks avoids such rigidity.

The *soft-linking* via pattern of events also helps to limit the number of tasks that are modified upon a change requirement. This is important especially for carrying out the modifications on running process instances, where the states of the tasks determine the legitimacy of modification. Understandably, modifying an already completed task is meaningless. Tasks that are already under execution may allow modifications depending on the properties that are modified (Section 6.5). However, it is possible to modify a future task or post-conditions of tasks that are still under execution in a process instance. Therefore, if the number of tasks that need to be altered is high for a given change (due to limitations of the language such as a direct linkage among tasks), then there is a higher probability that the change becomes invalid due to the involvement of an already completed task or a task under execution. Such inability to carrying out possible modifications would hinder the flexibility and thereby the business agility. The publisher-independent and subscriber-independent properties of events help to avoid a direct linkage among tasks and isolate the modifications as much as possible.

To elaborate, consider the scenario in which a new task *tNofityTowFailureToCustomer* needs to be dynamically inserted into a running process instance to handle an exception. This task shows a dependency with the existing task *tTow*. Suppose that *tTow* is already under execution or completed for this process instance. Due to the use of events as soft-links and the publisher-independent nature of events, the new task *tNofityTowFailureToCustomer* can be dynamically inserted without requiring any modifications to *tTow*. All that needs to be done is to let the task *tNofityTowFailureToCustomer* subscribe to the event *eTowFailed*, which is both publisher independent and subscriber independent. On the contrary, if these two tasks are directly linked, then it might be required to modify the *tTow* to specify *what the next possible task is*, which could be problematic as *tTow* is already complete or is being completed.

In conclusion, the loosely coupled tasks have improved the amount of flexibility that is required for modifying the running process instances. The loose coupling has been achieved by using the events as soft-links between tasks. The publisher-independent and subscriber-independent nature of events has made dynamic insertion/deletion of tasks and events possible at the process instance level. In Serendip, the flexibility offered by such loosely coupled tasks is used to describe adaptable organisational behaviours. The Serendip processes are, in turn, defined using these adaptable behaviours.

4.3 Behaviour-based processes

Service aggregators generate value by bringing the service providers and consumers closer, creating a service ecosystem [5]. While the service providers and consumers benefit from such a service ecosystem, an aggregator tries to increase its revenue through various custodianships. Aggregators need to address the varying requirements of different service consumer groups to exploit new business opportunities and thereby increase its revenue. Given the existence of an already aggregated composition of services, the aggregator always attempts to maximise the profit by increasing the reuse of its system, including the partner services. For example, the roadside assistance can be delivered as multiple packages by including different features using the same service composition of services as mentioned in Chapter 2.

Modular programming is a concept whereby a complete code is segregated into discrete units or modules, each of which maintains a responsibility for specific functions [247]. One of the main purposes of providing modularity is to improve code reuse. The current service orchestration approaches provide little support for increased reuse [248]. Usually a process is defined by wiring the available services to suit the business requirements of a customer or customer group. Redefining separate service orchestrations ground-up to suit the requirements of different consumer groups can be time-consuming and costly. Such inefficiencies may negatively impact on the prospect of quickly exploiting the market opportunity, which may appear and disappear in a short period of time. The reduced time-to-market is important in online marketplaces. Hence, the ability to reuse the existing services as well as already proven service orchestrations can increase the business agility [249].

Modularisation in service orchestration offers a better approach for increasing the reusability in service orchestration. Rather than specifying a lengthy and monolithic coordination, it is advisable to define small and reusable units of coordination. Later, larger and more meaningful and complete business processes can be constructed using such small units to address the demands of different service consumer groups.

This idea of modularisation has been explored in the past. Khalaf [250] attempts to create multiple fragments of a Business Process Execution Language (BPEL) process while maintaining the operational semantics. However, it does not actually promote the reuse of already proven service orchestration, rather it attempts to create several fragments. In contrast, Adams [146] attempt to improve the reuse of a fragmented process by defining a self-contained repertoire of subprocesses to handle exceptions in workflows via *Worklets*. A worklet is a self-contained (YAWL [103]) process fragment that will be selected and executed as a replacement for a particular *task* of a workflow. The worklets (process fragments) can be reused across multiple distinct *tasks* [143].

Although the use of process fragments is primarily for substituting selected tasks of a workflow, it makes an important contribution in terms of promoting process modularisation and reuse. Larger processes can be recursively defined from these process fragment units. Such an arrangement can provide the much required agility and abstraction for a service orchestration.

4.3.1 Organisational behaviour

In Serendip, a complete behaviour of the organisation is represented as a collection of relatively independent units called *behaviour units*. A behaviour unit provides modularity by grouping related tasks together. For example, towing, repairing and taxi ordering are behaviour units of the RoSAS organisation that can be reused to fulfil the demands of multiple consumer groups.

As shown in Listing 4.6, the behaviour *bTowing* consists of tasks tTow and tPayTow. The pre- and post-event patterns among these tasks can define their dependencies as described in Section 4.2. As many behaviour units as required can be defined on top of the organisation structure during design time and runtime.

The organisation acts as a repository for defining and maintaining a pool of such behaviour units that will be referenced or used by different business process definitions. These behaviour units define how the underlying service infrastructure should be coordinated. A business process is a collection of behaviour units tailored towards fulfilling a business goal of a consumer or a consumer group. These business goals may be formulated to satisfy the business requirements of a particular service consumer group within the aggregator's business model. For example, some users of RoSAS may prefer to have additional services such as taxi drop-offs, accommodation and paramedic services for an extra cost, whereas others may prefer to have basic towing and repairing services for a lower cost. Subsequently, depending on the requirements, behaviour units can be reused across multiple business processes.

This means that multiple business processes can be defined to achieve multiple business goals upon the same organisational structure as shown in Figure 4.13. This gives the opportunity to address the requirements of different consumer groups in both a timely and cost-effective manner, compared to a ground-up building of different service orchestrations. The following properties of a behaviour unit underlie the aforementioned advantages.

```
Behavior bTowing{
  TaskRef TT.tTow {
    InitOn "eTowReqd * eDestinationKnown";
    Triggers "eTowSuccess ^ eTowFailed";
  }
  TaskRef CO.tPayTT {
    InitOn "eTowSuccess";
    Triggers "eTTPaid";
  }
}
```

Listing 4.6 A sample behaviour description, bTowing.

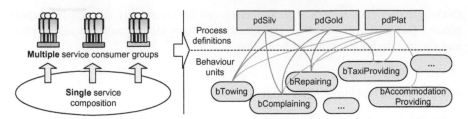

Figure 4.13 Organisational behaviours are reused across process definitions.

1. A behaviour unit defines an accepted organisational behaviour by grouping related tasks in a declarative manner. The tasks of a behaviour unit is executed without any direct and imperative ordering among them, but solely based on the satisfaction of their pre-conditions.
2. A behaviour unit is reusable. A single behaviour unit may be used across multiple process definitions.
3. A behaviour unit is self-contained and can express a well-identified behaviour of an orga-nisation independent of the processes that refer to it. The behaviour captures both the tasks (Section 4.2) and the constraints (Section 4.4) among them.

4.3.2 Process definitions

In Serendip, a *Process Definition* consists of a collection of references to existing behaviour units of the organisation. As mentioned, behaviour units are declarative and a collection of tasks, but they *do not have* the notion of start and end. Nevertheless, a process definition should have a start and end so that process instances can be initiated and terminated. Therefore, apart from a collection of references to behaviour units, a process definition should also specify the start and end conditions of the process. This is important for two reasons.

1. It gives the designer the ability to specify different start/end conditions for different pro-cess definitions, although they may share the same behaviour units.
2. The enactment engine can allocate and deallocate resources for process instances depend-ing on the fulfilment of these start and end conditions.

As shown in Listing 4.7, the sample process definition *pdGold* specifies the con-dition of start (CoS) and condition of termination (CoT), along with a number of references (BehaviorRef) to existing behaviour units. According to the definition, a new process will start when a complaint or request is received as indicated by the event *eComplainRcvdGold*. The process will continue as specified by the referenced behaviour units, *bComplaining*, *bTowing*, *bRepairing* and *bTaxiProviding*. The pro-cess will terminate when the member is notified of the completion of handling the case as indicated by the event *eMMNotifDone*.

Similarly, another process definition (Listing 4.8) can be defined sharing (some of) the existing behaviour units. However, if the defined behaviours are not

```
ProcessDefinition pdGold {
    CoS "eComplainRcvdGold";
    CoT "eMMNotifDone";
    BehaviourRef bComplaining;
    BehaviourRef bTowing;
    BehaviourRef bRepairing;
    BehaviourRef bTaxiProviding;
}
```

Listing 4.7 A sample process definition, pdGold.

```
ProcessDefinition pdPlat {
    CoS "ePlatComplainRcvdPlat";
    CoT "eMMNotifDone";
    BehaviorRef bComplaining;
    BehaviorRef bTowing;
    BehaviorRef bRepairing;
    BehaviorRef bTaxiProviding;
    BehaviorRef bAccommodationProviding;
}
```

Listing 4.8 A sample process definition, pdPlat.

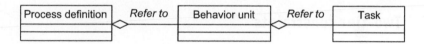

Figure 4.14 Meta-model: process definitions, behaviour units and tasks.

sufficient to achieve the goal, new behaviour units can be defined over the organisation and accordingly referenced by the new process definitions.

The relationship between process definition, behaviour unit and Task is captured in the meta-model shown in Figure 4.14. As shown, the behaviour unit captures a unit of organisational behaviour by collecting a set of related tasks together. Process definitions refer and reuse a set of behaviour units to achieve a specific goal.

In summary, behaviour-based process modelling provides the following advantages.

1. *Abstraction*: Behaviour units provide an *abstraction* of underlying task complexities. A behaviour unit may encapsulate a single or a number of tasks and the dependencies among them. Such an abstraction is important for adapting high-level business requirements as a feature-based customisation of a service composition, where the behaviour unit corresponds to a feature. As such, features can be added or removed from certain process definitions depending on user requirements by adding and removing behaviour units.
2. *Capturing commonalities*: Processes defined upon the same application or service organisation can show many commonalities. Behaviour units facilitate the capture of these commonalities by allowing many process definitions to reuse or share a single behaviour unit.

3. *Agile modifications*: Process definitions reference behaviour units. To change a feature that appears in multiple process definitions, only a single behaviour unit needs to be modified, instead of updating the multiple process definitions repetitively. For example, if the towing protocol needs to be patched, there is no need to repeatedly modify an array of business process definitions that use towing. An update in the behaviour unit *bTowing* would automatically be available for all the referenced process definitions.

Nevertheless, it should be noted there are also some associated drawbacks with behaviour reuse and sharing. For example, suppose the aggregator patches/modifies a particular behaviour unit to facilitate a business requirement of a particular process definition. Because the same behaviour is reused in different process definitions, such an upgrade or patching might potentially harm the objectives of other sharing process definitions. This could challenge the integrity of the service composition and thereby the business. In addition, certain changes might be specific to a particular process definition (for a particular consumer group). Because the same behaviour unit is reused, such specific changes might not be possible. Therefore, despite the benefits, the reuse of behaviours has some inherent drawbacks. In next two sections (i.e., Sections 4.4 and 4.5), we discuss the solutions to these drawbacks of behaviour reuse.

4.4   Two-tier constraints

A service orchestration is a coherent environment in which the service consumers and service providers as business entities achieve their respective goals via their integration by a service aggregator. However, changes are inevitable. Therefore, during the runtime, the organisational behaviours, as described by behaviour units in Serendip, need to be altered to facilitate various change requirements. Irrespective of the source, the runtime changes need to be carried out both in the process definition level and in the process instance level [77, 251]. It is a challenge for a service orchestration to maintain its integrity amidst such changes. Therefore, it is important that the process modelling approach provides suitable measures to ensure that the changes are carried out within a safe boundary.

In this section, we discuss the importance of such a boundary for a safe modification and how to define one without unnecessarily restricting the possible modifications.

4.4.1   *The boundary for a safe modification*

A clearly defined boundary for safe modification not only safeguards the integrity of the organisation or composition but also helps to increase the confidence level when applying changes. Such confidence allows a service aggregator to further optimise the business processes without being held back by the possibility of possible violations of business constraints. In a service composition, optimisations need to be carried out to satisfy the business requirements of the service consumers and service providers.

For example, some service consumers may need faster and rapid completion of towing, repairing and other assistances. Certain assistance processes might need to deviate from the originally specified time period depending on the severity of the accident and the unforeseen customer requirements. Fulfilling such requirements can increase the reputation of RoSAS as the service aggregator. Inability to cater for the customer requirements may damage its reputation. However, the providers of bound services are also autonomous businesses and have their own limits in delivering services. Furthermore, the collaborations need to maintain certain temporal and causal dependencies between tasks. An adaptation from a service consumer point of view may lead to breaking certain dependencies, hindering the collaborations and impacting on the service delivery in the long run.

Similarly, an adaptation requested by one of the collaborating services might also impact on the customer goals. Thus, the service aggregator needs to support the adaptability in a careful manner. The *possible adaptations* need to be facilitated but *without compromising the integrity* of the composite from the perspectives of the consumers, partner services and aggregator. Consequently, the problem of supporting adaptations should be considered as one of finding a solution to meet customer demands within a safe boundary, as symbolised in Figure 4.15. Therefore, we define the boundary for safe modification in terms of 'a set of constraints formulated from the business requirements of the aggregator as well as the consumer and partner services of a service orchestration to avoid invalid modifications.'

The use of constraints in business process modelling has been extensively explored in the past. Condec [73, 150] is a constraint-based process modelling language that attempts to use constraints for business process modelling. In Condec, there is no specific flow of activities; instead, the activities are carried out as long as the execution adheres to the defined constraint model. The constraint model defines the constraints that should not be violated at a given time. This ensures the integrity while providing increased flexibility for the runtime execution. Regev et al. [76] also see the flexibility as the ability to change without losing the identity. The identity of a business is defined via a set of 'norms' and 'beliefs'. Here, a norm is a feature that remains relatively stable and a belief is a point of view from a particular observer [252].

We also agree that defining such constraints when modelling business processes is essential to ensure their integrity. However, this book moves a step further by

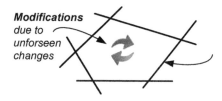

Figure 4.15 Boundary for safe modification.

$$CS_{global} = \left\{ \bigcup_{i=1}^{k} CS_{PDi} \right\} \bigcup \left\{ \bigcup_{j=1}^{m} CS_{Bj} \right\}$$

where

CS_{PDi} ($i = 1, 2, 3, \ldots, k$) is the set of constraints defined in the ith process definition PD_i.
CS_{Bj} ($j = 1, 2, 3, \ldots, m$) is the set of constraints defined in the jth behaviour unit B_j.

4.4.3   Benefits of two-tier constraints

To elaborate the benefits of having two-tier constraints, consider that six constraints (c1, c2, ..., c6) are defined within *the* scope of two process definitions (*pdGold* and *pdPlat*) and three behaviour units (*bRepairing*, *bTaxiProviding* and *bAccommodationProviding*), as shown in Figure 4.17. Assume there is a modification proposed to *pdGold* due to a change requirement in the gold service consumer group to change the way the taxi assistance is provided. Consequently, the behaviour unit *bTaxiProviding* needs to be modified. However, another process definition *pdPlat* also uses the behaviour unit *bTaxiProviding*.

Therefore, the change in the *pdGold* has an impact on the objectives of pdP*lat*. Consequently, the applicable *minimal set of constraints* that needs to be considered when identifying the impact of the modification include all the constraints defined in *bTaxiProviding*, *pdGold* and *pdPlat*. Therefore,

$CS_{msc} = \{c2, c5, c6\}$
$CS_{global} = \{c1, c2, c3, c4, c5, c6\}$

There is no requirement to consider the other constraints, i.e., c1, c3 and c4. Hence, such a scoping of constraints and the explicit linkage between process definitions and behaviour units avoid unnecessary restrictions and considerations in modifications in contrast to a global set of constraints. Only the applicable *minimal set of constraints* (CS_{csp}) is considered, which is always less or equal than the global set of constraints (CS_{global}).

The use of two-tier constraints also helps to identify the affected process definitions and behaviour units. This helps the change impact analysis processes. In this example, the process definitions *pdPlat* and *pdGold* and behaviour unit *bTaxiProviding* are affected. The other process definition *pdSilv* and the rest of the

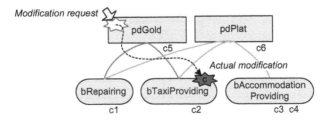

Figure 4.17 Process-collaboration linkage in constraint specification.

behaviour units are not affected. When violation happens as identified by impact analysis, a software engineer can pinpoint and perform corresponding actions only on the exact sections that are affected in a large service orchestration. Possible actions would be to discard the change or relax some constraints. Such a capability is possible due to the consideration of explicit linkage between the process definitions and behaviour units in the two-tier constraint validation process (see Section 6.4).

4.5   Behaviour specialisation

The concept of organisational behaviour modelling introduced in Section 4.3 can be used for capturing the commonalities among business processes that are defined upon the same service composition. Many processes can reuse the same behaviour unit to avoid redundancy of specification. It also helps to reduce the effort of ground-up modelling of new processes in addressing different consumer groups.

4.5.1   Variations in organisational behaviour

In general, we cannot assume that a defined behaviour unit can fully satisfy the expectations of all the consumer groups. The reality is that there are likely to be some slight variations in the expected organisational behaviours of a behaviour unit from different customers or customer groups. Furthermore, such variations can be unforeseen. Not reflecting these variations can make IT processes incorrect or insufficient in capturing real-world business processes. For example, although the towing behaviour is used across multiple processes, there can be some variations in the way the actual towing dependencies should be specified to cater to the requirements of different consumer groups. For platinum members (*pdPlat*), the *tTow* task may need to be delayed until the taxi picks up the motorist, whereas for silver members (*pdSilv*) there is no such dependency because they are not offered the taxi service (*bTaxiProviding*) at all (Figure 4.13). Introducing the event-dependency *eTaxiProvided* for *tTow* in a common behaviour unit *bTowing* can cause problems in executing a *pdSilv* process because there will *not* be any triggering of event *eTaxiProvided*. However, not introducing such a dependency might not capture the true dependencies as required by the process *pdPlat*.

One naive solution to this issue would be to model two separate behaviour units (*bTowingSilv*, *bTowingPlat*) targeting these two business processes. These two behaviour units duplicate all the tasks associated with the towing behaviour, but with *tTow* having different pre-conditions in the two behaviour units, as shown in Figure 4.18. The *bTowingPlat* specifies the pre-condition for *tTow* as '*eTowReqd* * *eDestinationKnown* * *eTaxiProvided*', whereas *bTowingSilv* specifies '*eTowReqd* * *eDestinationKnown*' as the pre-condition. Then, two process definitions *pdPlat* and *pdSilv* can refer to these separate respective behaviour units.

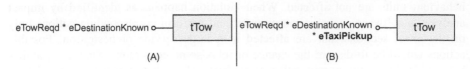

Figure 4.18 Variations in separate behaviour units: (A) bTowingSilv and (B) bTowingPlat.

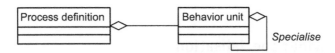

Figure 4.19 Meta-model: behaviour specialisation.

```
Behaviour bTowing2 extends bTowing {
   TaskRef TT.tTow  {
      InitOn "ePickupLocKnown * eDestinationKnown * eTaxiProvided"; //Overrides
   }
}
```

Listing 4.11 A specialised behaviour unit overriding a property of a task.

This solution, however, requires duplicating all the other tasks and dependencies in both behaviour units, even with a slight deviation of a pre-condition of a single task. Such duplication can hinder the efficiency of performing modifications. As such, both behaviour units would then need to be modified with a patch or an upgrade to the towing behaviour. Assuming that there are also such slight variations in the other processes such as *pdGold*, the number of duplicate behaviours can grow significantly each time a variation is required in a shared behaviour, hindering the ability of capturing commonalities. Therefore, an *improved solution* is required to avoid the unnecessary duplications while allowing such variations.

We further improve the behaviour-based process modelling (Section 4.3) with the *behaviour specialisation* feature, which can be used to support variations. The *behaviour specialisation* feature allows a behaviour unit (the *child*) to specialise another behaviour unit (the *parent*) by specifying the additional tasks or overriding existing properties of tasks. This addition to the meta-model is shown in Figure 4.19. This feature makes it possible to form a *behaviour hierarchy* within the organisation. The new behaviour is called a child of the already defined parent. Therefore, for the given example, the behaviour variation required by the *pdPlat* can be addressed by extending or specialising the behaviour unit *bTowing* as shown in Listing 4.11. Note that the InitOn property of the task *tTow* (of *child*) is respecified to override the parent's InitOn property. As the child, bTowing2 will inherit all the other nonspecified tasks and the properties from *bTowing*, the parent. The process definition, *pdPlat*, which requires this specialised version of towing, can

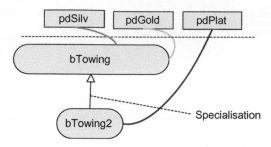

Figure 4.20 Process definitions can refer to specialised behaviour units.

```
Behavior btTowing3 extends bTowing {
  TaskRef CO.tAlertTowDone {
    InitOn "eTowSuccess";
    Triggers "eMemberTowAlerted";
  }
}
```

Listing 4.12 A specialised behaviour unit introducing a new task.

change its reference from *bTowing* to bTowing2 while the other process definitions (*pdSilv* and *pdGold*) can still refer to *bTowing* as shown in Figure 4.20.

Apart from overriding properties of tasks, new tasks can also be introduced. For example, if a gold member is required to be alerted when the towing is complete, then a new task *tAlertTowDone* can be introduced by specialising the behaviour unit as shown in Listing 4.12.

A behaviour unit can be either *concrete* or *abstract*. The aforementioned behaviour units are concrete units that fully specify their behaviour. In contrast, an abstract behaviour unit may not specify a complete behaviour due to lack of knowledge. Hence, abstract behaviour units cannot be directly referenced by a process definition. The purpose of abstract definitions is to act as a parent that can capture the commonalities among a set of variations expected by child behaviour units. For example, when a taxi is provided, a payment needs to be made. This payment can be made in various forms, e.g., using credit or debit. Assume that at the time of defining the behaviour unit, the payment protocol is unknown. The tasks such as placing a taxi order and providing a taxi are common to all behaviour units. However, a process definition should not refer to such a partially defined behaviour unit because the payment details are missing. In this case, it is best to define the common tasks in an *abstract parent* behaviour unit whilst the specialised payment procedures are specified in *child* behaviour units. Listing 4.13 shows a single abstract parent behaviour unit *bTaxiProviding* capturing the commonalities in taxi-provision while the two child behaviour units extend the parent to specify variations. Marking the parent behaviour unit *abstract* will prevent a process definition from referring to it.

```
//Parent behaviour unit is marked abstract, because how to perform the payment is unknown
abstract Behavior bTaxiProviding{
  TaskRef CO.tPlaceTaxiOrder {
    InitOn "eTaxiReqd";
    Triggers "eTaxiOrderPlaced";
  }
  TaskRef TX.tProvideTaxi {
    InitOn "eTaxiOrderPlaced";
    Triggers "eTaxiProvided";
  }
}
//Child behaviour unit, specialising the parent to specify how to perform credit-based payments
Behavior bTaxiProvidingCreditBased extends bTaxiProviding {
  //Payment is carried out after a credit check
  TaskRef CO.tCreditCheckForTaxiPay {
    InitOn "eTaxiProvided";
    Triggers "eTaxiCreditCheckSuccess ^eTaxiCreditCheckFailed":
  }
  TaskRef CO.tPayTaxi {
    InitOn " eTaxiCreditCheckSuccess ";
    Triggers "eTaxiPaid";
  }
  //Other tasks if any
}
//Child behaviour unit, specialising the parent to specify how to perform debit-based payments
BehaviorbTaxiProvidingDebitBased extends  bTaxiProviding {
  //Payment is carried out directly via debit
  TaskRef CO.tPayTaxi {
    InitOn " eTaxiProvided ";
    Triggers "eTaxiPaid";
  }
}
```

Listing 4.13 An abstract behaviour unit.

4.5.2 Specialisation rules

To ensure consistent and correct behaviour, behaviour specialisation needs to follow a set of rules. These rules are similar to the specialisation rules used in object-oriented programming [56−59], but are systematically applied to behaviour-based process modelling.

When a process definition *pdProcessDef* refers to a behaviour unit *bChild*, which specialises the behaviour unit *bParent* in a *behaviour hierarchy* as shown in Figure 4.21 a number of rules apply:

Rule 1. All tasks/constraints specified in *bParent* but not specified in *bChild* are *inherited* from *bParent*. All the tasks/constraints specified in *bChild* but not specified in *bParent* are recognised as newly specified *local* tasks/constraints of *bChild*. The inherited and locally specified tasks/constraints are treated the same way.

Rule 2. If there are tasks/constraints common to both *bChild* and *bParent*, then the common tasks/constraints of *bParent* are said to be overridden by those of *bChild*. The commonality is understood via the task/constraint identifier, i.e., if both *bChild* and *bParent* use the same identifier for the task/constraint, the parent's task/constraint is overridden by the child's.

Rule 3. When a task of a child (*bChild.tTask*) overrides a task of a parent (*bParent.tTask*):
   a. The attributes specified in Task *bParent.tTask* but not specified in *bChild.tTask* are inherited by *bChild tTask*.
   b. If there are attributes common to both *bChild.tTask* and *bParent.tTask*, then the attributes of *bChild.tTask* take precedence.

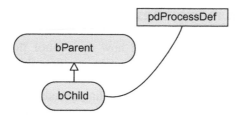

Figure 4.21 Rules of specialisation.

Rule 4. When a constraint of a child (*bChild.cCons*) overrides a constraint of a parent (*bParent.cCons*), the constraint expression of *bChild.cCons* takes precedence.

Rule 5. All the attributes of tasks of a concrete behaviour unit need to be fully defined (inherited or locally). If not, then the behaviour unit should be explicitly declared abstract.

4.5.3 Support for unforeseen variations

Identifying commonalities and allowing variations in business processes has been discussed in the past. Many approaches have been proposed to address this requirement [42, 66–68, 149, 193, 203]. These approaches help to identify the commonalities and variations to a certain extent. For example, the VxBPEL language extension for BPEL attempts to allow a process to be customised based on variability points [67]. However, the variability points are fixed and only the parameters are selected during the runtime. Likewise, the aspects/rules viewed via pointcuts [193] in the AO4BPEL [68, 190] represent the volatile parts, whereas the abstract process that defines the join-points represents the fixed part. Similarly [203], the variability points represent the volatile parts while the provided master process represents the fixed part.

These approaches nonetheless suffer from a common weakness, i.e., there is an assumption that the fixed part and the volatile part can be well-identified at the design time. This might be possible in certain business scenarios. However, such design-time identification cannot be applied to business environments where the commonalities and variations need to be identified or adjusted during the runtime. In contrast, we do not rely on such an assumption of fixed and volatile parts. The behaviours are defined without an explicit declaration of fixed and volatile parts. All the properties of each behaviour unit are considered to be potentially volatile. They can be modified or further extended using *behaviour specialisation* to suit the business requirements. As shown, the towing behaviour can be further extended by overriding its properties to support its variations in the future without an explicit declaration of fixed and volatile parts. This is beneficial for the service aggregator, who might not be able to foresee all the variations upfront.

For example, to perform the task *tTow*, a request needs to be sent from role TT to its player. This request needs certain data, including pickup location and destination. These data need to be extracted from the interactions *mOrderTow* and *mSendGarageLocaiton*, defined in CO_TT and GR_TT contracts, respectively, to the role TT. When the towing is completed (i.e., the tow task is executed), the bound player will send a response. The response needs to be transformed into response interactions of the aforementioned *mOrderTow* and *mSendGarageLocaiton* interactions.

Figure 4.26 illustrates the scenario described. We use the syntax $<$contract_id$>.<$interaction_id$>.<$req/res$>$ to uniquely identify a role−role interaction. Here, contract_id is the contract identifier and interaction_id is the interaction identifier. The suffix req/res indicates whether the interaction is from either the obligated role (request) or its partner in contract (response), respectively. We also use the $<$role_id$>.<$task_id$>.<$req/res$>$ to uniquely identify a role−player interaction. Here, a role_id is the role identifier and task_id is the task identifier. The suffix req/res indicates whether the interaction is from a role to player (request) or the player to role (response).

As shown, there is a transformation (T1) to create the interaction from TT role to its player. In addition, there are two transformations (T2, T3) to create the role−role interactions from the interaction from player to TT role.

TT.tTow.Req $= f_{T1}$ (CO_TT.mOrderTow.Req, GR_TT.mSendGarageLocation.Req);
CO_TT.mOrderTow.Res $= f_{T2}$ (TT.tTow.Res);
GR_TT.mSendGarageLocation.Res $= f_{T3}$ (TT.tTow.Res)

Listing 4.14 shows the task definition of *tTow* defined in the TT role. The clause *UsingMsgs* specifies the interactions that are being used to create the request to perform *tTow* as well as the transformation function. It also specifies what are the resulting interactions upon the completion of the task and what are the transformations to be used. The current implementation supports EXtensible Stylesheet Language (XSLT) transformations as default transformations. The details and the sample transformation files (XSLT) are available in Section 7.1.3.

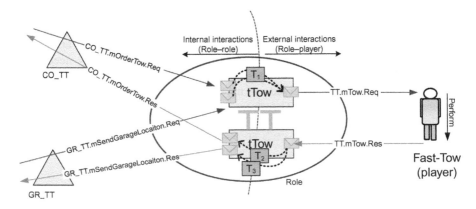

Figure 4.26 Tasks associate internal and external interactions.

```
Role TT playedBy binding1{
  Task tTow {
        UsingMsgs CO_TT.mOrderTow.Req, GR_TT.mSendGarageLocaiton.Req trans t1.xsl;
        ResultingMsgs CO_TT.mOrderTow.Res trans t2.xsl, GR_TT.mSendGarageLocaiton.
        Res
                                                               trans t3.xsl;
  }
}
```

Listing 4.14 Task definition specifies the source and resulting messages/interactions.

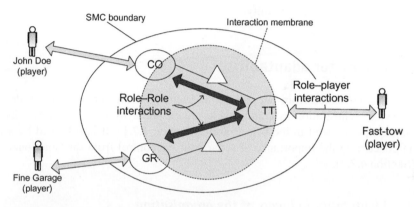

Figure 4.27 Formation of the interaction membrane.

4.6.3 Benefits of membranous design

A task associates and separates the internal interactions with external interactions via transformations as shown in the previous section. Each role defines a number of tasks. Therefore, all the tasks defined in all the roles of the organisation form an *interaction membrane* for the organisational self-managed composite (SMC), as illustrated in Figure 4.27. The core processes and information content are maintained within the boundary of the membrane and the concerns such as the message formats and delivery mechanisms are handled outside the membrane (yet inside the SMC/organisation boundary).

Such a membranous design helps to address the challenges mentioned previously. The message delivery is synchronised with the well-defined processes. The processes are internal to the organisation and reflect ways to achieve organisational goals. The information content of interactions can be altered and the complex interactions can be defined to conjoin and split messages to participating players. The core processes are separated from the underlying interactions to provide the stability upon frequent changes in underlying players or their interface. The message delivery concerns are also separated from the core processes to isolate them from changes in the underlying message delivery mechanisms. This is a separate concern that should be addressed by the message delivery mechanism (further details on message delivery mechanism are available in Section 7.2.5).

In conclusion, the organisation maintains its processes and the information content separate from the surrounding environment. Obviously, the environment is influential in preparing the processes and information content. Nevertheless, the representation inside the organisation is independent from the environment. This principle of the organisation is vital for an adaptive service orchestration design. An orchestration of services is not a isolated environment but consists of a number of partner services that interact via each other. The changes to these partner services are unforseen. Therefore, having such a membranous design to isolate the processes and information content of the service orchestration from the surrounding environment is vital to achieve adaptability.

4.7 Support for adaptability

The concepts presented from Section 4.2 to Section 4.6 are fundamental in designing a service orchestration as an adaptable organisation. In this section, we discuss the adaptability allowed in the organisation (Section 4.7.1). It is followed by a discusson concerning the importance of separating the control from the functional system (Section 4.7.2).

4.7.1 Adaptability in layers of the organisation

In Section 4.1.2, we have presented the different organisational layers of a service orchestration in Serendip (Figure 4.6). All these layers collectively achieve an adaptive service orchestration. In order to provide the benefit of a truly adaptable service orchestration, it is important that each aspect in these layers support adaptability. We discuss those adaptable aspects of the layers during both design time and runtime. An illustration is presented in Figure 4.28, where an adaptation point indicates the addition, deletion and modification of the properties of the entity.

- At the process level, the properties of process definitions such as CoT, CoS and constraints (indicated by 1.1) and the references to behaviour units (1.2) can be dynamically modified.
- At the behaviour level, the behaviour unit, which specifies when to perform tasks, can be dynamically modified to change the constraints (2.1) and the task dependencies (2.2).
- At the tasks level, in order to define how to perform the task, the task definition (3.1), the references to internal interactions (3.2), external interactions (3.3) and the transformations (3.3) can be modified. The internal message formats (3.5) and external message formats (3.6) can also be altered.
- At the contracts level, the contracts (4.1), interaction terms (4.2) and the interpretation rules (4.2) are modifiable.
- At the roles level, the roles (5.1) can be added or removed. In addition, the player bindings (5.2) can be changed to dynamically bind or unbind players to roles.
- Finally, at the player level, new candidate players can be included and existing candidate players can be excluded from the organisation (6.1).

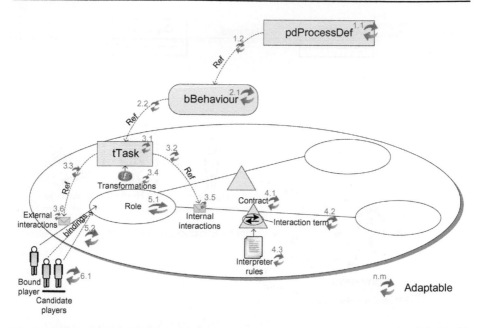

Figure 4.28 Adaptability in the organisation.

4.7.2   Separation of control and functional process

In order to carry out adaptations to an organisation-based service orchestration, there should be a decision-making entity with a decision-making process that determines the adaptations in the organisation. This *decision-making process* or the control aspect of the organisation should be separated from the functional processes of the organisation [82, 230, 258].

The work of this book applies the concept of *organiser* [81] to separate the control from the functional process. The elements in each layer of the organisation are subject to runtime regulation and reconfiguration *only* via the organiser. The organiser is a special role that is responsible for managing the composition. Each ROAD composite has only one organiser role. Just like other functional roles, the organiser role is played by a player such as a software system or a human or a combination of the two. The difference between the organiser role and the functional roles concerns the scope of control [83]. Furthermore, the organiser player may operate remotely in a distributed environment just like any other players playing functional roles. The relationship between the organiser and the organisation is shown in the meta-model given in Figure 4.29.

The work of this book does not intend to provide *self-adaptive* capabilities for service orchestrations. As pointed out by Salehie and Tahvildari [259], a self-adaptive software is a closed-loop system with a feedback loop aiming to adjust itself to changes during its operation. In contrast, our work keeps the loop open at the point of making decisions; hence, it does not provide *self-adaptive* capabilities,

Figure 4.29 Meta-model: the organiser.

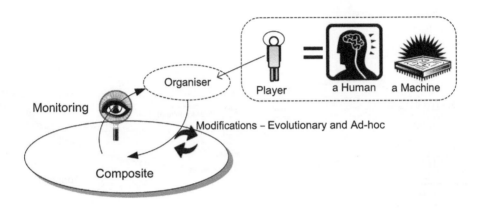

Figure 4.30 Organiser player.

although it provides the structural mechanism for self-adaptability through the organiser role and player. We consider that the decision-making capabilities that close the loop is external to the system (through the organiser player) and should be implemented in a domain-specific manner.

From the service orchestration point of view, the organiser can be seen as an entity that is responsible for making decisions and adapting the service orchestration. The question of *how the process adaptations are managed* is exogenous to the organisation [82]. This is vital as the complexity of *adaptation decision making* can be varied depending on the business domain. The complexity associated with the management decision making should be separated from the functional system by design. For example, the organiser player as shown in Figure 4.30 can be a human or an intelligent software system that makes complex decisions. The organiser itself can be formed of several subsystems that interact with each other in making decisions. Rule-based approaches and control-theoretic approaches are examples of approaches that could be used in designing the organiser player as a software system. The factors such as frequency of process changes, criticality and repetitiveness of change decision making can be influential in choosing the organiser player. Furthermore, the organiser player can also be changed during the runtime. A business that employs a human to make decisions may replace the human with a machine (or may keep both) due to management complexity and workload. For these reasons, it is important to separate the decision-making process from the functional process.

From the service orchestration point of view, the changes that result from a decision-making process can be either evolutionary or process instance-specific modifications. The service orchestration modelled as an organisation accepts and realises the change requests depending on their feasibility. The feasibility is determined by an impact analysis process, based on the scope of the modification, the current status of processes as well as the constraints imposed on the organisation. The interrelatedness of process goals and collaboration goals plays an important role in the impact analysis as discussed in Section 4.4. If a modification is feasible, then the organisation accepts and realises it; otherwise, it is rejected.

4.8 Managing complexity

Proper management of the complexity of a service orchestration is paramount to sustainable adaptability. If the complexity is not managed properly, then the service orchestration can become unusable in the long run. Necessary adaptations could be omitted because of a lack of confidence. In addition, the adaptations can be time consuming and error prone. The design of a service orchestration plays an important role in managing the complexity.

In the previous section, we have discussed the importance of separating control and functional processes in the service orchestration design and how this contributes to managing the complexity. In addition, there are three further design concepts of the organisational approach that help manage the complexity of a service orchestration, i.e., *hierarchical and recursive composition, support for heterogeneity* and *explicit representation of service relationships via contracts*.

4.8.1 Hierarchical and recursive composition

ROAD supports the *hierarchical and recursive* breakdown of complex systems [83, 260]. Using this concept, a large and complex service orchestration can be subdivided into manageable smaller units of orchestrations as shown in Figure 4.31.

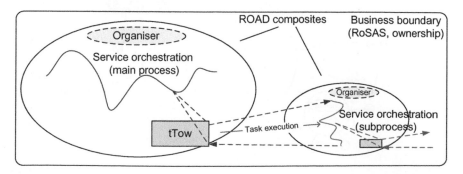

Figure 4.31 Reducing a complex orchestration into manageable suborchestrations.

A task can be executed by a player that is designed as another Serendip orchestration. How the task is executed and managed in the second composite is not a concern of the main composite. The organiser of the subcomposite can reconfigure and regulate its own (sub-)orchestrations, while the organiser of the main composite can reconfigure and regulate the main service orchestration. As such, the functional concerns are also separated.

For example, suppose that coordinating the towing activities is a rather complex process. It is no longer just a matter of ordering a towing service from a bound external player. Apart from the external towing services, there are tow-coordinating officers from RoSAS itself to handle the towing operations. In this sense, towing itself is a complex process that could be used by the main roadside assistance process. Rather than introducing this complexity into the main roadside assistance process, a subprocess (subsystem) can be introduced to hide that complexity from the main orchestration, as shown in Figure 4.31. RoSAS owns and manages both composites, but the concerns are now separated into two different systems. The main orchestration manages the *roadside assistance process*, whereas the suborchestration handles all the concerns associated with the *towing process*. Both composites have their own organiser roles. Depending on the requirement, the organiser roles of both composites could be played by the same player or different players who interact with each other.

Similarly, the other tasks of main orchestration can be further expanded and defined as suborchestrations as shown in Figure 4.32. The suborchestrations can also have another level of suborchestration if required, forming a hierarchy of service compositions. Figure 4.32 also shows that the boundary of ownership is not the same as the boundary of orchestration organisation. Such an ownership is defined by who controls the composite. As such, the same business can define and manage multiple composites in the hierarchy.

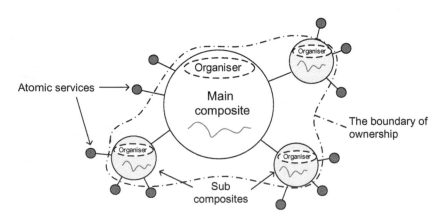

Figure 4.32 A hierarchy of service compositions.

4.8.2 Support for heterogeneity of task execution

Integration of heterogeneous distributed systems is one of the promises of SOA. Therefore, the support for *heterogeneity* is important in a service orchestration approach. The support for *heterogeneity* allows a defined service orchestration to function without requiring specific knowledge about how the players are implemented and managed. In heterogeneous environments, the players are implemented using various technologies and their implementations will vary over the time.

The design of the core service orchestration should be independent of the implementation and behaviour of the participating service as shown in Figure 4.33. Otherwise, the changes in the implementation and behaviour of the participating service can add to the complexity of the core service orchestration.

In order to support this requirement, Serendip does not specify any detail about the execution of tasks by the players. The core service orchestration assumes the execution of a task as an outsourced activity. Only the outcome of the task is used to determine the cause of executions via events as supported by the Serendip language. This allows any implementation (player) to be used to execute the task supporting the heterogeneity. The task could be executed by a locally deployed Java component/library, or it could be executed by a remote Web service. Irrespective of the player's implementation, the core execution could be defined.

Apart from the control flow, the data flow is highly dependent on the player. Different message exchange protocols, e.g., SOAP [261], REST [262] and XML-RPC [263], could be used by the players. In addition, even within the same protocol, different encodings, e.g., SOAP 1.1 versus SOAP 1.2, could be used. Moreover, different data formats, e.g., currencies, data time, etc., could be used. These concerns are handled separately from the core service orchestration. Further details on how the data transformations are carried out is available in Section 5.4.

4.8.3 Explicit service relationships

One of the important aspects of service orchestration is the interactions among the partner services. These interactions need to be modified to suit the evolving business requirements. The aspects such as obligations and the evaluation conditions of these interactions do change. A monolithic representation of these interactions can increase the complexity of the service orchestration. Therefore, it is necessary to

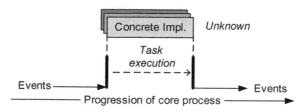

Figure 4.33 Implementation of task execution is unknown to core orchestration.

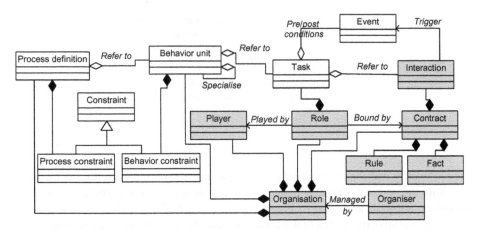

Figure 4.36 Serendip meta-model.

4.10 Summary

In this chapter we have introduced *Serendip*, a novel approach to business process modelling. It is that achieves adaptive service orchestration. It treats or views a service composition as an adaptive organisation, which has a structure that provides the required abstraction of the underlying services and their relationships. Upon such an adaptable structure, business processes are modelled.

The structural and process concepts of service orchestration modelled as an organisation are placed into six layers providing the logical abstraction for the organisation-based orchestration. The structural aspect consists of players, roles and contracts. The process aspect comprises the task, behaviour and process definitions. The adaptability at all these layers in the organisation collectively enables and contributes to the realisation of an adaptive service orchestration.

In Serendip, the loose coupling among tasks achieved by events improves the runtime adaptability; the behaviour-based process modelling and specialisation captures the behavioural commonalities and variations between processes and enables business agility; the two-tier constraints facilitate the analysis and localisation of change impacts and control the adaptations without unnecessary restrictions; and the interaction membrane isolates internal and external data flow concerns. Based on its set of basic concepts of the Serendip meta-model, the *SerendipLang* service orchestration modelling language is designed to support and realise the meta-model. We have also discussed how the Serendip approach can improve the adaptability of a service orchestration while managing the complexity that the adaptability requirements can introduce.

Serendip Runtime

5

In the previous chapter, we introduced the Serendip meta-model, language and underlying concepts, which enable adaptive service orchestration. In this chapter, we introduce a novel service orchestration runtime called *Serendip Runtime* designed to support the enactment of Serendip service orchestrations.

Instead of designing a new service orchestration runtime, an existing service orchestration runtime or an enactment engine could have been used. For instance, the Serendip language descriptions could be translated into an executable language such as WS-BPEL for enactment purposes. A popular BPEL engine such as Apache ODE [264] or Active BPEL [197] could have been used as the runtime platform. However, such an alternative would not provide the basis for fully exploiting the true benefits of the Serendip approach in supporting process adaptation. The resulting BPEL scripts from the translation do not have adaptability properties exhibited at the Serendip language level because WS-BPEL was not designed with adaptability in mind. The runtime BPEL engine does not support the required adaptability either. The loosely coupled tasks and event-driven nature of the Serendip language should be supported by a specifically designed runtime engine to facilitate the adaptability features of the language and approach.

A Serendip orchestration is designed as per the *role-oriented adaptive design* (ROAD). The newly introduced process layers are a natural extension of ROAD concepts as explained in Chapter 4. To implement these concepts, the Serendip runtime is also an extension the ROAD framework to providing the process support required. This chapter presents a detailed view of how the Serendip runtime is designed and how it achieves runtime orchestration of services according to the Serendip approach.

First, the design expectations for such an orchestration runtime are stated in Section 5.1.1. Second, the core components of the Serendip runtime are introduced in Section 5.1.2 to fulfil these expectations. Third, the details about how the Serendip runtime functions are explained from Section 5.2 to Section 5.5 by clarifying different aspects of the runtime platform, including process life-cycle management, event processing, data synthesis and synchronisation and dynamic creation of process graphs.

5.1 The design of an adaptive service orchestration runtime

This section presents an overview of the Serendip runtime. We first discuss the design expectations, clearly identifying the additional requirements that should be

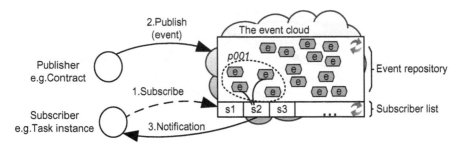

Figure 5.4 The event cloud.

Table 5.1 **Types of event publishers**

Publisher	Purpose	Example
Contract	To record the interpreted events (via contractual rules)	Contract CO_TT interprets message *CO_TT.mOrderTow.Req*, to generate event *eTowReqd*
Organiser	To add events to the Event Cloud	The organiser adds event *eMMNotifDone* to process instance pdGold034 to terminate the instance, because the motorist did not send the notification as obliged to

In Serendip, an event record is a tuple $<eid, pid, timestamp, expiration>$ where *eid* is the *event identification* and *pid* is the *process instance identification*. The *timestamp* captures when the event is fired and the *expiration* captures when the event eventually expires. By default, all events expire when the process instance (denoted by *pid*) is complete. The event cloud consists of two main collections, i.e. an *event repository* and a *subscriber list* as shown in Figure 5.4.

- *Event record repository* is used to keep the records of events. Adding events to the repository is known as *publishing*. Event records are published by the internal components of the ROAD composite. These components are known as *publishers*, as shown in Figure 5.4. A typical example of a publisher is a contract. A contract publishes events by interpreting the role−role interactions (Section 5.3.2). Events records are garbage-collected when they expire. Table 5.1 lists the different types of event publishers.
- *Subscriber list* is used to maintain a list of subscribers interested in events (or event patterns to be precise). Subscribers need to be maintained for notification purposes. When a new event is added, the event cloud checks for the interested event patterns of these subscribers and notifies those whose event patterns are matched. Subscribers can be added or removed at any time. At the time of a process enactment, for example, the task instances of a new process instance can be dynamically added to the list of subscribers. When the process instance is complete, its subscribers are removed. Table 5.2 lists the different types of subscribers.

Table 5.2 Types of event subscribers

Subscriber	Purpose	Example
Task	To identify when a task become do-able, i.e. to detect if its pre-event pattern is met	Task *tTow* of process instance *pdGold001* subscribes to Event Cloud to match event pattern, *eTowReqd* * *eDestinationKnown*
Enactment engine	To identify when a new process should be enacted, i.e. to detect when the *CoS* of each process definition is met	The engine subscribes to Event Cloud to detect the *CoS* event patterns of all the process definitions such as *eGoldRequestRcvd*
Process instance	To identify when a process instance should be terminated, i.e. to detect if the CoT event pattern is met	Process instance *pdGold001* subscribes to Event Cloud to detect *CoT* event pattern, *eTTPaid* * *eGRPaid* * *eMMConfirmed*
Adaptation script scheduler	To identify when to execute a scheduled adaptation script (Section 6.3.3)	An adaptation script S1 is dynamically scheduled to make a pre-condition of a task change from original definition if event *eTowFailed* has occurred in process instance *pdGold034*. The scheduler subscribes to the event *eTowFailed* of process instance *pdGold034*
Organiser	To receive alerts upon interested events	The organiser (role/player) wishes to be alerted when *eTowFailed* has occurred for process instance *pdGold034*

The use of such a *publish—subscribe*-based mechanism in *event cloud* enables loose coupling among the tasks to be executed. As described in Section 4.2.1, tasks of a Serendip process are loosely coupled, for example *tTow* and *tPayTT* do not relate to each other directly by design. Changes can be carried out on tasks to deviate them from the original process definition. As mentioned in expectation 4, the runtime should be ready for such late deviations in process instances. There are two important characteristics of the event cloud that facilitate this requirement.

1. Event cloud does not maintain subscribed event patterns but rather the subscribers.
2. Subscribers can be dynamically added or removed from the event cloud.

Event cloud does not maintain the event patterns of the subscribers. Instead, only a list of subscribers is maintained. Event cloud queries the subscribers to get the most up-to-date event pattern when a new event is received. This characteristic is useful to allow late changes for a subscriber. For example, the task *tPayTT* of process instance *pdGold001* can modify the pre-event pattern to deviate from the original event pattern, which is specified in its original process definition of *pdGold*. There is no need to specifically update the event patterns in the event cloud upon such changes.

Subscribers can be dynamically added or removed from the event cloud. In this way, the adaptations (e.g. new task insertions and removals) can be carried out while the process is running (Section 6.2). For example, consider an *ad hoc* change, where a new task *tNofityTowFailureToCustomer* is added into the instance *pdGold001* to handle the event *eTowFailed*. To support this change, a new task instance is first created and added to the process instance *pdGold001*. Once the task is added to the instance, the task is subscribed to the event cloud by the process instance.

The following section describes how these events are published in the event cloud via rule-based contracts.

5.3.2   Event triggering and business rules integration

Business rules technology is gaining popularity due to its expressiveness and inference capabilities [269]. In the past, business rules have been extensively used in knowledge-based systems and expert systems [176, 269–272]. Business rule integration [179, 269] with BPM has added many advantages. These include better de-coupling of the system, ease of understanding, reusability, manageability by non-technical staff and improved maintainability [179, 180]. Section 3.4.3 has presented a number of such approaches that integrate business rules into processes to improve their adaptability. Apart from the support for adaptability, rule-based message interpretation allows the specification of complex message interpretation logic.

According to the Business Rules Group [273], '*A business rule is a statement that defines and constrains some business. It is intended to assert business structure or to control or influence the behaviour of the business.*' According to this definition, business rules control the way a business behaves. As such, use of business rules is a natural choice for controlling and interpreting the interactions in a service composite to control the runtime behaviour of the business model as realised by a service orchestration. Nonetheless, a monolithic representation of business rules in a service composite can cause problems in terms of modularity and adaptability. Inappropriate modularity can cause confusion in writing or improving the rules that represent the assertions and constraints of a business. A lack of support for adaptability can cause problems when a business evolves and the specified assertions and constraints are no longer valid. Therefore, the business rules need to be specified with proper modularity and support for adaptability.

In this work, we integrate business rules with the Serendip orchestration runtime via ROAD contracts. Our aim is to clearly separate the process-level concerns from the complex message interpretation concerns. In a service orchestration, the message interpretation needs to be based on the existing relationships among the partner services. These relationships can be dynamically changed during the runtime. It follows that the processes running on the composite should also select the paths of executions in response to these changing service relationships.

A ROAD composite uses contracts to explicitly represent the relationships among the roles in the composite [81]. A contract represents a well-defined relationship between two roles. The players bound to the roles such as Web services need to interact according to the defined contracts. Contracts also have a memory during the runtime. In this memory, a contract maintains a set of facts that represents the contract state and a set of rules that represents a set of assertions of the relationships. The messages that pass through the contract are interpreted according to facts (i.e. *contractual facts*) and the rules (i.e. the *contractual rules*) maintained in the contract (memory). The facts are dynamically modified by the rules. This work uses these contractual rule-based interpretations to trigger events, exploiting the following advantages.

- *Modularity*: Contracts provide the modularity to specify the facts and rules for validating and interpreting the role−role interactions. The end result of this validation and interpretation step can be used to determine the course of the process flow.
- *Adaptability*: The memory of the contract represented by the facts and rules are dynamic. The facts and rules can be dynamically updated during the runtime to reflect the change to the relationship between the two services.

For example, roles CO and TT need to interact according to the interaction terms defined in the CO_TT contract and the relevant messages have to go through the CO_TT contract. As such, the *modularity* provided by the contract helps to specify all the interactions between CO and TT. The interactions include how to order the tow service and how to pay for the tow service. In addition, the CO_TT contract captures facts and assertions (rules) that allow evaluating these interactions.

The CO_TT contractual memory can be updated to reflect the changing evaluation conditions that determine a successful towing. For example, a new rule can be dynamically inserted to calculate whether the towing has been done in a remote or a metropolitan area. A fact can be updated (by rules) to record the number of requests from the case officer to tow truck for a given day. This provides the required *adaptability* to evolve the contractual rules to comply with the changing business requirements.

One of the key advantages of using ROAD is its ability to interpret events in terms of defined *service relationships*. This means that not only the message but also the *current context of the service relationship* can influence the final outcome of the interpretation of interaction. The *current context of the service relationship* can be derived from the facts maintained in contract memory. For example, suppose that according to the contract between roles CO and TT, a *bonus payment* needs to be made for every Nth tow request. In this case, whether the bonus payment should be made is a decision based on the current context of the service relationships rather than a decision solely based on the passing message. A fact e.g. *TowCount* in contract memory that is continuously updated according to contractual rules, would serve this purpose. An event *eTTBonusAllowed* can be triggered if the condition ($TowCount > N$) is true. A task *tPayBonus* may have the event *eTTBonusAllowed* as the pre-event pattern to perform the actual payment. As such, the contractual rules integration allows not only *message-based interpretation* but also a *service relationship-driven interpretation* as well.

Figure 5.5 shows a message exchange between the roles CO and TT via the *CO_TT* contract. Figure 5.5A shows that the tow request (#1) from role CO to role TT is

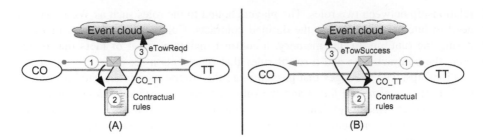

Figure 5.5 Message interpretation.

interpreted (#2) according to the rules defined in CO_TT contract. Consequently, the event *eTowReqd* is triggered and recorded in the event cloud (#3). Figure 5.5B shows that the response from role TT to role CO is interpreted again, according to the rules defined in the CO_TT contract. Subsequently, the event *eTowSuccess* (or *eTowFailure* otherwise) is triggered and recorded in the event cloud.

In conclusion, the complexity of the evaluation conditions/assertions is captured in contracts. The enactment engine is only concerned about the outcomes of the evaluation, i.e. triggered events. While benefiting from a powerful *service relationship-driven message interpretation*, this design decouples the process execution from the complexity of interpreting interactions as captured in the contracts.

5.4 Data synthesis of tasks

In Section 4.6, we have described how the *data synthesis and synchronisation* mechanism is designed to form a membrane (*the interaction membrane*) around the composite. The membrane is the border in which transformations between *internal messages* (due to *role−role interactions*) and *external messages* (*role-player interactions*) take place. An external interaction is composed possibly from internal interactions when a service invocation needs to be formulated. Conversely, an external interaction can cause further internal interactions. Transformations need to be carried to propagate data across the membrane. The membrane isolates the external interactions from the (internal) core processes (and vice versa) to provide organisational stability. In order to support this concept, the design of the Serendip runtime needs to address a number of challenges.

1. The request to complete a task needs to be composed from the data derived from a single or possibly multiple internal messages. In the case of multiple messages being used, they can arrive in any order. The runtime should accommodate such *unpredictability in internal message ordering*.
2. Multiple processes can run simultaneously. Multiple internal messages of the same type (e.g. *CO_TT.mOrderTow.Req*) but belonging to different process instances (e.g. *p001, p002*) can arrive at the role simultaneously. The message synthesis mechanism of the runtime should be able to deal with such *parallelism*.

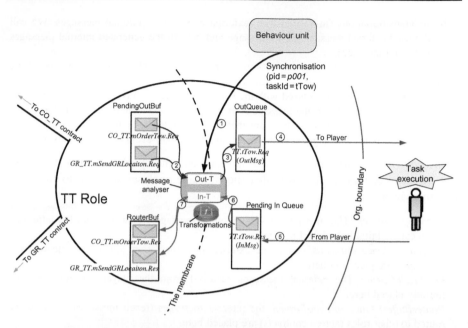

Figure 5.6 Data synthesis and synchronisation design.

3. Sending a request to the player needs to be synchronised according to the task dependencies defined in the behaviour units (e.g. *bTowing*) of the organisation. The message synthesis mechanism should provide support for such *synchronisation*.
4. The response from the player may be used to create a single or multiple internal interactions. The responses (to multiple requests) may arrive in any order irrespective of the order in which the requests are made. For example, if towing requests are made to the *FastTow* service in the order of process instances $p001 \rightarrow p002$, the responses may come in the order of $p002 \rightarrow p001$. The runtime should be able to handle the *unpredictability in external message ordering*.

5.4.1 The role design

In order to address these challenges, the runtime is designed as shown in Figure 5.6, which gives a zoomed-in view of an instantiated role composition at runtime. As shown, a role instance contains four message containers to store the messages and a *message analyser*. The purpose of the message analyser is twofold, i.e. data *synthesis* and *synchronisation*.

1. *Synthesis* performs the data transformations across (in and out of) the membrane. The message analyser performs two types of data transformations. These two transformations are named according to the perspective of the composite.
   a. Out-Transformations (Out-T) transform internal messages to external messages. We call the used internal messages the source messages and the generated external message the out-message.

b. In-Transformations (In-T) transform external messages to internal messages. We call the used external message the in-message and we call the generated internal messages the result messages.

2. *Synchronisation*: Synchronises the out-transformation in the behaviour layer by specifying the ordering of task executions and the reception of source messages. Note that the in-transformation is not synchronised with the behaviour layer, because, as soon as a message is received from the player, the message is in-transformed to create the internal result messages. Nevertheless, runtime makes sure that the interpretation of result messages via the contracts (Section 5.3.2) trigger events conforming to the post-event pattern of a given task.

In order to support the two transformations and the synchronisation, there are four message containers in a role that the message analyser will use to pick and drop messages.

- *PendingOutBuffer:* The internal messages (source messages) flowing from the adjoining contracts are initially buffered in here.
- *OutQueue:* Once *out-transformed*, the external messages from role to the player (out-messages) are placed in here.
- *PendingInQueue:* The external messages received from the player (in-messages) are initially placed here.
- *RouterBuffer:* Once *in-transformed*, the internal messages (result messages) ready to be routed to other roles (across contracts) are placed here.

5.4.2 The transformation process

The complete message transformation process is detailed here.

Synchronisation step:
1. When the behaviour layer has identified that task T_i of process instance PI_j is ready for execution, the message analyser of the obligated role is notified.

Out-Transformation steps:
2. The message analyser picks the relevant source messages with the same process identifier PI_j from the *PendingOutBuffer* as specified in the task description T_i.
3. The message analyser performs the out-transformation to generate the out-message. This may include enriching the information of the message and transforming the message to the expected format. Then, the out-message is marked with the same process identifier PI_j and placed in the *OutQueue*.
4. The underlying message delivery mechanism (e.g. ROAD4WS for Web services [260]) delivers the message from the *OutQueue* to the player. Then, the player executes task T_i of PI_j.

In-Transformation steps:
5. The underlying message delivery mechanism receives the response (i.e. the in-message) from the player and places it in the *PendingInQueue*. The message delivery mechanism ensures that the in-message is marked with the same process identifier PI_j, e.g. via a synchronous Web service request.

6. The message analyser picks the messages from *PendingInQueue* and performs the in-transformation as specified in task T_i to create result messages.

7. The created result messages are marked with the same process identifier PI_j and placed in the *RouterBuffer* to be routed across the adjoining contracts (towards suitable roles). Then, these contracts trigger events by interpreting these messages as explained in Section 5.3.2. The runtime (via Event Observer, Section 7.1.2) makes sure that the triggered events conform to the post-event pattern of the corresponding task.

Let us consider a specific example scenario to clarify these steps using the task *tTow* of role TT. First, the behaviour layer determines that the task *tTow* of process instance *p001* has become do-able (step 1). The source messages of the task *tTow* (*CO_TT.mOrderTow.Req, GR_TT.mSendGRLocation.Req*) that belong to the same process instance (i.e. with *p001*) are then picked from *PendingOutBuffer* (step 2). Then, these source messages are transformed (step 3) to create the out-message (*TT.tTow.Req*), which is the message delivered to the player (step 4). When the task is complete (i.e. car has been towed) and the player responds, the response message or the in-message (*TT.tTow.Res*) is placed in the *PendingInQueue* (step 5). The underlying message delivery mechanism makes sure that the same *pid* of the request is associated with the response. Then *TT.tTow.Res* is picked and transformed to create two result messages, i.e. *CO_TT.mOrderTow.Res* and *GR_TT. mSendGRLocation.Res* (step 6). These result messages are again associated with the same *pid* of the in-message. Then, these result messages are placed in the *RouterBuffer* (step 7) to be routed across the relevant roles, i.e. CO and GR via adjoining contracts, i.e. CO-TT and GR_TT.

This role and transformation design has been able to address the aforementioned challenges.

Challenge 1: The *PendingOutBuffer* provides the storage for messages to be buffered. The messages are picked based on the synchronisation request rather than the order in which they arrive. This addresses the challenge of unpredictability in-message ordering.

Challenge 2: All the messages are annotated with the process instance identifier. Therefore, the same type of messages of different process instances can be uniquely identified. This addresses the challenge posed by the parallelism in process execution.

Challenge 3: The *message analyser* is synchronised with the behaviour layer of the organisation. The out-transformation is carried out only when the task becomes do-able. As such, the message synthesis mechanism enables the synchronisation required.

Challenge 4: The message transformations are carried out in an asynchronous manner within the composite. The message containers allow a separation between the role and the message delivery mechanism that serves the *Out/InQueues* outside the membrane. The role does not need to wait for the response from the player. The message analyser operates in an asynchronous manner whereas the message delivery (player service invocation) may operate in a synchronous or an asynchronous manner (Section 7.2.5). Multiple threads in the message delivery mechanism may spawn to serve the messages in the *OutQueue* as well as to insert messages in the *InQueue* when the player responds (the player implementation need to support multi-threaded serving). In this way, the responses from the player may arrive in any order different from the request order.

5.5   Dynamic process graphs

The Serendip behaviour units capture different organisational behaviours. The MPF maintains all the behaviour units. The task dependencies are defined in a declarative manner. The benefits of having such declarative behaviour specification were described in Section 4.2 and Section 4.3. Behaviour units are assembled to specify a process definition to fulfil a particular customer requirement. For example, the *pdGold* process definition assembles behaviour units *bComplaining, bTowing, bRepairing* and *bTaxiDropOff* for customers in the gold category.

However, such declarative descriptions can be difficult to model mentally. Process visualisation helps to identify the possible gaps and optimisation opportunities in the process definitions. In fact, one main goal of BPM is to visualise processes to understand how they *are actually* performed (lived) and how they *should be* performed (intended) [274]. Process graphs are provided as a visual aid to help software engineers to understand the flow of a process, as illustrated by Figure 5.7.

Apart from the benefit of visualisation, such a graph-based representation of a process helps to check the correctness of the defined process. Because a behaviour unit is reused potentially by several process definitions, there may reachability issues. Such issues with the correctness of a process definition can be visually as well as formally identified if the complete flow of the process is constructed.

Furthermore, such a graph construction cannot be static. The behaviour units can be changed during the runtime, affecting all the process definitions that share these behaviour units. For example, insertion of new task *tNofityTowFailureToCustomer* to the behaviour *bTowing* could affect all the referenced process definitions, i.e. *pdSilv, pdGold* and *pdPlat*. In some cases, completely new behaviour units can be linked to the process definitions to add more features during the runtime. For example, behaviour *bHotelBooking* can be dynamically added to process definition *pdPlat* to provide accommodation to stranded *platinum members*, if required. In addition, an individual process instance also can deviate from the original definition to accommodate *ad hoc* changes. These changes lead to changes in the complete flow of a process definition or a process instance. As the MPF maintains all these process models, there should be support from the MPF to dynamically reconstruct

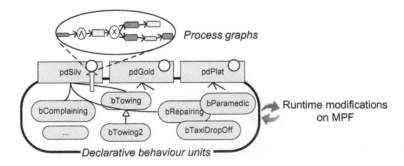

Figure 5.7 Generating process graphs from declarative behaviour units.

the process graphs incorporating the modifications. We describe in this section how the process graphs are dynamically constructed.

Due to the event-driven nature of task specifications and dependencies in Serendip, a suitable notation for the visual representation should also support events. The process modelling notation for event-driven process chains (EPC) introduced by Sheer [17] has been chosen in this book as the notation for process visualisation (EPC is also used in process modelling tools such as ARIS [275] and SAP R/3 [276]). An EPC graph consists of three main elements, i.e. *functions*, *events* and *connectors* (*AND, OR, XOR*). The directed *edges* connect these elements together into a directed graph forming a workflow. Serendip defines a process as a collection of declarative behaviour units. Each behaviour unit contains tasks and its pre-conditions and post-conditions (event patterns) define the control flow. These declarative behaviour units need to be transformed into as an EPC workflow model in the form of a process graph. Then, a suitable tool can be used to visualise these graphs.

The construction of an EPC process graph is carried out in two steps:

1. Construct *atomic graphs* for each task[2] of process.
2. Link all the constructed atomic graphs to form the *final graph* by mapping events.

Section 5.5.1 describes what an atomic graph is and how to construct pre-trees and post-trees as part of step 1. Section 5.5.2 describes how event-based mapping is used to link the atomic graphs together to construct a complete EPC workflow as part of step 2.

5.5.1 Atomic graphs

An *atomic graph* is a single EPC function with its pre-trees and post-trees constructed. Here, a *pre-tree* is a tree constructed of events and connectors, based on the pre-event pattern of a task. A *post-tree* is a tree constructed of events and connectors, based on the post-event pattern of a task. The EPC function corresponds to a Serendip-Task. An EPC event corresponds to a Serendip-Event specified in pre-events and post-event patterns of tasks. The EPC connector symbols (AND, OR, XOR) are used with their semantics as explained elsewhere [277] and are summarised in Table 5.3.

A sample atomic graph is shown in Figure 5.8. As shown, the pre-event pattern *eTowReqd * eDestinationKnown* would create one *AND connector* with *two incoming edges* for events *eTowReqd, eDestinationKnown* to form the *pre-tree* of task tTow. Similarly the post-event pattern *eTowSuccess ^ eTowFailed* creates the *post-tree* that has an *XOR connector* with two outgoing *edges* for events *eTowSuccess* and *eTowFailed*. The complexity of the *Pre-trees* and *post-trees* depends on the complexity of the specified event patterns.

---

[2]To mark the termination of a process definition, we insert an additionalTask with the identifier *<Pid>. tTerminate*. This additional task's pre-event pattern is the *CoT* of the process definition and the post-event pattern is an event with identifier *e<Pid>End*. This ensures the visualisation captures the termination condition of the process definition.

Table 5.3 EPC connectors

Pattern	Join		Split	
	Symbol	Description	Symbol	Description
OR		Any incoming branch, or a combination of incoming branches, will initiate the outgoing branch		One or more outgoing branches will be enabled after the incoming branch finishes
XOR		One, and only one, incoming branch will initiate the outgoing branch		One, and only one, outgoing branch will be enabled after the incoming branch finishes
AND		The outgoing branch is initiated only after all the incoming branches have been executed		Two or more outgoing branches are enabled after the incoming branch finishes

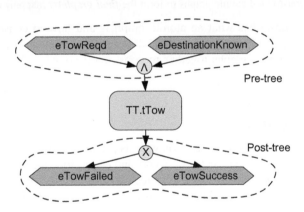

Figure 5.8 An atomic EPC graph.

The algorithm that constructs an atomic graph for a given task is listed in Listing 5.1. The procedure *createAtomicGraph()* creates an atomic graph for a given task *T*. The function uses the grammar given in Listing 5.2 to construct an abstract syntax tree (AST). Two ASTs are generated, one for the pre-event pattern and one for the post-event pattern. Using the constructed ASTs, the pre-trees and post-trees are constructed using the procedure *construct()*, which recursively calls itself until all the nodes of the AST are processed.

5.5.2 Patterns of event mapping and construction of EPC graphs

For a given process, a task has dependencies on other tasks through events. These dependencies are represented as identical events in the constructed atomic graphs.

```
//The procedure to create an atomic graph.
PROC createAtomicGraph(Task T)
   G = new Graph(); //Create a new graph.
   F = new EPCFunction(); //Create a new EPC Function.
   G.addFunction(F);//Add the Function to the Graph
   //Abstract syntax trees are constructed by parsing the pre-and post-event patterns.
   AST preAST = parse(T.getPreEventPattern());
   AST postAST = parse(T.getPostEventPattern());
   //Create pre and post trees.
   construct(preAST, G, F, TRUE);
   construct(postAST, G, F, FALSE);
   RETURN G;
ENDPROC

//The procedure to construct an EPC graph G for a given AST.
// This function can be reused to construct both pre-and post-trees.
PROC construct(AST anAST, Graph G, Node node, BOOL isPreTree)
   EPCElement elem = NULL;
   SWITCH anAST.Type // Type of the root of the tree.
   CASE'OR'
      elem = new ORConnector();
      G.addORConnector(elem);
      BREAK;
   CASE'XOR'
      elem = new ANDConnector();
      G.addANDConnector(elem);
      BREAK;
   CASE 'AND'
      elem = new XORConnector();
      G.addXORConnector(elem);
      BREAK;
   CASE 'EVENT'
      elem = new Event(node.getId());
      G.addEvent(elem);
      BREAK;
   ENDSWITCH
   //Add edges
   IF (isPreTree)
      G.addEdge(elem, node);
   ELSE
      G.addEdge( node, elem);
   ENDIF
   //Recursively call for all the children;
   FOR (INT i=0  To anAST.getChildCount())
      construct(anAST.getChild(i), G, elem, isPreTree); //recursive call
   ENDFOR
ENDPROC
```

Listing 5.1 The algorithm to construct an atomic graph.

```
eventpattern :xorpattern  ;
xorpattern: orpattern ('^'orpattern)*  ;
orpattern:  andpattern ('|'andpattern)*  ;
andpattern: atom ('*'atom)*  ;
atom: ('('eventpattern ')') | event;
event: ('a'..'z' | 'A'..'Z' |'0'..'9')+  ;
```

Listing 5.2 EBNF grammar for event pattern.

For example, the *tTow* and *tPayTT* tasks show dependencies via event *eTowSuccess* as shown in Figure 5.9. Within the space of a process definition (or process instance), these identical event(s) need to be mapped and linked to construct the complete EPC graph. However, this mapping process needs to be carried out in a way that ensures the validity of the resulting EPC graph.

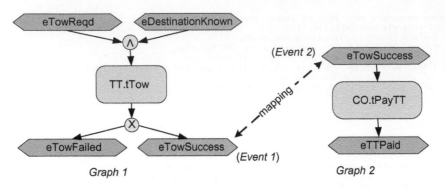

Figure 5.9 Mapping identical events.

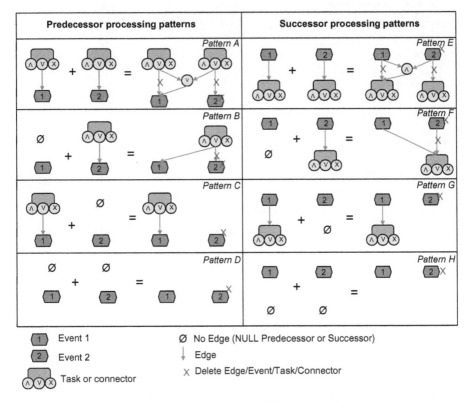

Figure 5.10 Predecessor and successor processing for merging events.

In order to carry out the mapping ensuring the validity of the final EPC graph that represents a process, we introduce a set of eight *event mapping patterns*, as shown in Figure 5.10. For a given event, it *may* have a successor, predecessor or both. When the mapping is carried out, the successors and predecessors need to be carefully arranged. Depending on the applicability for predecessors or successors, the patterns are categorised into two sets, *predecessor processing patterns* and *successor processing patterns*. These patterns need to be used as pairs in order to perform a single event mapping, e.g. pattern A + pattern G.

The selection of a pair is based on how the events predecessors and successors are organised for a given event.

1. A predecessor or a successor of an event can be a *connector* (AND, OR, XOR), *a Task* or a *Null/void* (∅).
2. An event cannot have another event as a predecessor or successor in the graph. Events always relate to each other via a *connector* or a *task*.

Column 1 of Figure 5.10 provides four patterns to process the *predecessors* of a mapping event, whereas *column 2* provides four patterns to process the *successors* of a mapping event. The objective is to create one graph out of two graphs with an identical event. For example, *eTowSuccess* in Figure 5.9 is the identical event in both atomic graphs. Let us call these two events event 1 and event 2 to uniquely identify them. Event 1 is the *eTowSuccess* in graph 1 and event 2 is the same event in graph 2. Each pattern provides what needs to be done for the two graphs (graph 1 and graph 2) when event 1 and event 2 need to be mapped or linked into one, as explained in Table 5.4.

A mapping is done by selecting a *pattern-pair*; one from *column 1* and one from *column 2*.

$$\therefore \text{A pattern-pair} = \{A, B, C, D\} \times \{D, E, F, G\}$$

The truth table for the pattern-pair selection is given in Table 5.5. Depending on the presence of a predecessor and a successor, a pair of patterns is selected according to the truth table. To elaborate how the pattern-pair selection works, let us take the mapping shown in Figure 5.9, where the two graphs 1 and 2 have an identical event identified by *eTowSuccess*. As mentioned, let us call *eTowSuccess* in graph 1 *event 1* and *eTowSuccess* in graph 2 *event 2*.

- Event 1 has a predecessor (connector *XOR*) but does not have a successor.
- Event 2 does not have a predecessor but has a successor (task *tPayTT*).

According to the truth table given in Table 5.5, the corresponding pair of patterns that should be applied is C + F, where the predecessor pattern is C and the successor pattern is F. By applying pattern C, the resulting graph deletes the event 2 and keeps the rest intact. By applying pattern F, the resulting graph creates a new edge from event 1 to the task *tPayTT*, as shown in Figure 5.11.

For a process definition or a process instance, all the identical events of all the graphs are iteratively linked to construct a complete EPC graph. The algorithm for this construction process is given in Listing 5.3. The EPC graphs ($G_{1...n}$) are the atomic graphs that correspond to the process tasks and are constructed as described in the previous section. The procedure *linkGraphs* links the graphs one-by-one until a single graph is constructed. It uses the procedure *linkTwoGraphs* to link only two

Table 5.4 The mapping patterns and the actions

Pattern		Description	Actions
Predecessor processing	A	Both Event 1 and Event 2 have a predecessor	The predecessors of identical events of Graph 1 and Graph 2 are kept by combining via an OR connector. New edges, i.e. predecessor 1→OR, predecessor 2→OR and OR→Event 1 are added. Event 2 and its edge from predecessor 2 are discarded. The edge of Event 1 from its predecessor is also discarded
	B	Event 1 does not have a predecessor, but Event 2 has a predecessor	The only predecessor of Graph 2 is connected to Event 1 via a new edge. Event 2 and its edge from predecessor 2 are discarded
	C	Event 1 has a predecessor, but Event 2 does not have a predecessor	Event 2 is discarded
	D	Neither Event 1 or Event 2 has a predecessor	Event 2 is discarded
Successor processing	E	Both Event 1 and Event 2 have a successor	The successors of identical events of Graph 1 and Graph 2 are kept by combining via an AND connector. New edges Event 1→AND, AND→successor 1, AND→successor 2 are added. Event 2 and its edge to successor 2 are discarded. The edge from Event 1 to successor 1 is also discarded
	F	Event 1 does not have a predecessor, but Event 2 has a successor	Only successor of Graph 2 is connected to Event 1 via a new edge. Event 2 and its edge to successor 2 are discarded
	G	Event 1 has a predecessor, but Event 2 does not have a successor	Event 2 is discarded
	H	Neither Event 1 or Event 2 has a successor	Event 2 is discarded

Table 5.5 **The truth table for pattern-pair selection**

Event 1 (Graph 1)		Event 2 (Graph 2)		Pattern-pair
Predecessor?	Successor?	Predecessor?	Successor?	
1	1	1	1	A + E
1	1	1	0	A + G
1	1	0	1	C + E
1	1	0	0	C + G
1	0	1	1	A + F
1	0	1	0	A + H
1	0	0	1	C + F
1	0	0	0	C + H
0	1	1	1	B + E
0	1	1	0	B + G
0	1	0	1	D + E
0	1	0	0	D + G
0	0	1	1	B + F
0	0	1	0	B + H
0	0	0	1	D + F
0	0	0	0	D + H

1, Present; 0, not present.

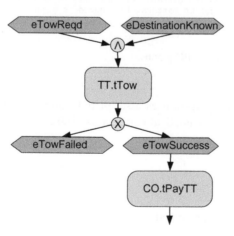

Figure 5.11 A linked graph.

graphs. The procedure *linkTwoEvents* uses the mapping patterns (Figure 5.10) to modify the graphs by mapping identical events as described. A constructed EPC graph is shown in Figure 5.12.

Finally, to ensure the correctness of the constructed EPC graph, it is validated using ProM (as indicated by the *verify()* function call), which has an EPC validator

```
//1. Iteratively link assembled EPCs
PROC linkGraphs(Graph [] {G₁, G₂, G₃…Gᵢ...Gₙ})
   Graph linkedGraph=G₁;  //Initialise with the first graph of the array
   FOR (INT i=2 TO n)
     Graph linkedGraph =  linkTwoGraphs(linkedGraph, Gᵢ);
   ENDFOR

   IF(verify (linkedGraph)) //Check for correctness.
     RETURN linkedGraph;
   ELSE
     RETURN NULL;
ENDPROC

//2. Link two Graphs
PROC linkTwoGraphs (Graph Gₓ, Graph Gᵧ)
   Graph Gₙₑw = New Graph(); //Create an Empty Graph
   COPY all the functions+events+connectors+edges of Gₓ, Gᵧ to Gₙₑw;
   INT Ne = Number of events of the graph Gₙₑw;
   FOR (INT i=0 TO Nₑ){
     Event eCur= Eᵢ; //current event is iᵗʰ event
     FOR (INT j=i+1 TO  Nₑ)
       Event eTemp = Eⱼ; //temporary event is jᵗʰ event
       IF (eTemp.identifier == eCurIdentifier)THEN
        //We have a match. Link two events
        Graph Gₙₑw = linkTwoEvents(eCur, eTemp, Gₙₑw);
       ENDIF
     ENDFOR
   ENDFOR
   RETURN Gₙₑw;
ENDPROC

//3. Link Two events
PROC linkTwoEvents(Event Event1, Event Event2, Graph Gₘₐₚ)
   //Select a pair of mapping patterns as indicated in Table 5.5.
   //Link according to mapping patterns introduced in Figure 5.10 to Modify Graph G.
   RETURN Gₘₐₚ;
ENDPROC
```

Listing 5.3 Algorithm to link EPC graphs.

plug-in [278, 279]. The plug-in uses a set of reduction rules and a Petri-Net-based analysis to determine the syntactical correctness [280].

5.6 Summary

In this chapter, we have presented the key design details of the Serendip runtime. The motivation for designing such a runtime is to provide the required runtime adaptability for a service orchestration as defined using the Serendip concepts.

We first presented the expectations for an adaptable service orchestration runtime. Then, the core components of the Serendip runtime were introduced to fulfil these expectations. Later, the main mechanisms of the runtime were explained. These include how the Serendip process progresses, how the events are triggered based on service relationships, how the data are synthesised and synchronised and how the process graphs are constructed. These mechanisms are designed with the motive of supporting the adaptability required to realise Serendip processes.

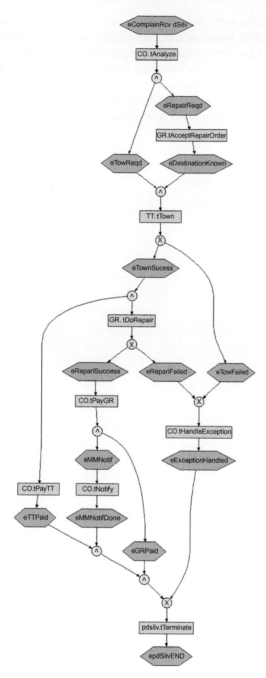

Figure 5.12 A dynamically constructed EPC graph for pdSilv process.

The publish—subscribe mechanism supports late change of task dependencies. The subscribers such as task instances can perform late modifications locally to its event patterns to allow *ad hoc* deviations. The progression of processes is based on events that are triggered by dynamically changing contracts. The design of the role as well as the message transformation process addresses a number of challenges, including message ordering and process correlation issues. Dynamic process graph generation provides the up-to-date graph-based representation for visualisation as well as validation purposes.

Adaptation Management 6

Modern organisations are required to respond to changing business requirements and exceptional situations more effectively and efficiently than in the past [281]. Process-aware information systems (PAIS) [282] facilitate this requirement to a certain extent by leveraging IT support to design and redesign business processes. Unexpected changes to the requirements emerge when the business processes are already instantiated or in operation. Providing business process support for well-identified exceptional situations is somewhat less challenging, because they can be captured in the initial process design. Alternative process flows may be pre-included in the process definitions, which is also known as *flexibility by design* in the literature [63]. However, the unexpected exceptional situations need to be handled during the runtime while the system is in operation and the processes are running. This is more difficult than applying changes to static process definitions.

Two types of changes that need to be supported by a PAIS are identified by van der Aalst [55, 84, 141, 251].

1. *Ad hoc changes*: These changes are carried out on a case-by-case basis. Usually, they are applied to provide a case or process-instance specific solution.
2. *Evolutionary changes*: These changes are carried out in a broader and relatively more permanent manner. All future cases or process instances reflect the changes.

Heinl et al. [59] in his terminology also identifies these two categories of changes as *instance adaptation* and *type adaptation*, respectively. In addition, a few other works have also highlighted the difference and the importance of supporting these two types of changes in a PAIS [110, 169, 283, 284]. A service orchestration needs to be designed in such a manner that it provides support for both *ad hoc* and evolutionary changes.

According to Regev et al. [76], flexibility is the ability to continuously balance between change and stability without losing identity. From this perspective, the changes need to be carried out in a manner that they do not lead to erroneous situations. The composition, both prior to and after the adaptations, needs to be stable and ensure the expected goals are achieved. This is applicable for both evolutionary and *ad hoc* changes, where even an *ad hoc* change should not violate organisational goals.

Adapting running process instances is more challenging than adapting static process definitions. The running process instances can be in different states at a given time. The adaptations on running process instances need to be carried out only when they are in suitable states. The suitability of a state also varies depending on the kinds of adaptation (i.e. what is adapted).

For these reasons, runtime changes to service orchestrations need to be carefully carried out. Proper management (IT) support is essential. We refer to this support as *adaptation management*, and we refer to an IT system that provides such support as *an adaptation management system*.

This chapter presents how the *adaptation management system* of the Serendip framework is designed. This work adopts and further extends the ROAD architecture [81] to manage the adaptations in a service orchestration. The ROAD architecture introduces the guidelines for architecting and managing a software composite structure. This includes changes to the structural aspects of the composite such as contracts, roles and players, which have been extensively discussed previously. The concerns associated with managing such changes in the composite structure are beyond the scope of this book and we refer to other works [82, 83] for more details. The content of this chapter focuses only on managing process adaptations in a service composition. First, a detailed discussion of process management and different adaptation phases is introduced. Second, the basic concepts of a design of an adaptation management system and the potential challenges are discussed. Later, a detailed description of the adaptation management system that addresses these challenges is presented.

6.1   Overview of process management and adaptation

To understand the *adaptation management* in the context of service orchestration, it is necessary to understand the life cycle of business process management (BPM) and its phases. Section 6.1.1 provides some previously presented views of BPM life cycle and phases. Section 6.1.2 will further refine these views to provide a more detailed and expanded understanding of process management and adaptation.

6.1.1   Process modelling life cycles

Weber [285] presented a traditional business process life cycle of a PAIS consisting of four phases, as shown in Figure 6.1A. During the *design* phase, the high-level business requirements are designed as a process or a workflow. During the *modelling* phase, the design is translated into an executable model. Then, the model is executed during the *execute* phase. Finally, the executed processes are monitored at the *monitor* phase. The feedback may be used to redesign the processes and the cycle continues.

A similar view was taken by van der Aalst et al. [7]. As shown in Figure 6.1B, the BPM life cycle has four stages, *process design*, *system configuration*, *process enactment* and *diagnosis*. Initially, the processes are designed in the *process design* phase. During the *system configuration* phase, these processes are implemented. Then, the implemented processes are enacted using the configured system at the *process enactment* phase. These enacted processes are analysed to identify possible

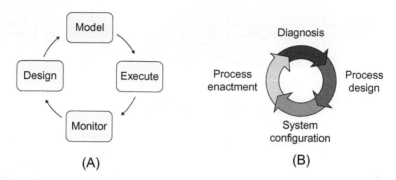

Figure 6.1 (A) Process life cycle, cf. Ref. [285] and (B) BPM life cycle, cf. Ref. [7].

improvements in the *diagnosis* phase. This view is an extension of the workflow management stages, which does not contain a phase for *diagnosis*.

Although these two views of a process life cycle have slight differences in terms of the defined stages or phases, both highlight two important aspects of IT process support. That is, the IT process support is always subject to *iterative refinements*. The existing process executions or enactments provide feedback to shape the future designs of the process. Furthermore, both views assume that the process adaptation (refinement/redesign) is a *management activity or concern*. Nonetheless, these views have the following limitations.

1. There is no clear distinction between the process definition adaptation and the process instance adaptation in these views [55, 110]. The views focus mainly on the process definition adaptation. In an operational environment, the same process definition can be used for different process instances that may require individual and different adaptations. These adaptations are not a complete redesign of the process concerned and are carried out within a scope of a process instance.
2. These views assume that adaptation at the process definition level is a design time activity. There is no representation for *runtime adaptations* at the process definition level. This is understandable as the traditional BPM systems require an offline (re)design of the definitions/schemas before being (re-)deployed in an enactment engine. On the contrary, contemporary systems require adapting the process definitions or schemas while the system is up and running without complete redeployment. Such a capability is essential for modern applications functioning in a competitive business environment, where a temporary shutdown of an orchestration engine can be costly to the businesses, if not catastrophic.

6.1.2 Adaptation phases

This book presents a more detailed view of process management and adaptation support than other views presented in the literature. As illustrated in Figure 6.2, this view also assumes that the process refinement is an *iterative activity*, and that the process design/redesign is a *management activity* that should be based on the feedback provided by monitoring the process execution. As such, this view does not

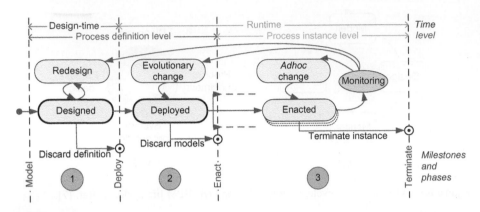

Figure 6.2 Process adaptation phases.

contradict the previously presented views in Figure 6.1. However, this view clearly distinguishes the process definition adaptation from the process instance adaptation, addressing the first limitation. It also shows that the adaptations on process definitions are no longer a complete design-time-only activity, but they also can be a runtime activity, addressing the second limitation. These two explicit representations are vital to understand the phases of adaptation management in an adaptive service orchestration.

As shown in Figure 6.2, process adaptation has *three phases* between *four milestones*. The four milestones are marked according to the activities of *model*, *deploy*, *enact* and *terminate* (shown by vertical bars). Between these four milestones, there are three phases known as *designed* (*1*), *deployed* (*2*) and *enacted* (*3*). An understanding of these three phases and milestones is necessary to determine the type of adaptation that should be carried out in a service orchestration. Let us clarify these phases and milestones in detail.

At the beginning, an initial design is drafted to reflect the business requirements. This involves business analysts and software engineers. It should be noted that an IT process design is just to achieve a close approximation of the real-world business requirements. Therefore, the design is subject to numerous revisions until the design is accepted as 'close enough'. This forms phase 1 or the *designed phase*. Once a process definition is *designed*, then it is *deployed* on a suitable platform, e.g. an orchestration engine. Upon deployment, many process instances can be enacted from the same definition. This is phase 2 or the *deployed phase*. Then, the enacted business process instances are executed during phase 3 or the *enacted phase*. These instances are individually monitored and adapted to instance-specific business requirements and unexpected exceptions until they terminate.

The monitoring is a continuous activity that is carried out during phase 3. Monitoring provides the feedback to carry out three different types of adaptations in all three phases. Therefore, unlike the views presented in Figure 6.1, this view (Figure 6.2) does not consider monitoring as a completely different phase. Instead, monitoring is considered as an activity carried out during the enactment phase by observing how running processes behave. *Business process monitoring* and *change mining/analysis* are important aspects of process adaptation, and much work has been done in this area [283, 286]. As shown, the output from the monitoring closes the feedback loop in three different locations.

During phase 3, the process instances are subject to *ad hoc changes* [55, 84, 141] to deviate from the original definition. These changes are not permanent and affect only a particular process instance. However, if the outcome demands a common and systemwide adaptation, then *evolutionary changes* are carried out on the loaded definitions or their internal representation (models maintained at runtime). Such changes affect the future process instances but do not require a redeployment of service orchestration descriptions. The loaded runtime process models that represent the process definitions can be dynamically modified to reflect the changes in phase 2. However, in a worst case scenario, a complete system/process *redesign* is required and the system's ability of handling such changes may be beyond the change capabilities offered at phase 2. Such drastic changes are required to be carried out during phase 1.

This view shows that the process definition level change is no longer a complete design time activity. Usually, there is confusion in referring *process runtime changes* to *process instance-level changes*. In modern PAIS, meanings of these two are not identical. During runtime, both process definitions and instances can be changed. The system design should support performing such changes *on the fly* with minimal or no interruptions to the system's ongoing operation. Therefore, of the adaptations in the three phases, this book focuses on the adaptations in phase 2 and phase 3, i.e. evolutionary and *ad hoc* adaptations at runtime, respectively. Design time modifications at phase 1 are beyond the scope of this book.

6.2   Adaptation management

The adaptations of a service orchestration need to be managed to assure that the objectives of service providers, aggregator and consumers are achieved. When there is a change in the way that the services collaborate, the service orchestration needs to be adapted. Nonetheless, adaptations cannot be carried out at will. Instead, they should be carefully managed. Therefore, the middleware for service orchestration should provide mechanisms to manage the adaptations. Based on the overview provided in the previous section, this section describes how the adaptations are managed in the Serendip framework.

6.2.1   Functional and management systems

Human organisations such as hospitals or universities consist of both functional and management systems. The *functional system* continuously performs business functions, whereas the *management system* manages the behaviour of the functional system. To elaborate, for example, treating patients is defined in the functional system of a hospital, which includes functionalities such as diagnosis, treatment and keeping medical records. The functional system also defines a number of roles such as doctors, nurses and clerks to perform these functions/duties. However, the management system (the authority) of a hospital continuously manages the functional system. Concerns such as what roles should exist, who should play these roles and how roles should interact with each other are determined by the management system.

Adopting such a managed-system viewpoint, a Serendip service orchestration also includes both functional and management systems. A service orchestration deployed in an orchestration engine serves the incoming requests. In order to serve the requests, a number of roles are defined. The service orchestration uses external partner services to play the functional roles. The service orchestration defines *when* and *how* to invoke these partner services. However, the management system decides *when* and *how* to reconfigure and regulate the service orchestration to optimise its operations. The concerns such as what roles should exist, how the service relationships are changed, what process definitions are modified and how a particular process instance should deviate are the decisions that the management system takes. Both functional and management systems run in parallel.

It is important that the functional and management concerns are separated [48]. Serendip will follow this separation of functional and management systems by adopting the concept of *the organiser*.

6.2.2 The organiser

The role-oriented adaptive design (ROAD) separates the management concerns from the functional concerns via a special role called the *organiser* in a service composite. The *organiser* reconfigures and regulates its composite [83]. An organiser player manages the composite via the organiser player and can either be a human or an intelligent software system, which is automated or semi-automated. The organiser player (*the management system*) should be separated from the service orchestration (*the functional system*). For a simple service orchestration, the organiser can be a human monitoring the processes and performing the adaptations. For a more sophisticated service orchestration that requires machine intelligence, the design of the organiser can be a complex software system with or without human involvement.

The work presented in this book uses *the organiser* [82, 83, 287] concept and further extends it to support process monitoring and adaptation. In this work, the organiser not only reconfigures and regulates the structure but also changes the behaviour or processes of the organisation. The behaviour units can be dynamically added, removed or changed to reflect the changing business requirements. Such modifications do not require any pre-configured tunable points, as is the case with many existing alternatives [67, 68, 149]. We believe that such configured tunable points are not flexible enough in dynamic operating environments, as they require foreseeing the changing business requirements. Ability to change without requiring pre-configured tunable points helps the decision-making entity (a software system or human) to better reflect the changes in business requirements in the IT process support.

In the existing ROAD framework, a set of operations is provided via the organiser role and is exposed to the organiser player for it to reconfigure and regulate the service composite structure. The organiser player can add/remove/modify the contacts/roles/player bindings of the composite via the organiser role interface. This book extends the available operations of the organiser role to provide the support for process-level modifications. That is, the organiser can change the process definitions as well as process instances of the organisation via this extended set of operations. For example, *updatePropertyOfTask(String pid, String taskeId, String property, String value)* is an operation that performs an *atomic adaptation* to change a property, e.g. pre-conditions, of a task. The complete list of operations is listed in Appendix C.

Based on our experience, process-level adaptations can be more challenging than the structural adaptations. Running process instances have a relatively shorter lifetime compared to the composite structure and can change their states quickly. The adaptations need to be carried out systematically to ensure such properties as atomicity, consistency, isolation and durability (i.e. the ACID properties) [288]. Achieving such sound adaptations requires an adaptation engine in the runtime framework.

6.2.3 The adaptation engine

In Section 5.1.2, we briefly introduced the *adaptation engine*, which is a core component of the Serendip framework that provides adaptation support systematically and reliably. Each deployed and instantiated composite will have its own instance of an *adaptation engine*, which is running in parallel to the *enactment engine*.

As shown in Figure 6.3, the *adaptation engine* belongs to the management system while the *enactment engine* and the *model provider factory* belong to the

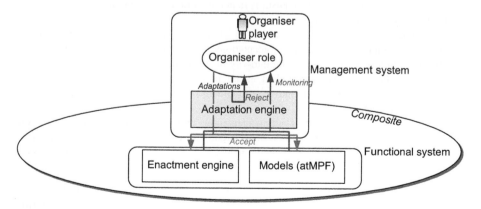

Figure 6.3 Separation of management and functional systems.

functional system. The management decisions taken by the organiser player are realised in the functional system via the adaptation engine. If the decision is not safe
to be carried out, then the adaptation engine will reject the adaptations and provide
possible reasons. For example, if the organiser player decides to make a process
instance deviate from the original process definition, then that decision must get the
consent of the adaptation engine. If the deviation is not safe, e.g. due to a violation
of a *behaviour constraint*, then the deviation is rejected. In addition, the adaptation
engine provides operations for *monitoring* the functional system.

One of the main reasons to place an adaptation engine between the organiser
player and the functional system is to address a number of process adaptation management challenges that can occur during the runtime. Just providing a set of operations via the organiser interface does not address these challenges. In practice,
when a human is the organiser player, he/she may not be able to determine the safe
states (Section 6.5) of running process instances to carry out the adaptations.
Furthermore, if the organiser player is remotely located over a network, then the
network delays can make the adaptation decision invalid due to process state
changes over the period of time delay.

6.2.4   Challenges

There are a number of adaptation challenges that should be addressed by the design
of the adaptation engine. They are:

1. The organiser and the service orchestration can be decentralised. Therefore, there should
   be a mechanism to adapt the service orchestration in a decentralised manner.
2. A single logical adaptation may involve multiple adaptation steps. Therefore, there should
   be a mechanism to carry out multiple steps of an adaptation in a single transaction. This
   is important for both efficiency and for avoiding false alarms due to process validation
   carried out in inconsistent states.
3. Manually performing the adaptations on running process instances that are executed
   speedily can be difficult. A mechanism is required from the adaptation engine to schedule
   and automate the future adaptations.
4. Adaptations can be frequent, and manual validation can be inefficient. Therefore, it is necessary to automate the validation of adaptations. In addition, the adaptations need to be
   carried out in a way that ensures the integrity of process definitions and underlying organisational behaviours. The interlinked nature of process definitions and organisational
   behaviours needs to be taken into consideration while performing the adaptations to
   ensure the integrity.
5. For phase 3 adaptations, i.e. the runtime adaptations on a process instance, the state of the
   running process instance needs to be considered. The validity of an adaptation of a process instance depends not only on the defined constraints but also on the state in which
   the process instance is currently in.

To address the *first challenge*, the work of this book extends the operation-based
adaptation mechanism of the existing ROAD framework to achieve the adaptation
support for processes. The details are discussed in Section 6.3.1.

In order to address the *second challenge*, this book proposes a *batch mode adaptation* mechanism on top of the existing *operation-based adaptation*. In batch mode adaptation, a number of atomic operations are carried out in a single logical transaction prior to process validation. The batch mode adaptation is described in Section 6.3.2. The adaptation scripts that support batch mode adaptation is described in Section 6.3.3.

In order to address the *third challenge*, a script scheduling mechanism that improves the scheduling capabilities of the adaptation mechanism is introduced. The script scheduling is described in Section 6.3.4 and the complete adaptation mechanism is described in Section 6.3.5.

In order to address the *fourth challenge*, an automated process validation mechanism is introduced in Section 6.4. This mechanism uses the two-tier constraints described in Section 4.4. Such validation is applicable for both process instances and process definitions.

Finally, the *fifth challenge* is addressed by performing *state checks* before adaptations, as described in Section 6.5. State check is a mechanism to ensure that a process instance is in a stable position to carry out the adaptations.

6.3   Adaptations

Adaptations on service orchestration are carried out during the runtime on process definitions and on process instances, i.e. at phase 2 and phase 3, as introduced in Section 6.1.2. Serendip supports two main modes of adaptations called *operation-based adaptations* and *batch mode adaptations*, which are discussed in detail.

6.3.1   Operation-based adaptations

Adaptations of a ROAD composite are carried out via the exposed operations of the organiser. For example, if a role needs to be added, then the *addRole()* operation of the organiser role is invoked by the organiser player.

This book extends the available set of operations of the organiser role in order to perform the adaptations on the newly introduced process layers. An overview of the types of operations available in the organiser interface is given in Figure 6.4. First, all the operations can be divided into *monitoring operations* and *adaptation*

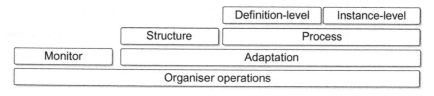

Figure 6.4 Types of operations in organiser interface.

operations. The monitoring operations allow the monitoring of the organisation while the adaptation operations allow adapting the organisation.

The adaptation operations can be further divided into two sets, i.e. operations that adapt the *structure* and operations that adapt *processes* of the organisation. While we use the operations for structure adaptations available in ROAD framework, we introduce new operations to perform process adaptations. Depending on whether the adaptations are carried out in process definitions (phase 2) or in process instances (phase 3), the process adaptation operations can be further divided into two sets, i.e. *instance-level* adaptation operations and *definition-level* adaptation operations. For example, *addTaskToProcessInst()* is an adaptation operation that performs an instance-level adaptation, whilst *addBehaviorRefToProcessDef()* is an adaptation operation that performs a definition-level adaptation. The full list of operations of the organiser role is available in Appendix C.

These operations allow a decentralised organiser player to manipulate the service orchestration. A suitable deployment technology such as Web services can be used to expose these operations of the organiser role as Web service operations. This is discussed further in Section 7.2. Each adaptation would lead to an integrity check. Depending on the outcome of the integrity check, a feedback is sent to the organiser player, e.g. as a Web service message.

In some cases, multiple operations are required to complete a process adaptation and to bring the service orchestration from one valid state to another. The operation-based adaptations alone cannot fulfil this requirement. Consequently, a batch mode adaptation is introduced.

6.3.2 Batch mode adaptations

Figure 6.5 shows the fundamental difference between operation-based adaptation and batch mode adaptation. After a single transaction (invocation of adaptation operation or operations), the adaptation engine performs an automated validation to ensure the integrity of the orchestration (Figure 6.4). Depending on the validation result, the change is either accepted or rejected. As shown in Figure 6.5A, the operation-based adaptation performs validations after each adaptation operation (i.e. each operation is treated as a transaction). In contrast, a batch mode adaptation as shown in Figure 6.5B performs a number of adaptation operations before an

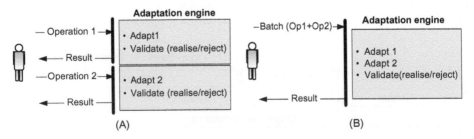

Figure 6.5 (A) Operations-based adaptation and (B) batch mode adaptation.

integrity check. Furthermore, the adaptation is performed in a single transaction, which is efficient when the organiser player and the organisation are decentralised in a networked environment.

The primary use of batch mode adaptation is to avoid *false alarms*, which is a practical problem with operation-based adaptations. For some change requirements, it is necessary to carry out a number of adaptations in the orchestration to bring the orchestration from one valid state to another. For example, consider an adaptation that imposes a new event dependency between two tasks *tTowPay* and *tRecordCreditPay*. When a task *tRecordCreditPay* subscribes to event *eTTPaidByCredit*, another task *tTowPay* of the process should trigger this event. This requires a number of atomic operations. If the validation is carried out after one atomic operation, e.g. modify the pre-event pattern (preEP) of *tRecordCreditPay,* then it would trigger a false alarm because the *eTTPaidByCredit* is not triggered by any other task.

The batch mode adaptation ensures the ACID properties in adaptation transactions, similar to transactions in database systems [288]. The ACID properties (atomicity, consistency, isolation and durability) are well known for their ability to guarantee a safe transaction, which is a single logical unit of operations on a database. Similarly a *batch adaptation* is a single *logical unit of adaptations* in a Serendip composite and it may consist of a number of atomic adaptation actions (Section 6.3.5). A failure in a single command of a batch adaptation would result in a failure in the complete transaction (atomicity). A batch adaptation should bring the service orchestration from one valid state to another valid state (consistency). No two batch adaptations should interfere with each other during the execution (isolation). The adaptation engine ensures that these adaptations are carried out in sequence to support the isolation property. Once a batch adaptation is carried out, it will remain committed in the service orchestration at either the process definition level or the instance level (durability).

In order to support batch mode adaptations, the work of this book uses *adaptation scripts*. The adaptation scripts can be executed via the organiser operation *executeScript()*. A script can be used to order a number of atomic adaptation operations in a single transaction. This allows a number of adaptation operations to be performed prior to an integrity check. The following section introduces adaptation scripts.

6.3.3 Adaptation scripts

In order to support the batch mode adaptation, the *Serendip framework* provides a scripting language (*Serendip adaptation scripts*) to issue a number of adaptation commands in a single transaction. Appendix D presents the syntax and details of the language.

An adaptation *script* specifies a number of *commands* scoped into possibly multiple *blocks*. A *script* corresponds to a single transaction, i.e. all the commands specified in the script (enclosed by blocks) need to be committed in a single transaction. A failure of a single command is a failure of the complete script. A *block* is

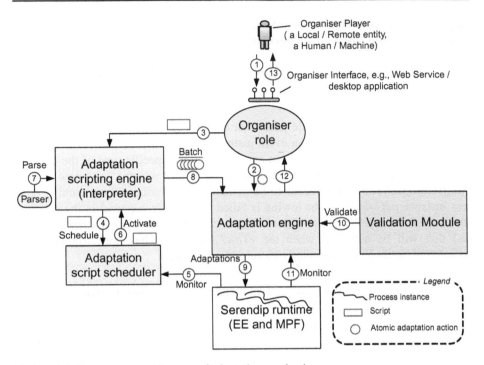

Figure 6.6 The runtime architecture of adaptation mechanism.

- *Organiser role* acts as a proxy for an organiser player to reconfigure and regulate the service orchestration as discussed in Section 6.2.2.
- *Adaptation engine* provides the process adaptation support in a timely, consistent and accurate manner as discussed in Section 6.2.3. It accepts atomic adaptation actions, which are single-step adaptations in the functional system corresponding to an adaptation command, e.g. *updateTaskOfProcessInst*.
- *Adaptation scripting engine* interprets and schedules adaptation scripts, supports batch mode adaptations and uses a script parser to parse the scripts.
- *Adaptation script scheduler* schedules adaptation scripts and listens to the Serendip runtime to identify when to issue the scheduled script.
- *Validation module* performs validations on adaptations to be discussed in Section 6.4.

The organiser player can use the organiser role interface to perform either operation-based or batch mode adaptations (1). The operation-based adaptations are directly issued to the adaptation engine (2). In contrast, the batch mode adaptation has to go through the *adaptation scripting engine* (3).

The *adaptation scripting engine* can either schedule the script (4) or interpret the script immediately (8), depending on *when* the script should be executed. Scheduling scripts is accomplished via the *adaptation script scheduler*. If there is at least one scheduled script, then the scheduler continuously listens (5) to the triggered events in the enactment environment in order to identify when to activate the scripts (6). The *adaptation script scheduler* subscribes to the event cloud, which

Table 6.1 **Adaptation modes and paths of execution**

Adaptation mode		Path of execution
Operations-based		$1-2-9-10-11-12-13$
Batch mode	Non-scheduled	$1-3-7-8-9-10-11-12-13$
	Scheduled	$1-3-4-5-6-7-8-9-10-11-12-13$

maintains the triggered events. The *adaptation scripting engine* parses (7) and inter-prets the adaptation scripts to create an array of *atomic adaptation actions* (8). These *atomic adaptation actions* are understood by the adaptation engine.

Irrespective of whether the adaptation actions are from *operations* or from *batch mode*, the adaptation engine understands and executes *atomic adaptation actions*. This arrangement provides a unified and consistent interface to carry out adaptations. The adaptation engine carries out adaptation requests sequentially in a single thread to ensure that no two adaptations will interfere with each other (*isolation*).

Prior to the adaptation, suitable backups are made in order to make sure the roll-backs are possible upon failure (*atomicity*). For example, if a process instance needs to be deviated from, the models and the instance status are backed up. If adaptation of the instance fails, then the backed-up process instance is restored. For phase 3 adaptations, the engine also needs to perform a state check (Section 6.5). Upon these pre-checks, the adaptations are carried out (9). If the adaptation is a phase 2 adaptation, then the models correspond to the definitions maintained in the MPF are changed. If the adaptation is a phase 3 adaptation, then, first, the process instance is paused (to be resumed after the adaptations) and the models corresponding to the process instances in MPF are adapted.

The adaptation engine performs a validation (10) to identify the impact of change (Section 6.4). This ensures that adaptation only takes the service orchestration from one valid state to another (*consistency*). Once the adaptation is successful, the change is committed (*durability*). Otherwise, the change is rejected and the backup is restored.

Apart from the adaptation commands, the monitoring commands are accepted by the adaptation engine and executed by reading the Serendip runtime (11, 12 and 13). These monitoring commands, e.g. *getCurrentStatusOfProcessInst*, let the orga-niser monitor the Serendip runtime. Table 6.1 summarises the different adaptation modes and corresponding paths of execution as shown in Figure 6.6.

6.4 Automated process validation

McKinley et al. [291] have identified two major types of approaches for dynamic software composition as *tunable software* and *mutable software*. The *tunable soft-ware* allows fine-tuning of the identified crosscutting concerns to suit changing environmental conditions. In contrast, *mutable software* allows changing even the imperative function of an application dynamically. However, the authors have also stated that, '*While very powerful (mutable software), in most cases the developer must constrain this flexibility to ensure the system's integrity across adaptations*'. This is so in the sense that tunable software naturally ensures the system's integrity by explicitly specifying and allowing *what can be tuned*. In contrast, mutable software needs an explicit mechanism to ensure the system's integrity.

Although this categorisation has been made with respect to software systems in general, it is also applicable to process adaptations. The approaches such as AO4BPEL [68], MoDAR [149] and VxBPEL [67] allow the change of crosscutting concerns of a process in a *tunable* manner. These approaches explicitly specify what can be tuned. In contrast, Serendip allows changes to the service orchestration without any requirement for pre-identified tunable points. While this provides a greater degree of flexibility, it comes with the risk of possible violations to process integrity upon adaptations. Therefore, Serendip needs to explicitly provide a mechanism to ensure the integrity of the service orchestration.

Serendip provides a two-tier constraint validation mechanism at the behaviour unit level and the process level, as discussed in Section 4.4. The *linkage* between process definitions and behaviour units is used to determine the minimal set of constraints to perform the validation. In addition, the impacts of the changes can also be identified. This section further extends the discussion in Section 4.4 to clarify how the Serendip runtime supports this concept.

6.4.1 Validation mechanism

The adaptations upon a service orchestration can be frequent and the complexity of the adaptations can be high. A manual validation can be time consuming and error prone. Therefore, it is important that the continuous adaptations are supported by an *automated and formal change validation mechanism* to protect the integrity of the service orchestration. To formalise and automate the change validation, it is necessary that task dependencies and constraints are mapped into formal specifications. This book uses some of the work by van der Aalst [245] and Gardey et al. [292] to conduct the formal mapping.

Figure 6.7 presents an overview of the *change validation mechanism*. First, all the *task dependencies* are mapped (T_d) to a *dependency specification*. Second, the minimal set of constraints (as identified in Section 4.4.2) are mapped (T_c) to a *constraint specification*. The dependency specification is being used by the constraint mapping process to ensure the consistency among the two specifications. Details about the preparation of dependency specification and constraint specification are given in Section 6.4.2 and in Section 6.4.3, respectively. Finally, a model checker validates the dependency specification against the constraint specification. The result can indicate if the validation is successful. If not successful, then the result identifies the violations that cause the failure.

6.4.2 Dependency specification

The dependency specification is prepared as a time Petri-Net (TPN) [292, 293]. A Serendip process definition potentially refers to a number of behaviour units. The

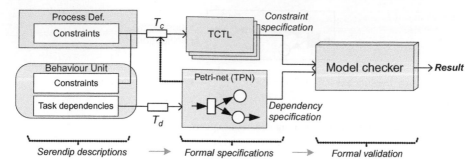

Figure 6.7 Change validation mechanism.

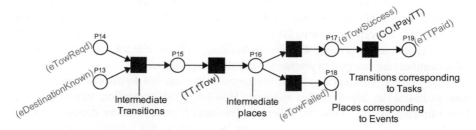

Figure 6.8 Preparing the dependency specification.

task dependencies of all the behaviour units of a process definition in its EPC representation are mapped to a TPN. A TPN is a Petri-Net [80, 99] that associates a time/clock with each transition. The mapping mechanism reuses the rules introduced in Refs. [245, 294].

A sample mapping is shown in Figure 6.8. As shown, the *tasks* are mapped to *Petri-Net transitions* and *events* are mapped to *Petri-Net places*. Moreover, if a task is associated with a performance property (e.g. time to execute), then the corresponding *transitions* are annotated with the cost value. In addition, there can be many *intermediary transitions and places* that can be produced due to the connectors such as XOR, AND and OR according to the transformation rules provided.

6.4.3 Constraint specification

The constraints can be specified in both behaviour units and process definitions levels (Section 4.4). These constraints are specified in the CTL/TCTL [80] language, making the T_c mapping straightforward compared to T_d (Figure 6.7). However, the mapping T_c requires observing the generated *dependency specification* to ensure the consistency between the two specifications. The *event identifiers* used in the constraint expressions are mapped to the equivalent *places* of the generated Petri-Net.

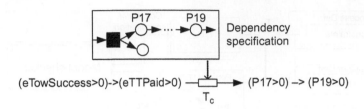

Figure 6.9 Preparing the corresponding constraint specification.

To elaborate, suppose the constraint expression '*(eTowSuccess > 0)->* *(eTTPaid > 0)*' needs to be mapped into the constraint specification in CTL/TCTL. The expression refers to two events *eTowSuccess* and *eTTPaid*. Suppose the places of the generated Petri-Net corresponding to these two events *eTowSuccess* and *eTTPaid* are P17 and P19, respectively. Then, the constraint specification will include the consistent TCTL expression as shown in Figure 6.9. Similarly, all the relevant constraints (for the modifications) are mapped to prepare the constraint specification.

Note that the validation scheme presented is the default Petri-Net-based validation available in the Serendip runtime. However, the validation module of the Serendip runtime is extensible. When the business requires a more domain-specific validation, custom validation plug-ins can be added to the runtime. For example, the validation mechanism can be extended by a business rules [176] plug-in, which allows the specification and enforcement checking of domain-specific business rules beyond the capabilities offered by the default Petri-Net-based validation module. Furthermore, there are other validation techniques and tools available [212, 295] that can be easily plugged into the Serendip runtime to extend its domain-specific validation capabilities.

6.5   State checks

The validity of the phase 3 adaptations depends not only on the violation of business constraints (Section 6.4) but also on the state of the process instance. A state check is carried out prior to every atomic adaptation action to ensure that the adaptation is carried out in a state-safe manner.

At a given time, a process instance can be in any of the states shown in Figure 6.10A. When a process is enacted, the process instance is in the *active* state. A process instance in the *active* state can be either *paused* or *terminated*. A *paused* process instance can become *active*, should the operation need to be resumed. A process is *terminated* when it is naturally completed or aborted, i.e. a forced completion.

A process instance consists of many tasks that are executed during the phase 3. Figure 6.10B shows the states of a task in a process instance. All the tasks of a

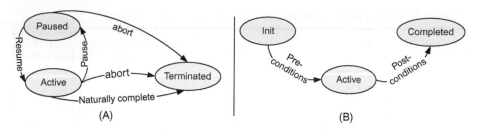

Figure 6.10 States of (A) a process instance and (B) a task of a process instance.

process instance are at the *init* state until the pre-conditions are met. Once the pre-conditions are met, the task is in the *active* state, which indicates that the obligated role player is performing the task. Once the post-conditions are met, the task is considered to be *completed*.

Prior to any process instance-specific adaptation, the process instance must be in the *paused* state (except for operation *updateStateOfProcessInst*, which is used to change the process instance state, e.g. to pause a process instance). If the process instance is in the active state, then the engine temporarily *pauses* the process instance throughout the complete adaptation transaction. When the process instance is *paused*, the service orchestration can still receive the messages related to the process instance from the players. However, the sending of messages (service invocations) is delayed until the process instance *resumes* its operations.

Table 6.2 summarises adaptation actions and their relationships with the state of process instance and task. For example, the *addTaskToProcessInst* or *removeTaskFromProcessInst* operations are carried out only when the process state is *paused* and the task state is *init*. This is same for the *updateTaskOfProcessInst* operation, which updates a property of a task, except when the property is *postEP*. The postEP of a task of a process instance could be modified even if the task is currently in the *Active* state.

The operation *updateStateOfProcessInst* is allowed when the process instance is either *active* or *paused*. The other operations, i.e. *addConstraintToProcessInst*, *removeContraintFromProcessInst*, *updateContraintOfProcessInst*, *updateProcessInst*, *addNewEventToProcessInst* and *removeEventFromProcessInst*, are allowed when the process instance is paused. The task status is not applicable (N/A) for these operations because they are not modifying a specific task.

While the process instances are adapted, the structure is stable. The adaptation engine does not perform parallel adaptations (e.g. tow adaptation scripts) to ensure the *isolation* property [288], as described in Section 6.3.5. Therefore, it is not possible for the organisational structure to be changed while a process instance is adapted, unless specifically included in the same script.

6.6 Summary

In this chapter, we have shown how the adaptation management system of the Serendip framework is designed. The objective of the adaptation management

Table 6.2 State checks for different adaptation actions

Operation	Allowed process instance status	Allowed task status
addTaskToProcessInst	Paused	Init
removeTaskFromProcessInst	Paused	Init
updateTaskOfProcessInst when @prop = preEP	Paused	Init
updateTaskOfProcessInst when @prop = postEP	Paused	Init/active
updateTaskOfProcessInst when @prop = pp	Paused	Init
updateTaskOfProcessInst when @prop = obligRole	Paused	Init
updateStateOfProcessInst	Paused/active	N/A
addConstraintToProcessInst	Paused	N/A
removeContraintFromProcessInst	Paused	N/A
updateContraintOfProcessInst	Paused	N/A
updateProcessInst @prop = CoT[a]	Paused	N/A
addNewEventToProcessInst	Paused	N/A
removeEventFromProcessInst	Paused	N/A

[a]Updating CoS is not applicable for a process instance.

system is to systematically carry out the phase 2 and phase 3 adaptations to a service orchestration.

An overview was initially presented explaining the different adaptation phases of a service orchestration. We further extended the previous models of process life cycle management. Based on this extended model, we presented the adaptation management system of the Serendip framework.

The adaptation management system clearly separates the functional and management systems of a service composite. We further extend the organiser role of the ROAD framework and provide the runtime support for adaptations via the adaptation engine. In designing the adaptation engine, several challenges have been addressed. To address these challenges, various design decisions have been made and are reflected in the design of the Serendip adaptation management system.

To support process modifications that may involve multiple adaptation operations, the batch mode adaptation mechanism is introduced. The batch mode adaptations adhere to the ACID properties (atomicity, consistency, isolation and durability). A scripting language has been designed to support the batch mode adaptations. A scheduling mechanism has also been introduced to schedule and automate the adaptation scripts. The complete adaptation mechanism supports both operation-based and batch mode adaptations (scheduled and otherwise).

Manual verification of adaptations is inefficient and impractical. To ensure the business constraints are not violated during adaptation, an automated validation mechanism has been introduced. This mechanism supports the two-tier constraint specification for processes (as described in Chapter 4). The validation mechanism uses a Petri-Net-based formal validation tool to automate the integrity checking of process adaptations, where a dynamically generated Petri-Net for a process is validated against the TCTL constraints *on the fly*.

Phase 3 adaptations require additional state checks to ensure that the adaptations are carried out only when the process instance is in a safe state. Adaptations may be allowed/disallowed depending on the state a process instance is in. The state transition models for process and task states were also presented and the relationships between different process/task states and the plausibility of Phase 3 adaptations discussed.

Part Three

Part Three

The Serendip Orchestration Framework

7

Chapter 5 has presented the design of the Serendip runtime to support adaptive service orchestration, whilst Chapter 6 has showed how the adaptations are managed. These two chapters have collectively presented the architectural underpinnings to improve the runtime adaptability of service orchestration. In this chapter, we present the implementation details to show how those design concepts are implemented in *the Serendip orchestration framework.*

The current implementation of *the Serendip orchestration framework* primarily supports and uses the Web services technology. It uses the *Apache Axis2* [296, 297] as the Web service engine. The issues of transport layer protocols, message processing and security are handled by the Axis2 engine. This ensures that the implementation conforms to the existing Web services standards such as SOAP [261] and WSDL [38]. In addition, this work uses the existing ROAD framework [81] and further improves its capabilities with added process support, as discussed in Chapter 5. These two major decisions to reuse the ROAD framework and Apache Axis2 implementations have significantly reduced the effort of implementing the framework.

To reuse existing the ROAD framework and Apache Axis2, we need to develop a range of new components for the overall Serendip framework. The message routing, message transformation and deployment mechanisms are developed by extending the ROAD framework to provide better adaptability as required at the orchestration layer. The Apache Axis2 runtime is extended to support the *service composite deployment* [260], which is in addition to Axis2' existing *service deployment*. Importantly, the changes are introduced as extensions, and no changes are made to the Axis2 code base. This ensures the compatibility with Axis2 code base. The extension is implemented as another layer on top of Axis2, has additional capabilities beyond the behaviour of Axis2-core [297, 298] and is called as ROAD4WS [260]. Such an extension evades the need of maintaining a dedicated version of Axis2 to support this work.

The *Serendip orchestration framework* can be divided into three main parts, i.e. the *deployment layer, orchestration layer* and the *tool support*, as shown in Figure 7.1. Collectively, these three parts provide the service orchestration support. The orchestration layer, called the *Serendip-Core*, is implemented to be independent from the deployment environment and currently supports only Web services. The motivation of making the core independent is to allow other future deployment environments to reuse the *Serendip-Core*. The ROADfactory, which is the core implementation of the ROAD framework, has been improved and extended with the

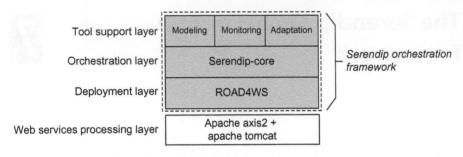

Figure 7.1 Layers of framework implementation.

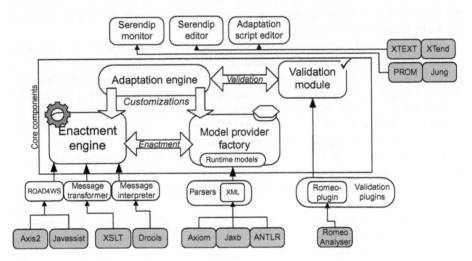

Figure 7.2 Serendip framework implementation and related technologies.

process support to implement the Serendip-Core. The *Web services deployment layer* is the ROAD4WS extension to Apache Axis2. The *tool support* layer includes various tools implemented to support software engineers in modelling, monitoring and adapting Serendip orchestrations. An overview of all the technologies used and different modules are given in Figure 7.2. The external software and tools used are shaded in the figure. We introduce these existing technologies in upcoming sections as we discuss the relevant components of the Serendip framework.

The rest of this chapter is organised as follows. Section 7.1 provides details on how the Serendip-Core is implemented, highlighting important aspects. Section 7.2 describes the deployment environment, i.e. ROAD4WS. Finally, Section 7.3 provides details on the tool support provided for modelling, monitoring and adapting service orchestrations.

7.1   Serendip-Core

The Serendip-Core is the central implementation of the *Serendip orchestration framework*. It consists of a number of interrelated components that support modelling and enacting adaptive service orchestrations. It is important that the Serendip-Core implementation delivers sufficient support for the underlying service orchestration philosophy described in the previous chapters of the book. Consequently, certain specific principles were followed at the implementation level. This section discusses those implementation principles.

One of the key considerations behind the Serendip-Core implementation is to implement an adaptive service orchestration engine that is independent of the underlying deployment environment. The main reason for this design principle is to make the core framework reusable among an array of different deployment technologies. Besides, the deployment technologies and standards may evolve over time. For example, apart from SOAP/Web services, which is the currently supported technology (Section 7.2), other alternative technologies such as *RESTful Services* [262, 299, 300], *XML/RPC* [263], *Mobile Web services* [301] do exist. Therefore, it is important to have the Serendip-Core implemented in a deployment-technology neutral manner. To meet this requirement a couple of implementation decisions are made.

1. The event-based process progression in the engine does not depend on specific messages but rather only on events. This de-couples the engine operations with the underlying message mediation mechanisms and the employed technologies.
2. Another decision is that the adaptation, validation, message transformation and message interpretation mechanisms are implemented in an extensible manner. The validation mechanism could be extended further to support domain-specific constraint languages apart from the default TCTL expressions [80, 257]. Likewise, future alternatives can replace XSLT [182], which is used for realising message transformations. Drools engine [302] can also be replaced in the future by alternative message interpretation mechanisms.

The core framework is implemented by extending the ROADfactory 1.0, which is the implementation of the role-oriented adaptive design approach to software systems [81]. The ROADfactory 1.0 implementation supports the instantiation and management of ROAD composites, involving roles, contracts and message routing among different roles based on declarative interaction terms and contractual rules. However, it did not have business process support. For example, the ROADfactory 1.0 implementation did not have the concept of a process in its original message routing and synchronisation mechanism. Moreover, it did not have the concept of task defined in roles. Therefore, it was not possible to use ROADfactory 1.0 in its original form for this implementation. Instead, the ROADfactory 1.0 implementation is modified to support the newly introduced process concepts. For example, the message routing and message synchronisation are required to be carried out within a context of a process instance. Furthermore, in order to support the event-driven nature of the coordination layer, the contractual message evaluation and routing mechanism needs to be modified. In addition, the concept of task and how it is used to synthesise and synchronise the internal and external interactions have been introduced. The complete implementation (including support for Serendip, i.e. the work of this book) is now known as the ROADfactory 2.0.

It should be noted that the framework implementation is large and a detailed explanation is beyond the space allowed in this book. Therefore, the next few sections present only the important implementation details of the framework. For more details about the implementation of this book, please refer to the ROAD 2.0 documentation,[1] which is an integration of both Serendip and ROAD 1.0.

7.1.1 The event cloud

The Serendip enactment engine is event-driven. The tasks become do-able when its pre-conditions, specified as patterns of events, are met. As tasks are completed, more events are triggered, which make more tasks do-able. To record and manage these events, the event cloud component is used in the enactment engine implementation.

The implementation of the event cloud is carried out according to the publish/subscribe architecture [303, 304] as discussed in Section 5.3. The publish/subscribe architecture is used to de-couple how the information is published from how the information is used. The data from a publisher that capture the information are not specific to a particular subscriber. Such de-coupling provides more flexibility in adding and removing publishers and subscribers with minimal effect.

The implementation of event cloud and associated classes are shown in Figure 7.3. The *EventCloud* is an object maintained in the enactment engine to keep event records. The organiser instance (only one for the composite) and the contract instances (many) can publish events to the event cloud as discussed in Section 5.3.1.

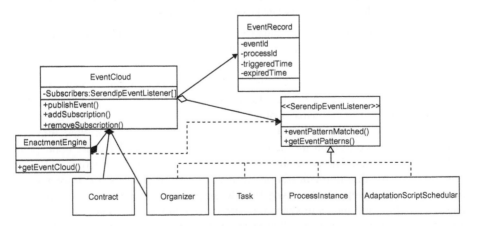

Figure 7.3 Class diagram: event cloud implementation.

[1]http://www.swinburne.edu.au/ict/research/cs3/road/implementations.htm.

Apart from *EventRecords*, the *EventCloud* also maintains a list of subscribers. The subscribers of these types can be dynamically subscribed to or removed from the list. All subscribers must implement the *SerendipEventListener* interface. The interface specifies two methods, *getEventPatterns()* and *eventPatternMatched()*. The *EventCloud* uses the former method to retrieve the event patterns that the subscriber is interested in and the latter method to call the action as implemented locally in the subscriber. Table 7.1 presents what these patterns are and the defined actions when the event patterns are matched.

In order to evaluate the event patterns, a library called *event pattern recogniser* has been implemented using the ANTLR parser generator [305]. The event cloud uses the *event pattern recogniser* to evaluate the patterns based on recorded events. The parser allows the creation of a *binary tree* [306] based on the event pattern expressions. The tree is constructed using the same grammar used to create the pre-tree of an atomic graph as described in Section 5.5.1. The interior nodes of the tree consist of operators (AND = *, OR = |, XOR = ^), and the leaf nodes consist of events as shown in Figure 7.4. During the pattern evaluation, the events are replaced with true/false values depending on the whether the event has been triggered. Finally, the tree is traversed (depth-first), evaluating each node until the top-most node is evaluated, which produces the outcome of either *true* or *false*.

Table 7.1 Subscribed event patterns and subsequent actions

Subscriber type	Subscribed event pattern	Action when event pattern matches
Task	Pre-event pattern	Notifies the obligated role to perform the task (e.g. invoke a player service)
Enactment engine	Condition of start of all the process definitions	Enacts a new process instance of a relevant definition according to CoS
Process instance	Condition of termination	Self-terminates upon CoT
Adaptation script scheduler	Event pattern that should trigger a script	Executes the script
Organiser	Event patterns that the organiser player is interested in	Unknown

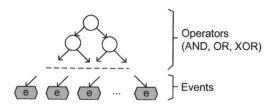

Figure 7.4 A binary tree to evaluate event patterns.

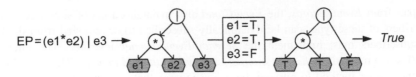

Figure 7.5 Example event-pattern evaluation.

Figure 7.5 shows an example where the event pattern '(e1*e2)|e3' is converted to a binary tree. Suppose events e1 and e2 have been triggered but e3 has not been triggered. As the next step, the tree is annotated with true/false values. The tree traversal produces the outcome, *true*, which indicates that the event pattern has been matched.

7.1.2 Interpreting interactions

Serendip processes progress based on triggered events. These events are triggered by interpreting the interactions between roles according to the defined service relationships (Section 5.3.2). In order to interpret such interactions and trigger events, the work of this book uses declarative rules specified in Drools rule language [176].

From the implementation point of view, there are many advantages of integrating Drools [176, 307] as the business rules engine. First, Drools supports *Java Specification Request for Java Rules Engines* (JSR94 API) [308], which is the standard Java runtime API to access a rules engine from a Java platform. Second, Drools engine is implemented based on the RETE algorithm [309]. RETE is a decision-making algorithm, which is asymptotically independent from the number of rules that are being executed [310]. This improves the efficiency of decision-making at the Serendip runtime and thereby the overall process execution. Third, Drools framework is rich with tool support to write and execute business rules. Fourth, the language is expressive and easy to follow. Fifth, Drools supports XML-based rules syntax as well. This is an advantage if the interchangeability of rule files is a requirement. Finally, Drools is free and has a strong user and developer community, which helps a Serendip user to quickly learn and use the language.

Apart from these advantages, Drools is capable of maintaining a *long-lived and iteratively modifiable contract state*, which is important to represent the *state of contract*. The state of contract keeps *facts* that capture the current context/state of the service relationship and *rules* that specify how to interpret the interactions according to the current context of the service relationship. Drools allows dynamically inserting these facts (Java objects) and rules (Drools rules) into the state called a *stateful knowledge session* [311]. *Stateful knowledge session* is long-lived and can be iteratively modified during the runtime (in contrast to its counterpart, the *stateless knowledge session*). A contract state is thus represented as a *stateful knowledge session* in Drools. When a contract is instantiated, a *stateful knowledge session* is instantiated. As the roles bound by the contract interact, this *stateful knowledge session* is updated. When the contract needs to be removed, the *stateful knowledge session* is '*disposed*' [311].

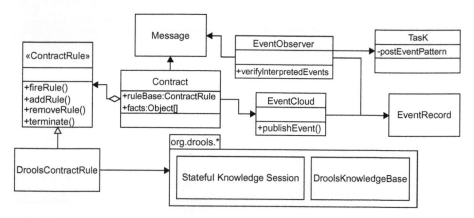

Figure 7.6 Class diagram: contract implementation.

Figure 7.6 shows the classes associated with the Drools implementation. As shown, any rule implementation to be integrated with the core framework has to implement the *ContractRule* interface. Accordingly, the *DroolsContractRule* implements the interface as the Drools plug-in for the framework to interpret the messages using Drools rules. A contract maintains its contract rules (a rule base) during the runtime. New rules can be added and existing rules can be removed from the rule base. Eventually, the rule base is deleted when no longer required, i.e. when the contract is removed. When a message needs to be interpreted, the specified rules are fired via the *fireRule()* method.

The events that trigger as part of evaluation of result messages of a task should adhere to the post-event pattern of the task. A runtime entity called an *EventObserver* associated with the task determines whether the fired events adhere to the post-event patterns of a given task of a given process instance by analysing the collective outcome of all the triggered events. For example, both of the events *eTowSuccess* and e*Tow*Failed should be triggered as part of a single rule evaluation upon completion of task *tTow*, because its post-event pattern is '*eTowSuccess XOR eTowFailed*'. When a task is completed, an instance of *EventObserver* is created and shared by reference to all the result messages. When a result message is interpreted, the *EventObserver* collects the triggered events and marks that result message as interpreted. Upon completion of interpretation of all the result messages, the *EventObserver* determines whether the triggered set of events adheres to the post-event pattern of the task. Finally, the resulting event records are published in the *event cloud*.

Drools rules are condition-action rules [176]. Therefore, a Drools rule contains two main parts, i.e. the *when* and *then* parts, which are also referred to as the left-hand side (LHS) and right-hand side (LHS).

* The *when* part specifies a certain condition to trigger the rule. This condition may be evaluated as true or false based on the properties of facts in the *stateful knowledge session* [307]. Here, a fact means a Java object, such as a message inserted into the *stateful knowledge session*, or the number of requests over the contract being maintained.

```
/** 1. The rule to evaluate the interaction orderTow on the request path **/
rule "orderTowRequestRule"
  when
    $msg : MessageRecievedEvent(operationName == "orderTow", response == false)
  then
    $msg.triggerEvent("eTowReqd");
end

/** 2. The rule to evaluate the interaction orderTow on the response path **/
rule "orderTowResponseRule"
  when
    $msg : MessageRecievedEvent (operationName == "orderTow", response == true)
  then
    //If everything is OK trigger success event
    $msg.triggerEvent("eTowSuccess");
    //If something is wrong with the interaction trigger the failure event
    //$msg.triggerEvent("eTowFailed");
end
```

Listing 7.1 Two rules to interpret interaction *orderTow* specified in CO_TT.drl.

• The *then* part specifies what needs to be done if the condition is evaluated to true. The business logic of the contract to inspect and interpret messages is written here.

Listing 7.1 shows a sample rule file that interprets the interaction *orderTow* of contract CO_TT. The first rule interprets the '*request*' message from case officer to tow truck for the operation '*orderTow*'. This condition is fulfiled by evaluating the two properties of the message *operationName* and *isResponse* in the *when* part of the rule. In this case, *operationName* is '*orderTow*' and *isResponse* is *false*, stating that *the request of orderTow interaction* will trigger this rule. The *then* part of this rule contains the business logic, i.e. the event, *eTowReqd*, that should be triggered.

The second rule is to evaluate the message in the response path. In this rule, either of the *eTowSuccess* or *eTowFailed* events is triggered depending on the response.

7.1.3   Message synchronisation and synthesis

Section 5.4 presented how the internal interactions between roles are used to compose external interactions and vice versa. This section provides how the current implementation supports these transformations using the Default *XSLTMessageAnalyser*. The *XSLTMessageAnalyser* is an XSLT-based [182, 312] implementation to transform XML-based messages such as SOAP messages exchanged among Web services. XSLT transformations are dynamically loaded and executed. This allows the message synthesis logic to independently evolve from the rest of service orchestration logic.

XSLT has been chosen due to the many advantages it offers. XSLT is a well-established and popular standard to transform XML documents [313]. Different parts of a SOAP message could be referred using XPath inside an XSLT descriptor [183]. Complex transformations can be written using high-level constructs, which are more resilient compared to the use of low-level custom transformation using, e.g. DOM/ SAX [314]. XSLT is platform-independent. It also has good tool support and is well-understood within the community.

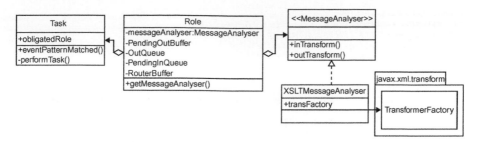

Figure 7.7 Class diagram: message synchronisation implementation.

```
Task tTow {
        UsingMsgs CO_TT.mOrderTow.Req, GR_TT.mSendGarageLocaiton.Req;
        ResultingMsgs CO_TT.mOrderTow.Res, GR_TT.mSendGarageLocaiton.Res;
}
```

Listing 7.2 A sample task description.

Let us elaborate how the message synchronisation and synthesis mechanism has been implemented using XSLT. As shown in Figure 7.7, the *XSLTMessageAnalyser* implements the generic *MessageAnalyser* interface, which consists of two methods, *inTransform()* and *outTransform()*. A role maintains a *MessageAnalyser*[2] for this purpose. When a task of the role becomes do-able, the *outTransform()* method will be called; when a message is received from the player, the *inTransform()* method will be called. Any *MessageAnalyser* can use the buffers and queues of the role to select and place messages (Section 5.4). The *XSLTMessageAnalyser* uses the javax. xml.transform.TransformFactory to perform the transformations.

Listing 7.2 shows the task description of *tTow* that specifies what internal messages are used to extract the information (i.e. clause *UsingMsgs*) for constructing the request to the player. The given example uses two messages, *CO_TT. mOrderTow.Req* and *GR_TT.mSendGarageLocaiton.Req*. The task description also specifies what internal messages are generated (i.e. clause *ResultingMsgs*) from the player response, i.e. *CO_TT.mOrderTow.Res, GR_TT.mSendGarageLocaiton.Res*.

Depending on the task description, a number of template XSLT transformation files are generated by the Serendip Modelling Tool, i.e. one template for the out-transformation and one each for result messages. The transformation file for the out-transformation of *tTow* is given in Listing 7.2. As shown, the two messages *CO_TT.orderTow.Req* and *GR_TT.sendGRLocation.Req* can be accessed via the specified XSLT parameters. Within an XSLT, a developer can use XPath expressions [315] to refer to the specific parts of these messages, i.e. the information to be extracted. Likewise, Listing 7.3 shows the XSLT transformation to create the internal message *CO_TT.orderTow.Res* from the player response to the task *tTow*.

[2]The current implementation only supports an XSLT Message Analyser.

```
<xsl:stylesheet version="2.0"
    xmlns:xsl="http://www.w3.org/1999/XSL/Transform"
xmlns:soapenv="http://schemas.xmlsoap.org/soap/envelope/"
    xmlns:q0="http://ws.apache.org/axis2">
    <xsl:output method="xml" indent="yes"/>
    <xsl:param name="CO_TT.orderTow.Req"/>
    <xsl:param name="GR_TT.sendGRLocation.Req"/>
    <xsl:template match="/">
        <soapenv:Envelope xmlns:soapenv="http://schemas.xmlsoap.org/soap/envelope/">
            <soapenv:Body>
                <q0:tow xmlns:q0="http://ws.apache.org/axis2">
                    <pickupLocation>
                        <xsl:value-of select="$CO_TT.orderTow.Req/soapenv:Envelope/
soapenv:Body/q0:orderTow/pickupInfo"/>
                    </pickupLocation>
                    <garageLocation>
                        <xsl:value-of select="$GR_TT.sendGRLocation.Req/soapenv:Envelope/
soapenv:Body/q0:sendGRLocation/content"/>
                    </garageLocation>
                </q0:tow>
            </soapenv:Body>
        </soapenv:Envelope>
    </xsl:template>
</xsl:stylesheet>
```

Listing 7.3 XSLT file for out-transformation, tTow.xsl.

7.1.4 The validation module

The Serendip framework provides an in-built process validation mechanism based on Petri-Nets [99] and TCTL [253, 254], as discussed in Section 6.4. This section provides more specific implementation details on how the validation module works.

The Petri-Net-based validator is implemented using the *Romeo model checker* tool.[3] *Romeo* supports analysis of time Petri-Net and is developed by the *real-time systems team at IRCCyN.*[4] It also provides the support for validating TCTL constraints. The *Romeo model checker* is free and widely used (Listing 7.4).

As part of the integration effort, a Java plug-in has been developed to integrate Romeo with the Serendip-Core. The classes associated with the plug-in have been shown in Figure 7.8. *RomeoPNValidation* defines the *SerendipValidation* interface. The adaptation engine keeps a reference to the validation module and calls the plug-in when validation is required. The plug-in transforms the task dependency specification into a Petri-Net model using the *PetriNetBuilder*. The *PetriNetBuilder* uses the ProM framework [278] as a library for this purpose. Then, the generated Petri-Net model is translated into a Romeo-compatible representation (see Listing 7.5 for an example fragment from the process instance *pdGold001*).

Likewise, the *CTLWriter* class has been implemented to translate the TCTL constraint expressions into Romeo-compatible representation (see Listing 7.6 for an example of TCTL-based specification for constraints of process instance *pdGold001*). The Romeo tool does not provide a Java interface. Therefore, when the

---

[3]http://romeo.rts-software.org/
[4]http://www.irccyn.ec-nantes.fr/?lang=en

```
<xsl:stylesheet version="2.0"
   xmlns:xsl="http://www.w3.org/1999/XSL/Transform"
xmlns:soapenv="http://schemas.xmlsoap.org/soap/envelope/"
   xmlns:q0="http://ws.apache.org/axis2">
   <xsl:output method="xml" indent="yes"/>
   <xsl:param name="tTow.doneMsg"/>
   <xsl:template match="/">
      <soapenv:Envelope xmlns:soapenv="http://schemas.xmlsoap.org/soap/envelope/">
         <soapenv:Body>
            <q0:orderTowResponse xmlns:q0="http://ws.apache.org/axis2">
               <return>
                  <xsl:value-of
select="$tTow.doneMsg/soapenv:Envelope/soapenv:Body/q0:towResponse/return/orderTow
Response"/>
               </return>
            </q0:orderTowResponse>
         </soapenv:Body>
      </soapenv:Envelope>
   </xsl:template>
</xsl:stylesheet>
```

Listing 7.4 XSLT file for in-transformation, CO_TT_orderTow_Res.xsl.

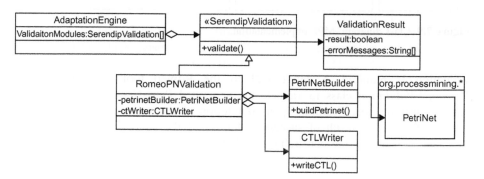

Figure 7.8 Class diagram: validation module implementation.

```
<?xml version="1.0" encoding="UTF-8"?>
<TPN name="pdGold001">
   <!--places (events or generated intermediary places) -->
   <place id="18" label="ComplainRcvd" initialMarking="0">...    </place>
   <place id="19" label="p1" initialMarking="0">...    </place>
   ...
   <!--transitions (tasks or generated intermediary transitions) -->
   <transition id="11" label="CO.Analyse" eft="0" lft="33"> ... </transition>
   <transition id="12" label="TT.Tow" eft="0" lft="33"> ... </transition>
   ...
   <!--arcs (generated connections between places and transitions) -->
   <arc place="18" transition="11" type="PlaceTransition" weight="1"> ... </arc>
   <arc place="19" transition="11" type="TransitionPlace" weight="1"> ... </arc>
   ...
</TPN>
```

Listing 7.5 Generated Romeo-compatible Petri-Net file.

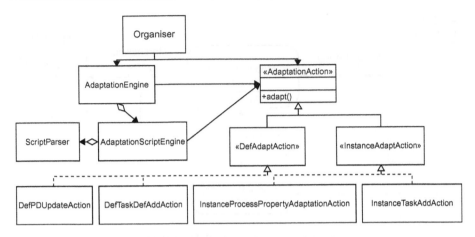

Figure 7.11 Class diagram: adaptation engine implementation.

present the details of how the adaptation engine is implemented and what the related technologies are.

- The implementation should provide a unified and consistent method to perform both operation-based and batch-mode adaptations.
- The implementation should be extensible. That is, future additions to the framework should be able to support additional types of adaptations, should the Serendip meta-model be extended, without requiring a change in the core adaptation mechanism.
- The implementation should provide an error recovery mechanism.

The related classes of the adaptation engine implementation are shown in Figure 7.11. The organiser refers to the adaptation engine to perform the adaptations. The adaptation engine can be used for both operation-based and batch-mode adaptations (Section 6.3). In both cases, the adaptation engine accepts *atomic adaptation actions*. These atomic adaptation actions are either from the *AdaptationSrcriptingEngine* or by the organiser role itself. Any atomic adaptation action should implement the interface *AdaptationAction*.

The *AdaptationAction* has two specialisations, i.e. *DefAdaptAction* and *InstanceAdaptAction*, for definition-level adaptations and process instance-level adaptations, respectively. The atomic adaptation actions,[6] e.g. *DefPDUpdateAction*, should implement either of these interfaces. Each atomic adaptation action specifies the pre-checks that are carried out prior to the adaptations and the actual adaptation steps by implementing the *adapt()* method. For clarity, Listing 7.7 shows a sample adaptation action. The adaptation engine performs these atomic adaptation actions sequentially by executing the *adapt()* method, as a batch or individually. The framework can be extended to support adaptations of future additions to the meta-model by adding more such adaptation actions without changing the core adaptation mechanism.

[6]Only four atomic adaptation actions are shown here for clarity,

```
public class InstanceTaskPropertyAdaptationAction implements InstanceAdaptAction{
    //Properties of Adaptation Action
    private String taskId;
    private String proeprtyId;
    private String newVal;
    //The constructor of Adaptation Action
    public InstanceTaskPropertyAdaptationAction(String taskId, String propertyId,String val ){
        this.taskId = taskId;
        this.proeprtyId = propertyId;
        this.newVal = val;
    }
    //The body of the Adaptation Action
    @Override
    public boolean adapt(ProcessInstance pi) throws AdaptationException {
        //Perform state checks(Optional). Throws exception if an error.
        //Perform adaptations. Throws exception if an error.
        return true;
    }
}
```

Listing 7.7 A sample adaptation action.

If an error occurs during the adaptation, an *AdaptationException* is thrown and caught by the adaptation engine. In such a case, the adaptation is aborted and the backup is restored to discard all the changes. If all the adaptation actions are successful, then the validation module (Section 7.1.4) is used by the adaptation engine to check the integrity of the adapted model(s) (Section 6.4). If the integrity check results in a constraint violation, then, again, the changes are discarded and the backup is restored. Otherwise, the changes are accepted as valid and the backup is discarded.

The adaptation engine uses a parser to parse an adaptation script and create adaptation actions. The lexer and parser for the scripting language are created using ANTLR [305]. The grammar for the scripting language is available in Appendix D. Once an adaptation script is received at the adaptation scripting engine, the engine uses the ScriptParser to create an abstract syntax tree (AST). The AST is an abstract representation of the parsed data in a tree structure. The root node is a type of *script* and the leaf nodes are *commands*. The *blocks* that define a scope for commands (Section 6.3.3) are the intermediary nodes of the tree. Then, the AST is used to create the instances of adaptation actions for each and every command of the tree.

7.2 Deployment environment

In order to deploy Serendip service orchestrations, we have extended the Apache Axis2 Web services engine. The extension is called ROAD4WS. In this section, we introduce Axis2 and explain how it is extended to provide support for adaptive service orchestration.

7.2.1 Apache Axis2

Apache Axis2 [297] is a free and open source Web services engine that provides functionalities to deploy and consume Web services. The modular design in the is created under AXIS2_HOME. Service orchestration descriptors such as RoSAS.xml (Appendix B) are placed inside this *road_composites* directory. This can be done while the Server (Tomcat) is running.

Once the descriptor is deployed, the descriptor is automatically picked up by ROAD4WS via the *ROADDeployer* and the structure of the composition is instantiated. This includes the creation of services interfaces (provided interface) for each and every role and the formation of the contracts among roles. The service interfaces are exposed according to the WSDL 2.0 standard [38]. Each and every operation of a role is exposed as WSDL operation [260]. These interfaces allow any WSDL 2.0 compatible client API to be used to invoke the role operations. Then, the orchestration engine, the adaptation engine, the model provider factory and the validation modules are instantiated for a given composite. In addition, the organiser interface or the organiser service proxy is generated for the organiser player to bind to. This interface is the gateway to the organiser role for the player to manipulate the service orchestration at runtime.

The signature of the address of a deployed proxy service is as follows: http://< HOST >:< PORT >/axis2/services/< ORGNISATION-ID > _ < ROLE-ID>.

Figure 7.14 shows that the role MM (member) of the RoSAS organisation (rosassmc) is deployed in the server under the endpoint reference (EPR) http://127.0.0.1:8080/axis2/services/rosassmc_mm. The service has only one operation, i.e. complain. The WSDL description and the message types can be viewed via the URL http://127.0.0.1:8080/axis2/services/rosassmc_mm?wsdl.

ROAD4WS dynamically adjusts the deployed interfaces depending on the runtime changes to roles and contracts. For example, new roles and contracts can be introduced, and existing roles and contracts can be modified or removed. ROAD4WS automatically detects these changes in the deployed composites and adjust the proxy services and their WSDL operations accordingly.

ROAD4WS supports the deployment of multiple composites. This allows the decomposition of a large service composite into smaller sub-composites in a hierarchical structure to separate the management concerns [81, 260]. For example, the *case officer* service can be played by another ROAD composite that defines its own processes and structures to manage the customer complaints or requests.

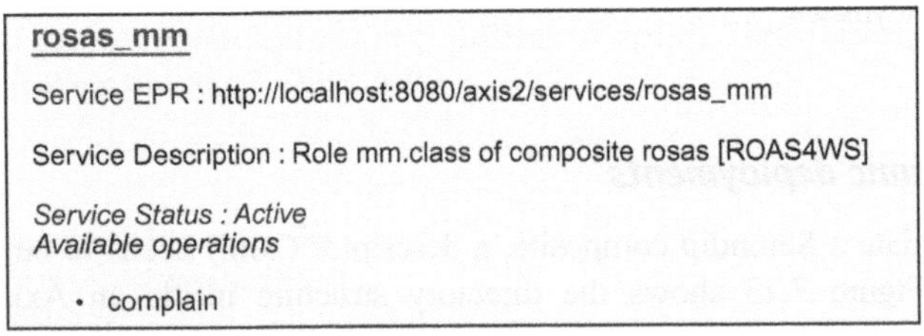

```
┌─────────────────────────────────────────────────────────────┐
│ rosas_mm                                                     │
│                                                              │
│ Service EPR : http://localhost:8080/axis2/services/rosas_mm  │
│                                                              │
│ Service Description : Role mm.class of composite rosas [ROAS4WS] │
│                                                              │
│ Service Status : Active                                      │
│ Available operations                                         │
│                                                              │
│   • complain                                                 │
└─────────────────────────────────────────────────────────────┘
```

Figure 7.14 Role operations exposed as web service operations.

7.2.4 Orchestrating web services

Once deployed and initiated, the composite is ready to accept service requests via the exposed service interfaces. For example, a client application installed in a motorist's mobile device may send a service request to the composite via the *rosassmc_member* interface (Figure 7.14). Then, the composite enacts the corresponding business process as described in Section 5.2. Subsequently, the bound partner services can exchange messages via the composite according to the process. The role-player's implementation can be either *Web services*, *Web service clients* or *a combination of both* as shown in Figure 7.15. For example, a mobile app installed in a client's mobile phone is a client-only player. A tow truck scheduling service can be a service-only player, which does not actively communicate with the composite but expects the composite to invoke the service upon a towing requirement. However, a job scheduling application at a garage is required to actively communicate with the composite (using a Web service client API such as Axis2 client API) and, hence, needs to act as both a client and a service.

The type of the player required is dependent on the type of interface that a role exposes. According to ROAD [81], there are two types of interfaces that a role may consist of, i.e. the *required* and *provided* interfaces.

1. *Required interface*: The interface that should be implemented by the player. This interface is generated if a role needs to invoke the player. The role (as a client) invokes the player (service) via this interface.
2. *Provided interface*: The interface provided by the role to the player. This interface is generated if the player requires invoking the role. The player (as a client) invokes the role operation (service) via this interface.

In ROAD4WS, these are represented as WSDL interfaces as mentioned in the previous section. During the runtime, the role and its bound player exchange messages via these required and provided interfaces.

Section 5.4 has explained how the service invocation requests are initiated based on task descriptions. In addition, Section 7.1.3 has explained how the external SOAP messages are composed via XSLT transformations. To complete tasks, the messages need to be exchanged with bound players or services, which usually reside in a distributed environment. This requirement has been addressed by extending the

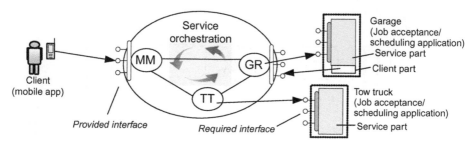

Figure 7.15 Orchestrating partner web services.

Axis2 SOAP processing mode [297]. Figure 7.16 shows how the implementation has extended the *Axis2 message processing model* to intercept messages. The left side of the figure shows how an incoming message (SOAP) is handled, whilst the right side shows how the outgoing messages are handled.

The message is initially processed by a *transport listener* such as HTTP or TCP Transport Listener [297] in Axis2. Then, the message has to pass through a pipe of handlers, e.g. WS-addressing handlers and WS-security handlers, depending on the Axis2 configuration [298]. For example, if WS-addressing is enabled, then the corresponding handler will interpret the WS-addressing headers [22]. If WS-security features are enabled, then the messages will be processed for security requirements [322]. The *ROAD message receiver* that is placed after these handlers dispatches the message to the appropriate service composite, e.g. RoSAS.

This design is accompanied by two challenges that need to be addressed:

1. The descriptors are dynamically loaded. It is not possible to configure a static message receiver.
2. The messages that target default services should not be intercepted. That is, only the messages targeting ROAD composites should be intercepted.

To address both of these challenges, each operation of a dynamically created role interface (proxy service) is allocated with an instance of a *ROAD message receiver* at the time of instantiation. With such a design, both the dynamic deployment and the unnecessary interception of non-ROAD messages are avoided. Axis2 can still host the standard Web services and continue to dispatch messages to them.

When the message is received by the composite, it is directed to the appropriate role and contract. Within a contract, the message is interpreted, events are triggered and a service invocation request may be generated as described in Section 7.1.2 and Section 7.1.3.

When a message is ready to be sent to an external player or service from a role, the *ROAD message sender* picks up the message placed in the *OutQueue* (Section 5.4) of the role and places it on the outgoing path of the *Axis2 message processing model* by specifying the endpoint address of the player. Consequently, the message will go through another set of handlers in the outgoing path to the appropriate *transport sender*. Then, the *transport sender* makes sure that the message is sent to the specified external service (endpoint).

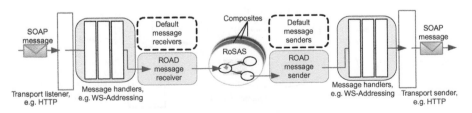

Figure 7.16 Message routing towards/from service composites.

As illustrated, the complete Serendip/ROAD service orchestration implementation provides the service orchestration capabilities to Axis2 users by hooking the implementation to the Axis2 runtime without any modifications to the Axis2 code base.

7.2.5   Message delivery patterns

The previous ROAD framework provides two types of message *delivery mechanisms*, i.e. *push* and *pull* [81]. The push mechanism is used to push the messages to the player from the role, whereas the pull mechanism is for a player to pull the messages from the role. The pull mechanism is useful when the player cannot provide a static endpoint but is willing to pull the messages when ready and required. A special synchronous operation called *getNextMessage()* is exposed in each of the provided role interfaces for a player to retrieve messages.

The work of this book further extends these *push* message delivery mechanisms as shown in Figure 7.17. A set of message delivery patterns is formed based on:

- What the message delivery mechanism is (*Push/Pull*).
- What the communication synchronisation mode is (*Asynchronous/Synchronous*).
- Who initiates the communication (*Role/Player*).

The patterns A through D are for push message delivery, whereas the pattern E is designed to support the pull mechanism of the previous ROAD framework. For all these patterns, the delivery mechanism in ROAD4WS works only with the queues outside the membrane of the composite (Section 5.4). The buffers inside the membrane are used for the internal communication of the composite only. This clearly separates the internal communication of the composite or organisation from the external communication. Figure 7.18 illustrates how the message delivery mechanism supports these patterns.

- *Pattern A*: Role sends a message to the player and does not wait for the response (the HTTP connection is not alive). First, the message is taken (1) from the *OutQueue* if available and then delivered (2) to the player (service) via the *ROAD message sender*.
- *Pattern B*: Player sends a message to the role and does not wait for the response (the HTTP connection is not alive). Message received (1) by the *ROAD message receiver* and then the message is placed (2) in the *PendingInQueue*.

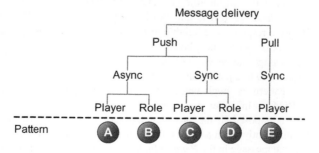

Figure 7.17 Message delivery patterns.

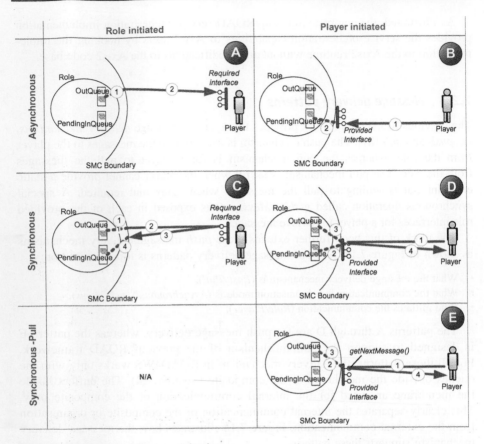

Figure 7.18 Message delivery mechanism.

- *Pattern C*: Role sends a message to the player and waits (busy wait) for a response (HTTP connection is kept alive). First, the message is taken (1) from the *OutQueue* and then delivered (2) via the *ROAD message sender* who waits for the response. When the response is received (3), it is placed (4) in the *PendingInQueue*.
- *Pattern D*: Player sends a message to the role and waits (busy wait) for a response. The player invokes an operation of the role (1). Then, the *ROAD message receiver* places (2) the message in the *PendingInQueue* and busily waits for response (HTTP connection is kept alive). When the response is available at the *OutQueue*, the message is collected (3) and sent as a response (4) to the player's request kept alive. The busy wait uses the properties of the message (i.e. *messageId* and the *isResponse*) to determine that the arrived message is a response to a request from the player or not.
- *Pattern E*: This pattern is implemented to support the pull-based message delivery mechanism in ROAD. In order to support this pattern, a special operation called *getNextMessage()* is exposed in the provided interface of the role. The *ROAD message receiver* behaves differently when a request from the player for this operation is received (1). Instead of placing the message in the *PendingInQueue* as in the case for pattern D, the *ROAD message receiver* checks the *OutQueue* of the role for any available push messages (2).

If available, then the message is collected (3) and attached in the response path to be sent back to the player (4). If not, then a fault message is sent back to the player as a response (4). This pattern is useful when the player cannot provide a static endpoint to the composite but still wants to process the messages arriving at the role it plays.

7.3 Tool support

The Serendip framework has a set of tools for the software engineers to model, monitor and adapt the service orchestrations in an effective manner. The tool support available can be divided into three categories depending on their use, i.e. *modelling, monitoring* and *adaptation*. Section 7.3.1, Section 7.3.2 and Section 7.3.3 describe in detail the tool support for those aspects, respectively.

7.3.1 Modelling tools

The motivation of the Serendip modelling tool is to allow a software engineer to model a Serendip orchestration based on the SerendipLang as presented in Chapter 4. The language conforms to the Serendip orchestration meta-model and concepts. However, the deployment environment (Section 7.2) accepts the ROAD descriptions in a unified format that is XML. In addition, there are a number of artefacts that need to be associated with a ROAD descriptor file, including the rules and transformation templates. To support orchestration modelling in Serendip and automatically generate the artefacts required for enactment, a modelling tool as an eclipse-based plug-in has been developed.

This plug-in modelling tool, called *SerendipLang Editor*, can be easily integrated with the eclipse development environment as an eclipse plug-in. It supports a software engineer to develop Serendip orchestrations in a comprehensive and effective manner. As shown in Figure 7.19, the tool consists of an editor with autocomplete support, context menu support, syntax and error highlighting capabilities.

When a Serendip descriptor or the source file, e.g. RoSAS.sdp (Figure 7.19), is saved in the editor, a deployable XML descriptor is automatically generated. In addition, the required artefacts [i.e. the contractual rule (*.drl) and XSLT (*.xsl) templates] are also automatically generated. Later, the rules templates (*.drl) can be edited to include the business policies (that evaluate and interpret the contractual interactions) using the *Drools IDE*.[12] The transformation templates (*.xsl) can be edited to include the message transformation logic using the *EclipseXSLT*[13] *editor*. Both the Drools IDE and the Eclipse XSLT editor are eclipse-based plug-ins that can be downloaded free. Finally, the complete set of artefacts can be deployed in ROAD4WS as described in Section 7.2.

---

[12]http://docs.jboss.org/drools/release/5.2.0.Final/drools-expert-docs/html/ch08.html
[13]http://eclipsexslt.sourceforge.net/

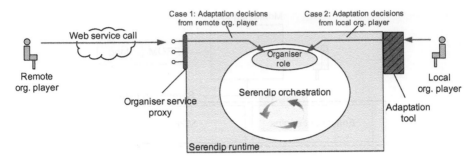

Figure 7.23 Remote and local organiser players.

In particular, this feature is useful for long-running processes. This work reuses the libraries of the ProM framework [278] with modifications to integrate with the Serendip.

7.3.3 Adaptation tools

During the runtime, adaptations on a Serendip orchestration are carried out via the organiser role as discussed in Chapter 6. The organiser player can be either remotely operating in a networked environment or locally located in the same server where the service orchestration is deployed. As shown in Figure 7.23, irrespective of where the organiser player is located, all the adaptation decisions need to go through the organiser role.

In the case of remotely located organiser player, the adaptations are carried out via the exposed operations of the organiser role's WSDL interface or the *organiser service proxy* (Section 7.2.3). The individual operations can be used to manipulate the service orchestration. Alternatively, more powerful script-based batch-mode adaptation mechanism (Section 6.3.3) can be used through the *executeScript()* operation. Any Web service invocation tool compatible with the WSDL standard, e.g. *Web service Explorer*[17] (available as an eclipse tool), can be used to invoke the operations of the organiser interface.

In the case of a locally located organiser player, the player can use the *Serendip adaptation tool* as a desktop application. Such a desktop application can share the Serendip runtime and allow speedy and efficient adaptation of the Serendip runtime without any network delays or burden of Web service calls. The *Serendip adaptation tool* can be initiated via the *Serendip monitoring tool* (Section 7.3.2). For example, if a software engineer is monitoring the progress of a process instance and needing to make the selected instance deviate from the original description, he/she can select the process and initiate the *adaptation tool*.

A screenshot of the *Serendip adaptation tool* is given in Figure 7.24. Once initiated, the adaptation script is written on the scripting window or loaded from a pre-written script file. The sample script shown is the sample adaptation script

---

[17]http://www.eclipse.org/webtools/jst/components/ws/M4/tutorials/WebServiceExplorer.html

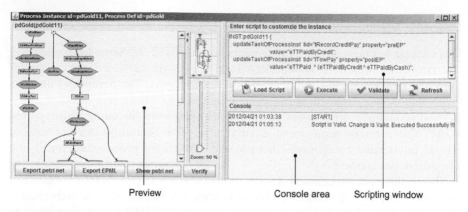

Preview   Console area   Scripting window

Figure 7.24 The adaptation tool.

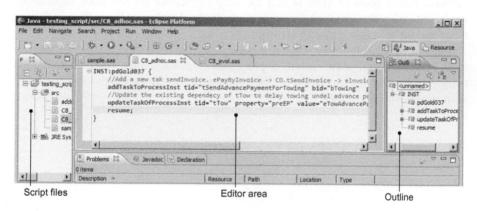

Script files   Editor area   Outline

Figure 7.25 Serendip adaptation script editor — an Eclipse Plug-in.

given in Section 6.3.3. Once the script is executed, the console area shows whether the execution is successful. If unsuccessful, then the possible reasons for failure due to syntax errors or constraint violations are shown in the *console* area. A preview of the new dependencies of the adapted process instance can also be seen as an EPC diagram in the *preview* area to the left of the screen.

In order to assist with the writing of adaptation scripts, an eclipse-based script editor called the *Serendip adaptation script editor* has been developed. A screenshot of the editor is given in Figure 7.25. This editor can be used to write adaptation scripts with error and syntax highlighting support. Once the script is written, it can be saved in the file system as a *.sas file. This file can be loaded by the adaptation tool (Figure 7.24) or the contents can be copied to the scripting window of the *adaptation tool* as described. Alternatively, if *the organiser* is remotely located, then the script content can be sent (e.g. via an FTP client) to the server and is executed via the *executeScript()* or *scheduleScript()* operations exposed in the organiser interface.

7.4   Summary

This chapter has presented the implementation details of the Serendip framework. The complete framework is separated into three main parts, i.e. the Serendip-Core, the deployment environment and the tool support. The Serendip-Core was implemented in a deployment-independent manner to ensure that the core could be used in multiple deployment environments apart from the currently supported SOAP/Web services deployment environment. The Serendip-Core consists of several interrelated components that provide support for process enactment and adaptation management.

The deployment environment known as ROAD4WS is developed by extending the Apache Axis2 Web services engine to provide the adaptive service orchestration capabilities. One of the important characteristics of ROAD4WS is its capability to support various message exchange patterns. Another important characteristic from the implementation point of view is that the adaptive service orchestration capabilities are introduced without requiring modifications to the Axis2 code base. The challenges faced and the solutions applied have been discussed.

Finally, the available tool support is presented. The tools have been developed to model, monitor and adapt Serendip processes. The tools have been implemented using a vast array of available technologies and also ensuring the compatibility with the existing standards.

Case Study

8

We presented an example business organisation in Chapter 2, i.e. RoSAS, that provides road-side assistance to motorists by integrating and re-purposing a number of services. RoSAS requires an adaptable service orchestration approach to provide the IT support for its business processes that may change in an unpredictable manner due to the nature of its operating environment. In this chapter, we present the RoSAS road-side assistance business as a case study to demonstrate how Serendip can be used to model, enact and manage service orchestrations that have inherent needs for unpredictable changes.

The objectives of this case study are as follows.

- To provide a thorough understanding of the Serendip language and its supporting Serendip orchestration framework.
- To show how the Serendip concepts can be applied to improve the adaptability of a service orchestration.
- To provide a set of guidelines to model and design a Serendip service orchestration and generate the deployment artefacts using the available tool support.

A Serendip orchestration separates its organisational structure from its processes. Firstly, Section 8.1 presents how the organisational structure is modelled to implement the RoSAS business scenario. Secondly, Section 8.2 presents how the processes are defined on top of the organisational structure. How the deployment artefacts (such as contractual rules and transformations templates) are specified is explained in Section 8.3. Overall, the first three sections provide a detailed analysis on how to design and implement a service orchestration using Serendip. Specific *guidelines* on how to use the Serendip concepts to model the service orchestration are presented. Then, these guidelines are clarified using the examples from the case study. The complete service orchestration descriptor for the case study is available in Appendix B.

Finally, in Section 8.4, the adaptation capabilities of the framework are introduced and are demonstrated through several adaptation scenarios from the case study to address specific adaptation requirements in a service orchestration.

A reader may find some of the discussions in this chapter are familiar, as the various fragments of the case study system have been used throughout the discussion of this book for further clarifications via examples. This chapter, however, aims to present the case study in a comprehensive manner to demonstrate how the Serendip approach can be systematically applied to a business scenario.

8.1   Defining the organisational structure

We follow a top-down approach to design the organisational structure. First of all, we design the higher level composite structure in terms of its roles and contracts in Section 8.1.1. The, the required interactions of the composite are specified in the defined contracts as described in Section 8.1.2.

8.1.1   Identifying roles, contracts and players

The first step of realising the RoSAS business scenario in Serendip is to draft a high-level design of the composite structure. This design provides an abstract representation of the roles and the relationships (i.e. the contracts) between the roles.

The following guidelines need to be followed to draft the high-level design.

G_811.1. For each representation requirement of a participating entity, allocate a new (functional) role R_i in the organisation.[1]

G_811.2. If a role R_1 needs to interact with or has an obligation to another role R_2, define a contract $R_1\_R_2$ between them.

Following these guidelines, in the RoSAS scenario, there are motorists (MM), case officers (CO), tow trucks (TT), taxis (TX) and garages (GR) as participants. A role should be allocated to each and every participant (G_811.1). For the RoSAS scenario, we define roles in the RoSAS composite as shown in Figure 8.1. Then, the contracts of the organisation need to be defined according to the requirements of interactions and obligations (G_811.2). For example, the case officer (CO) has to send a towing request to tow truck (TT), whom in response acknowledges the towing. Therefore, a contract CO_TT needs to be established. However, there are no interactions or obligations between the taxis (TX) and tow trucks (TT) for the given scenario. Consequently, there is no requirement to establish a contract between them (however, if TX and TT need to coordinate *towing of the car* and

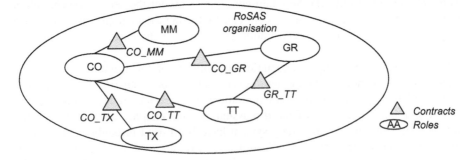

Figure 8.1 Design of the RoSAS composite structure.

[1]Definition of the organiser role is implicit.

picking up the motorist, then there could be a contract between TX and TT). The other relationships or contracts for the RoSAS business scenario are similarly defined. The high-level design for the RoSAS organisation is shown in Figure 8.1. The corresponding Serendip description is given in Listing 8.1.

A role is played by a player (see optional[2] clause *playedBy* in Listing 8.1). If the player requires receiving messages from the role, then the player should implement the *required interface* of the role (Section 7.2.4). For example, the task *tTow* of role TT needs to be accomplished by invoking the currently bound player's service endpoint. Therefore, there should be an endpoint specified in the player binding. However, the role MM does not require maintaining an active endpoint as the player is a client (Section 7.2.4) who is not actively contacted by the composite. In that case, it is not required to specify a player binding for role MM (Listing 8.1). The initial player bindings with their endpoints can be specified as shown in Listing 8.2. These player bindings can be dynamically changed during the runtime.

In this design, we do not allocate a role for each and every motorist (concrete player). Therefore, any number of motorists can communicate through the role MM. We assume that the identification of the exact player is carried out based on message contents (e.g. using a registration number). However, for a garage chain (concrete player), in this design we assign a concrete endpoint (e.g. Web service that accepts repair requests). For a given time, only a single player is bound to the

```
Organization RoSAS;

Role CO is a 'CaseOfficer'playedBy copb{.../*Role description*/...}
Role GR is a 'Garage'playedBy  grpb{.../*Role description*/...}
Role TT is a 'TowTruck'playedBy ttpb{.../*Role description*/...}
Role TX is a 'Taxi'playedBy txpb{.../*Role description*/...}
Role HT is a 'Hotel'playedBy htpb{.../*Role description*/...}
Role MM is a 'Member'{.../*Role description*/...}

Contract CO_MM{...}
Contract CO_TT{...}
Contract CO_GR{...}
Contract CO_TX{...}
Contract GR_TT{...}
Contract CO_HT{...}
```

Listing 8.1 Serendip description of the RoSAS composite structure.

```
PlayerBinding copb "http://127.0.0.1:8080/axis2/services/S6COService" is a CO;
PlayerBinding ttpb "http://136.186.7.228:8080/axis2/services/S6TTService" is a TT;
PlayerBinding grpb "http://136.186.7.228:8080/axis2/services/S6GRService" is a GR;
PlayerBinding txpb "http://136.186.7.228:8080/axis2/services/S6TXService" is a TX;
PlayerBinding htpb "http://136.186.7.228:8080/axis2/services/S6HTService" is a HT;
```

Listing 8.2 Player bindings.

---

[2]The grammar of the Serendip language is included in Appendix A.

garage. It should be noted that all these are design decisions based on the level of abstraction that should be captured and the communication requirements, i.e. whether RoSAS should initiate the communication (e.g. with garage) or respond to player requests (e.g. with motorists).

The high-level design of RoSAS defines the roles or organisational positions. Nevertheless, what actually defines a role in terms of its capabilities in the composite are its relationships with other roles. A role itself cannot explain the purpose of its existence. The relationships a role maintains with other roles collectively define its purpose of existence. For example, the purpose of role case officer is defined by its interactions with and obligations to members, tow trucks, garages and taxis. These relationships are captured by the relevant obligations of interactions (Section 8.1.2). The progression of processes in RoSAS (Section 8.2) is defined by how these interactions are interpreted by contracts to trigger events (Section 8.3.1) in terms of existing conditions of evaluations of service relationships. These events then act as pre-conditions to initiate the tasks defined in each role.

8.1.2   Defining interactions of contracts

A role interacts with adjoining roles to discharge their obligations. These interactions need to be captured in the contracts identified here.[3] This provides an explicit representation of service relationships among the participants of the composite. The following guidelines need to be followed to define interactions.

G_812.1. For a given contract, define two roles (role A and role B) and identify the possible interactions between the two roles. For each and every identified interaction, define an interaction term (ITerm).

G_812.2. For each interaction term (ITerm), define
  a. the direction of interaction (i.e. who initiates the interaction, either AtoB or BtoA)
  b. the data that should be part of the interaction (i.e. message parameters)
  c. whether the interaction is one way or two way (i.e. with or without a response).

The definition of the CO_TT contract is shown in Listing 8.3. It has two interaction terms (G_812.1), one to order a tow truck and another to send a payment for

```
Contract CO_TT{
    A is CO, B is TT; //The two roles bound by the contract,; refer to as A and B.
    ITerm orderTow (String:pickupInfo) withResponse (String:ackTowing) from AtoB;
    ITerm payTow (String:paymentInfo) from AtoB;
    ...
}
```

Listing 8.3 The contract CO_TT.

---

[3]Contracts also capture the rules (to evaluate the interactions) and facts (to represent the contract state). These are discussed in Section 8.3.1 in detail.

towing. The first term *orderTow* specifies the interaction between the CO and TT to order the towing as follows:

- The direction of interaction is *AtoB*, i.e. from CO to TT (G_812.2.a).
- There is a response (*withResponse*) for the interaction (G_812.2.b).
- The signature of request and response (G_812.2.c).

The second term *payTow* specifies the interaction between the CO and TT to pay for the towing as follows:

- The direction of interaction is again *AtoB*, i.e. from CO to TT (G_812.2.a).
- There is no response for the interaction (G_812.2.b).
- The signature of request and response (G_812.2.c).

The other contracts of the RoSAS composite can be similarly defined, and their details are given in Appendix B.

8.2   Defining the processes

Having defined the organisational structure, the next step is to define processes. In Serendip, more than one business process can be defined in a service composition to achieve multiple goals. These goals can arise due to the requirement of leveraging multiple service offerings as well as supporting the requirements of multiple tenants. RoSAS has identified three types of business offerings (packages) to its tenants depending on different road-side assistance requirements.

1. *Silver package*: Provides road-side assistance by offering towing and repairing the car.
2. *Gold package*: Provides road-side assistance by offering not only the towing and repairing of the car but also complementary taxi for the motorist to reach destination in the event of a breakdown.
3. *Platinum package*: Provides road-side assistance by offering towing, repairing, complementary taxi services and the option of complimentary accommodation.

For each of these packages, a process needs to be defined. However, prior to writing down the process definitions, the required organisational behaviours and the underlying tasks need to be defined. Section 8.2.1 describes the guidelines to identify and define organisational behaviours. Then, Section 8.2.2 describes how to define the tasks in (the roles of) the organisation. Based on these discussions, Section 8.2.3 describes how to define the business processes. In addition, Section 8.2.4 shows how to capture the commonalities and variations among the processes defined in an organisation.

8.2.1   Defining organisational behaviour

The organisational behaviour is represented by an array of behaviour units. While defining behaviour units, it is important to follow the guidelines here.

G_821.1. A behaviour unit needs to group related tasks so that a process definition can refer to such a relatively independent unit of functions in the organisation.

G_821.2. A behaviour unit needs to be defined by considering the possibility of re-use. This also helps in capturing the commonalities among multiple process definitions.

G_821.3. The task dependencies should be captured as event patterns via pre-event and post-event patterns.

G_821.4. If any, the constraints to protect the integrity of organisational behaviour need to be captured in behaviour units (Section 4.2.3).

The RoSAS business model requires that towing, repairing, taxi and accommodation-providing services are carried out as part of a complete road-side assistance process. In addition, there should be a way to complain about a car breakdown. These are the behaviour units of the organisation.

Each behaviour unit, as part of the captured organisation behaviour, defines the dependencies among tasks that should be performed by role players. For example, the role tow truck (TT) is obliged to perform the task *tTow* whilst the role case officer (CO) is obliged to perform the payment by executing task *tPayTT*. The towing behaviour unit groups such tasks and provides the required abstraction and encapsulation to be used in business processes (G_821.1, G_821.2). In general, we have the behaviour units of *bComplaining*, *bTowing*, *bRepairing*, *bTaxiProviding* and *bAccommodationProviding* as defined in Listing 8.4. Please refer to Appendix B to view all the behaviour units of the RoSAS organisation.

Task dependencies are captured by the event patterns (G_821.3). For example, behaviour unit *bTowing* specifies that *tPayTT* (of the role CO) will be initiated upon the event *eTowSuccess*, which is triggered by *tTow*. When *tPayTT* is completed, the event *eTTPaid* is triggered. Similarly, all the other task dependencies (via events) are captured in the relevant behaviour units.

Apart from the tasks, a behaviour unit also captures the behaviour constraints (G_821.4). These constraints ensure that the integrity of the behaviour is protected when there are runtime modifications (Section 4.4). For example, repairing behaviour (*bRepairing*) needs to ensure that a payment is made when a repair is completed. This is a constraint that should not be violated by any modification. Subsequently, this constraint is captured in the behaviour unit *bRepairing* as shown in Listing 8.4. The constraint (in TCTL [253]) specifies that the *eRepairSuccess* event must be followed by an event *eGRPaid*. Similarly other constraints of organisational behaviour are captured in respective behaviour units.

8.2.2 Defining tasks

The behaviour units as defined here refer to and orchestrate tasks that are performed by the roles and their corresponding players. These tasks need to be defined in the obligated roles. The guidelines here need to be followed in defining tasks.

G_822.1. For each task referred in a behaviour unit, define a task in the obligated role.

G_822.2. For a defined task, if required, specify what messages need to be used to perform the task. List these source messages under clause *UsingMsgs*.

G_822.3. For a defined task, if required, specify what messages would result in when the task is performed. List these resulting messages under the clause *ResultingMsgs*.

```
Behaviour bComplaining {
  TaskRef CO.tAnalyse {
    InitOn "eComplainRcvd";
    Triggers "eTowReqd * eRepairReqd";  }
  TaskRef CO.tNotify {
    InitOn "eMMNotif";
    Triggers "eMMNotifDone";  }
}
Behaviour bRepairing{
  TaskRef GR.tAcceptRepairOrder {
    InitOn "eRepairReqd";
    Triggers "eRepairAccept  *  eDestinationKnown";  }
  TaskRef GR.tDoRepair  {
    InitOn "eTowSuccess";
    Triggers "eRepairSuccess ^ eRepairFailed";  }
  TaskRef CO.tPayGR {
    InitOn "eRepairSuccess";
    Triggers "eGRPaid * eMMNotif";  }
  Constraint bRepairing_c1:"(eRepairSuccess>0)->(eGRPaid>0)";
}
Behaviour bTowing{
  TaskRef TT.tTow {
    InitOn "eTowReqd * eDestinationKnown";
    Triggers "eTowSuccess ^ eTowFailed";    }
  TaskRef CO.tPayTT {
    InitOn "eTowSuccess";
    Triggers "eTTPaid";  }
  Constraint bTowing_c1:"(eTowSuccess>0)->(eTTPaid>0)";
}
Behaviour bTaxiProviding{
  TaskRef CO.tPlaceTaxiOrder {
    InitOn "eTaxiReqd";
    Triggers "eTaxiOrderPlaced";  }
  TaskRef TX.tProvideTaxi {
    InitOn "eTaxiOrderPlaced";
    Triggers "eTaxiProvided";  }
  TaskRef CO.tPayTaxi {
    InitOn "eTaxiProvided";
    Triggers "eTaxiPaid";}
}
Behaviour bAccommodationProviding{
  TaskRef CO.tHotelBooking {
    InitOn "eAccommoReqd";
    Triggers "eAccommoReqested";  }
  TaskRef HT.confirmBooking {
    InitOn "eAccommoReqested";
    Triggers "eAccommoBookingConfirmed";  }
  TaskRef CO.tPayHotel{
    InitOn "eAccommoBookingConfirmed";
    Triggers "eHotelPaid";  }
}
```

Listing 8.4 Behaviour units of RoSAS organisation.

For example, the *tTow* task of the towing behaviour obliges or is to be carried out by the role TT (Listing 8.4). So, the task needs to be defined in role TT (G_822.1), as shown in Listing 8.5. In order to perform *tTow*, the interactions *CO_TT.orderTow.Req* and *GR_TT.sendGRLocation.Req* are used as source messages (G_822.2). TT carrying out *tTow* will result in the messages *CO_TT. orderTow.Res* and *GR_TT.sendGRLocation.Res* would result in (G_822.3). Similarly, all the tasks of all the roles can be defined.

```
Role TT is a 'TowTruck' playedBy ttpb{
  Task  tTow  {
    UsingMsgs CO_TT.orderTow.Req , GR_TT.sendGRLocation.Req;
    ResultingMsgs CO_TT.orderTow.Res,  GR_TT.sendGRLocation.Res;
  }
}
```

Listing 8.5 Task description.

8.2.3 Defining processes

A Serendip process is defined to achieve a business objective of a consumer
(or a consumer group). An organisation can have more than one process definition
to serve multiple objectives of multiple consumers. During the runtime the processes are enacted based on these process definitions. An important characteristic
of Serendip is that the common and single composite instance is reused to define
multiple processes. The commonalities are captured in terms of reusable behaviour
units within a single organisation instance. This is important to support the single-
instance multi-tenancy as required to develop SaaS applications [47, 89].

The guidelines here need to be followed in designing process definitions.

G_823.1. Define a new process definition to achieve the business objectives of each
consumer (consumer group).

G_823.2. For a given process definition
  a. Identify the behaviour units that need to be referenced.
  b. Identify the conditions of start (CoS) to enact process instances. No two
  process definitions should share the same CoS.
  c. Identify the conditions of termination (CoT) to terminate process instances.
  d. Identify the constraints that need to be imposed to protect the business goals.

G_823.3. Ensure the well-formedness of the defined process by constructing the process
graph via the Serendip runtime as described in Section 5.5.

In the RoSAS scenario, there are three types of consumer groups, silver, gold
and platinum. We design three process definitions to serve the requirements of
these three consumer groups (G_823.1). Let us call these three definitions *pdGold*,
pdSilv and *pdPlat* as shown in Listing 8.6.

The next step is to identify the behaviours that need to be referenced by
each process definition (G_823.2.a). The silver members require only towing
and repairing functionalities whilst the gold members require towing, repairing
and taxi functionalities as part of road-side assistance. In addition, the platinum
members require complimentary accommodation services in a suitable hotel.
These differences are captured in the process definitions *pdSilv*, *pdGold*
and *pdPlat*, respectively, in terms of the references to behaviour units.
Consequently, *pdSilv* only refers to *bComplaining*, *bTowing* and *bRepairing*;
pdGold refers to *bComplaining*, *bTowing*, *bRepairing* and *bTaxiProviding*; and
pdPlat refers to *bComplaining*, *bTowing*, *bRepairing*, *bTaxiProviding* and
bAccommodationProviding.

```
ProcessDefinition pdSilv   {
    CoS "eComplainRcvdSilv";
    CoT "(eMMNotifDone * eTTPaid * eGRPaid) ^ eExceptionHandled";
    BehaviourRef bComplaining;
    BehaviourRef bTowing;
    BehaviourRef bRepairing;
    Constraint pdSilv_c1: "(eComplainRcvdSilv>0)->(eMMNotif>0)";
}
ProcessDefinition pdGold   {
    CoS "eComplainRcvdGold";
    CoT "(eMMNotifDone * eTTPaid * eGRPaid * eTaxiPaid) ^ eExceptionHandled";
    BehaviourRef bComplaining;
    BehaviourRef bTowing;
    BehaviourRef bRepairing;
    BehaviourRef bTaxiProviding;
    Constraint pdGold_c1:"(eComplainRcvdGold>0)->(eMMNotif>0)";
}
ProcessDefinition pdPlat {
    CoS "eComplainRcvdPlat";
    CoT "(eMMNotifDone * eTTPaid * eGRPaid * eTaxiPaid * eHotelPaid) ^
eExceptionHandled";
    BehaviourRef bComplaining;
    BehaviourRef bTowing;
    BehaviourRef bRepairing;
    BehaviourRef bTaxiProviding;
    BehaviourRef bAccommodationProviding;
    Constraint pdPlat_c1:"(eComplainRcvdPlat>0)->(eMMNotif>0)";
}
```

Listing 8.6 Process definitions.

The intention of modelling reusable behaviour units, in fact, is to avoid the unnecessary redundancy that could be introduced otherwise. As an alternative solution, separate process definitions, without requiring a behaviour layer, could be defined for each customer group by directly referring to tasks. A service composition modelled in this way would lead to unnecessary redundancy due to overlapping task references and dependencies. Defining process definitions based on reusable behaviour units avoid such redundancy.

Once the references to behaviour units are determined, the *CoS* and the *CoT* for each process definitions need to be defined (G_823.2.b and G_823.2.c). The *CoS* is used by the orchestration engine to enact a new process instance of appropriate type. For example, if *eComplainRcvdSilv* is triggered, then the engine knows that a new process instance of *pdSilv* needs to be enacted. This event is triggered by the contractual rules in the CO_MM contract by interpreting the request from the motorist to case officer, which contains the member ID or any other form of identification. This means that the complexity of identifying the event to trigger (thereby type of definition) is handled by the rules (Section 8.3.1). In the process layer, the processes are enacted based on the events such as *eComplainRcvdSilv*. No two process definitions are allowed to have the same event as the *CoS* to avoid enactment conflicts. For example, if both *pdSilv* and *pdGold* has the same *CoS*, then the engine cannot determine which definition to use to enact a process instance. The *CoT* is specified using a pattern of events capturing the safe condition that a process can be terminated. For example, *(eMMNotifDone * eTTPaid * eGRPaid) ^ eExceptionHandled* is the *CoT* for process instance of *pdSilv*, which specifies either a combination of events *eMMNotifDone, eTTPaid and eGRPaid* or the event *eExceptionHandled* should be triggered.

Notably, *CoS* is an (atomic) event, whereas *CoT* possibly is an event pattern. The reason for this difference is that *CoS* is used by the enactment engine to instantiate a process instance. Usually, these initial events are triggered without a process instance identifier (*pId*) by the rules (later these events are assigned with the instantiated *pId* of the process instance by the engine). Therefore, it is not suitable to correlate two such *CoS* (initial) events, as such can lead to misinterpretations by the engine. However, *CoT* is used by a process instance within its scope to determine when it should terminate (and release resources and *self-destroy*). The events used in *CoT* are triggered with a specific pId and therefore can be correlated to form an event pattern.

Then, the process-level constraints that should be preserved need to be defined in the relevant process definitions. Similar to the behaviour constraints, the process constraints are specified in the TCTL language. For example, the constraint specified in the *pdGold* process states that the event *eComplainRcvdGold* should eventually be followed by *eMMNotif* event.

Finally, the well-formedness of the defined process needs to be ensured (G_823.3) as there can be problematic dependencies among tasks of defined behaviour units. These problems can be detected via an Event-driven Process Chain (EPC)-based well-formedness check (Section 5.5). If a *problematic dependency* is found, then that needs to be resolved first. For example, the task *tTow* specifies its pre-event pattern as *eTowReqd * eDestinationKnown*. Unless both these events are triggered by any of the referenced tasks, the tTow would not initiate. Yet, the event *eDestinationKnown* is *not* triggered within the behaviour unit *bTowing*. This is a *problematic dependency*. As shown in Listing 8.6, all the process definitions use behaviour unit *bRepairing* along with *bTowing* as a combination, so that the triggering of *eDestinationKnown* is always possible. If a new process definition is defined using *bTowing*, then at least one of the *other* behaviour units should contain a task that triggers the event *eDestinationKnown* (e.g. new behaviour that allows a motorist to report the destination address). It is advisable to limit the amount of dependencies on other behaviour units. However, to provide better flexibility, the dependencies are specified declaratively and are not limited within a behaviour unit with strict entry and exit conditions somewhat compromising the modularity of behaviour units. If required, events triggered in other behaviour units can be used. In fact, there should be at least one such dependency (otherwise the tasks of behaviour units are not connected to the rest of the process). However, it is not recommended to overly connect the tasks of two behaviour units. Such an over-connection may indicate a possible combination of the two behaviour units to a one.

8.2.4 Specialising behaviour units

Major commonalities and variations among the process definitions can be captured by referring to common behaviour units or by referring to different behaviour units as discussed in Sections 8.2.1 and 8.2.3. However, minor variations of the same behaviour can be captured using the *behaviour specialisation* feature (4.2.4) without leading to unnecessary redundancy.

In order to use the behaviour specialisation feature, the guidelines here need to be followed.

G_824.1. Common tasks need to be specified in the parent behaviour unit.

G_824.2. Tasks to be specialised need to be defined in the children behaviour units to allow variations of the same behaviour.

G_824.3. The process that requires slightly deviated behaviours needs to refer to the specialised child behaviour unit.

For instance, if the platinum members require that when towing is completed (i.e. when task *tTow* is completed), an update is sent to the motorist. In order to support this requirement, an alternative towing behaviour needs to be defined. The platinum process can refer to the alternative behaviour whilst the other processes can refer to the default towing behaviour.

As shown in Listing 8.7, the behaviour *bTowingAlt* extends the behaviour *bTowing* presented in Listing 8.4. The *bTowing* behaviour captures the common tasks for all three processes (G_824.1). The child behaviour (i.e. *bTowingAlt*) defines the specialised tasks (G_824.2). Then, the *pdPlat* process can replace the reference to *bTowing* with the *bTowingAlt*, as shown in Listing 8.8 (G_824.3). The other processes *pdGold* and *pdSilv* can still keep their references to *bTowing*. Such replacement can be done via adaptation operations similar to *Scenario 842.1* explained in Section 8.4.2.

Due to this specialisation, the *pdPlat* process contains *two inherited* tasks from the parent and *one additionally specified* task (*tAlertTowDone* from the child, i.e. the variation in the *bTowingAlt*). The behaviour variation and specialisation are illustrated in Figure 8.2.

```
Behaviour bTowingAlt extends  bTowing {
  TaskRef CO.tAlertTowDone {
    InitOn "eTowSuccess";
    Triggers "eMemberTowAlerted";
  }
}
```

Listing 8.7 Behaviour specialisation.

```
ProcessDefinition pdPlat   {
  ...
  BehaviourRef bTowing bTowingAlt; //The old reference has been replaced with the new
  ...
}
```

Listing 8.8 pdPlat uses the specialised behaviour.

the *eTowReqd* event by evaluating the request path (response=false) of the interaction *orderTow*. The second and third rules both[4] evaluate the response path (response=true) of interactions *orderTow*. However, in addition, the rule evaluates the message content (using a domain-specific Java library) to check if the content (e.g. of a SOAP [22] element) specifies whether the towing is successful. Depending on the outcome of evaluation (see clause *eval* in Listing 8.9) either the *eTowSuccess* or *eTowFailed* events are triggered. The fourth rule evaluates the one-way *payTow* interaction and triggers event *eTPaid*.

In addition to these rules, as discussed in Section 5.3.2, the current context of the service relationship also influences the final outcome of the evaluation. In Drools, facts (Java Objects) [311] can be used to capture the current context of the service relationship. These facts can be updated and used in the message interpretation process. Let us take the example described in Section 5.3.2, where bonus payments need to be made if the number of towing requests has exceeded a certain threshold value, e.g. 20. This is implemented via rules as shown in Listing 8.10. A fact called *TowCounter* has been declared to keep the number of towing requests made. The rule, *PaySomeBonus*, not only uses the attributes of an interaction message but also uses the attribute of the *TowCounter/fact* as a condition. If the conditions of the rule are evaluated as true, then the event *eTowBonusAllowed* is triggered and the counter is reset. The second rule, i.e. *IncrementTowCount*, increases the counter for every tow request. As mentioned in Section 7.1.2, the run-time (via Event Observer) makes sure that the triggered events conform to the respective post-event patterns of tasks.

The rules can also be used to evaluate process instance—specific conditions. This is vital for supporting runtime deviations of process instances to satisfy *ad hoc*

```
declare TowCounter
  count : int
end
rule "PaySomeBonus"
  when
      $msg : MessageRecievedEvent(operationName == "orderTow", response ==false)
      $tc: TowCount(count > 20)
  then
      $msg.triggerEvent("eTowBonusAllowed");
      $tc.setCount(0);//Reset
end
rule "IncrementTowCount"
  when
      $msg : MessageRecievedEvent(operationName == "orderTow", response ==false)
      $tc: TowCount(count < 20)
  then
      $tc.setCount($tc.getCount()+ 1);//Increment
end
```

Listing 8.10 Contextual decision making via rules.

---

[4]Drools rules are *condition-action* rules. In order to specify the *if-then-else* type of rules, capturing both *if* and *else* conditions in two different rules with opposing condition(s) is required.

business requirements. Such deviations may add additional events that should be triggered as part of task executions. For example, suppose that an additional bonus payment needs to be made to a specific process instance *pdGold034* due to a prior negotiation. Suppose that a new task has been added to the process instance with a pre-condition of event *eTTAdditionalPaymentAllowed*. However, unless this event is triggered, the task will not be initiated. Furthermore, the event needs to be triggered only for the process instance *pdGold034*.

In order to support this requirement, a new rule can be added to the CO_TT contract during the runtime, which will be triggered only when the *pId* of the message is *pdGold034*. This new rule can be inserted into the contract rule base (i.e. maintained in *Stateful Knowledge Session* — Drools [311]) via the adaptation operation *addContractRule()* (see Appendix C and Section 6.3). Once invoked, this operation will merge the new rule with the rule base maintained in the contract. Observably, the rule contains an additional condition, as shown in Listing 8.11. While other rules are common to all the process instances, this rule will be added only when the *pId* attribute of the message is equivalent to String *pdGold034*. Later, this rule can be removed if no longer required/when the process is terminated.

Contractual rules for other contracts of RoSAS can be similarly defined in respective rule files. Overall, the integration of *business rules* allows the specification of complex business logic to interpret the messages routed across the organisation over its contracts. Business rules separate the message interpretation concerns from the process or the control-flow concerns. The control-flow concerns can be captured in the processes while the more complex message interpretation and business decision-making concerns can be captured at the contractual rules.

Such benefits are common to many rule integration approaches proposed in the past [149, 179, 181, 184, 190]. While we learn from these approaches, we take a further step forward by capturing the business rules in terms of service relationships. In business environments, the relationships among collaborating services change over time and need to be represented in the design of the composition. The relationships maintain their own *state* and a *knowledge base* for decision-making purposes. In this approach, there is not only a separation of control flow from the decision-making process but also there are decision-making concerns separated across contracts. Separate contracts, e.g. CO_TT, CO_GR, maintain their own states and knowledge bases appropriately representing the relationships among services/roles.

The facts can be dynamically added, removed or modified to update the contract state to represent an up-to-date relationship. In addition, the rules can be dynamically added, removed or modified during the runtime to further extend these

```
rule "orderTowResponseAdditionalPayRule"
  when
    $msg : MessageRecieved(operationName == "orderTow", response==true, pId ==
  "pdGold034")
  then
    $msg.triggerEvent("eTTAdditionalPaymentAllowed ");
  end
```

Listing 8.11 A process instance—specific rule.

```xml
<?xml version="1.0" encoding="UTF-8"?>
<xsl:stylesheet version="2.0"
  xmlns:xsl=http://www.w3.org/1999/XSL/Transform
  xmlns:soapenv="http://schemas.xmlsoap.org/soap/envelope/"
  xmlns:q0="http://ws.apache.org/axis2">
  <xsl:output method="xml" indent="yes" />
  <xsl:param name="CO_MM.complain.Req" />
  <xsl:template match="/">
    <soapenv:Envelope xmlns:soapenv="http://schemas.xmlsoap.org/soap/envelope/">
      <soapenv:Body>
        <q0:analyze xmlns:q0="http://ws.apache.org/axis2">
          <memId>
            <xsl:value-of
select="$CO_MM.complain.Req/soapenv:Envelope/soapenv:Body/q0:complain/args0" />
          </memId>
          <complainDetails>
            <xsl:value-of
select="$CO_MM.complain.Req/soapenv:Envelope/soapenv:Body/q0:complain/args1" />
          </complainDetails>
        </q0:analyze>
      </soapenv:Body>
    </soapenv:Envelope>
  </xsl:template>
</xsl:stylesheet>
```

Listing 8.12 XSLT file to generate an invocation request.

knowledge bases to improve decision-making capabilities. The interpreted events act as the link between the control flow and the service relationships as represented by contracts. This design makes the well-captured and well-maintained service relationships an influential factor determining the next task(s) of a specified control flow of a service composition.

8.3.2 Specifying message transformations

The internal messages need to be translated to external messages and vice versa (Section 5.4) to enrich the message contents with additional information and ensure the compatibility of message formats. In the current implementation, these transformations are specified using XSLT [182] (Section 7.1.3). The guidelines here need to be followed when specifying such transformations.

G_832.1. For each task T defined in role R, specify a transformation $R.T.$; this transformation will create the *out-message* from a set of *source messages*.

G_832.2. For each *result message* (*rm*) defined in task T of R, specify a transformation $R.T.rm$; depending on the number of *result messages* of task T, one or more such transformations are required and they create these *result messages* from the single *in-message*.

The *Serendip modelling tool* helps to generate these transformation templates. The tool uses the following naming conventions for XSLT files for easy identification:

For out-transformations (G_832.1): <role_id> _ <task_id>.xsl
For in-transformations (G_832.2): <role_id> _ <task_id> _ <resultMsg_id>.xsl

The software engineer then has to complete the transformation logic. For example, let us take the task *tAnalyse*, which requires a case officer to analyse an incoming roadside assistance request (complaint). Listing 8.12 shows the out-transformation (G1)

```
<?xml version="1.0" encoding="UTF-8"?>
<xsl:stylesheet version="2.0"
  xmlns:xsl="http://www.w3.org/1999/XSL/Transform"
xmlns:soapenv="http://schemas.xmlsoap.org/soap/envelope/"
  xmlns:q0="http://ws.apache.org/axis2">
  <xsl:output method="xml" indent="yes" />
  <xsl:param name="Analyze.InMsg" />
  <xsl:template match="/">
      <soapenv:Envelope xmlns:soapenv="http://schemas.xmlsoap.org/soap/envelope/" >
          <soapenv:Body>
              <q0:orderTow xmlns:q0="http://ws.apache.org/axis2">
                 <content>
                     <xsl:value-of
select="$Analyze.InMsg/soapenv:Envelope/soapenv:Body/q0:analyzeResponse/return/orderT
ow"/>
                 </content>
              </q0:orderTow>
          </soapenv:Body>
      </soapenv:Envelope>
  </xsl:template>
</xsl:stylesheet>
```

Listing 8.13 XSLT file to derive a result message from a service response.

of the task *tAnalyse* specified in the file CO.Analyze.xsl. The source message indicated by the variable *$CO_MM.complain.Req* has been used to extract the data to generate the service request. An XPath expression has been used to copy the content from the source message to the SOAP request generated for the CO service. More details about XPath expressions and XSLT can be found elsewhere [312].

Similarly, the transformations to create result messages from an *in-message* are also generated (G2). For example, Listing 8.13 shows the transformation to create the *CO_TT.mOrderTow.Req* (the order tow request to tow truck), which is a *result message* created out of the information available in the response from CO after performing task *tAnalyze*. The transformations required by other tasks of RoSAS can be similarly defined.

Overall, the membranous design separates the external interactions from the internal interactions. The transformations defined in tasks collectively define a membrane that data in/out of the composition need to be crossed. The complexity associated with the external interactions (e.g. message syntax, transformation protocol) is separately addressed. This keeps the core orchestration simple and easier to manage.

8.4   Adaptations

RoSAS requires adapting its processes during the runtime. Chapter 6 has presented a few examples from the case study to demonstrate the adaptation capabilities of the framework. In general, there are numerous possible adaptations to the RoSAS processes at runtime. Instead of presenting a large number of possible adaptations, this section provides a systematic analysis of the possible types of adaptations using representative examples from the case study. In addition, the adaptations required for the structural aspects of the composites are assumed *given* in order to limit the discussion to the process adaptations, which is the focus of this book.

Firstly, the *operation-based adaptations* that need to be carried out from the case study are presented in Section 8.4.1. Secondly, to support the more complex adaptations required by the case study, the *batch-mode adaptations* are discussed in Section 8.4.2. Scenarios for both *evolutionary* and an *ad hoc* adaptations are considered in both sections. Section 8.4.3 analyses and demonstrates the importance of controlling the changes by considering example scenarios from the case study.

8.4.1 Operation-based adaptations

The individual operations of the organiser interface are used to perform *operation-based adaptations* (Section 6.3.1). In the following discussion, we present two adaptation scenarios that use operation-based adaptation. Scenario 841.1 is about an *evolutionary* adaptation whilst Scenario 841.2 is about an *ad hoc* adaptation.

Scenario 841.1 (*evolutionary, operation-based adaptation*): RoSAS requires the recording of the payments made to taxis and consequently requires a change to the current organisational behaviour coordinating the taxi service. This recording should be performed by the case officer after a payment is made.

Analysis: In order to perform this adaptation, a new task *tRecordPayTaxi* needs to be inserted into the behaviour unit *bTaxiProviding*. The task needs to have a dependency on the task *tPayTaxi*, i.e. the task *tRecordPayTaxi* should become do-able after *tPayTaxi* task is completed. Therefore, we will use the event *eTaxiPaid* as the pre-condition of *tRecordPayTaxi* to capture this dependency. Moreover, we will trigger an *eTaxiPayRecorded* event in order to mark that the task is completed. As mentioned, the case officer is obliged to perform the task. The *addTaskToBehaviour()* method of the organiser interface can be used to perform the adaptation as shown here (see also Appendix C for operation definition). Figure 8.3 shows the change as visualised in EPC graphs.

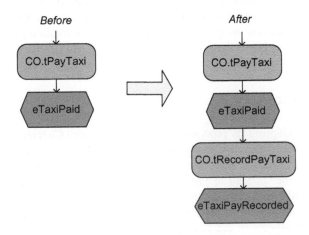

Figure 8.3 An evolutionary adaptation via operations.

addTaskToBehaviour ("bTaxiProviding", "tRecordPayTaxi", "eTaxiPaid", eTaxiPayRecorded", "CO", "2h");

This adaptation could be performed using the operation-based adaptation because the event *eTaxiPaid* has already been defined as a post-condition of task *tPayTaxi*. Operation-based adaptations are easy to execute in such scenarios. Had that been not the case, however, we would need to perform another adaptation action to add the event prior to adding this task. The batch-mode adaptation is useful in such scenarios where two adaptation actions can be carried out in a single transaction (Section 6.3.2).

Scenario 841.2 (*ad hoc, operation-based adaptation*): A platinum member, soon after sending the initial request for an assistance, requires the towing of the car to be delayed until the taxi picks her up due to bad weather. The already enacted process does not have such a dependency built-in between the two tasks. If possible, this dependency needs to be introduced.

Analysis: The current pre-condition to start the towing task *tTow* is (*eTowReqd* * *eDestinationKnown*). For this particular process instance (e.g. *pdPlat034*), a new dependency needs to be introduced, making the instance *pdPlat034* deviate from original definition. The pre-condition of *tTow* now should also include the event *eTaxiProvided*, i.e. the pre-condition of *tTow* after the adaptation should be (*eTowReqd* * *eDestinationKnown* * *eTaxiProvided*). In order to realise this deviation, the *updateTaskOfProcessInst()* operation in the organiser interface is used as shown here (see Appendix C for operation definition). Figure 8.4 shows the change as visualised in EPC graphs.

updateTaskOfProcessInst ("pdPlat034", "tTow", "preEP", "eTowReqd* eDestinationKnown * eTaxiProvided");

8.4.2   Batch-mode adaptations

The adaptations for these two scenarios were carried out using single operations. However, as mentioned in Section 6.4, operation-based adaptations have limitations when it comes to performing more complex adaptations. Hence, *script-based*

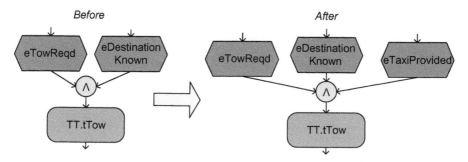

Figure 8.4 An *ad hoc* adaptation via operations.

```
INST:pdGold037 {
    //Update the dependency of existing  task
    updateTaskOfProcessInst  tId="tProvideTaxi" property="preEP"
value="eTaxiAdvancePaid * eTaxiOrderPlaced";
    //Add a new task
    addTaskToProcessInst tId="tSendAdvPayForTaxi" bId="bTaxiProviding"
preEP="eTaxiReqd" postEP="eTaxiAdvancePaid" obligRole="CO" pp="2h";
}
```

Listing 8.15 An adaptation script for an *ad hoc* adaptation.

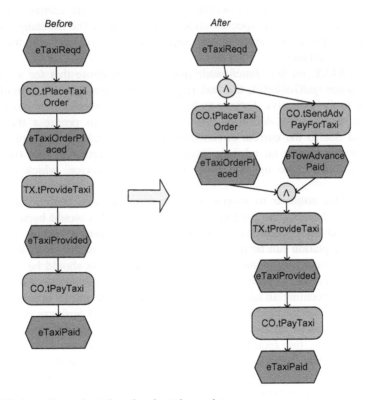

Figure 8.6 An *ad hoc* adaptation via adaptation scripts.

Firstly, the existing task *tProvideTaxi* of the process instance is updated by including the new pre-condition (*eTaxiAdvancePaid * eTaxiOrderPlaced*). This causes the *tProvideTaxi* task to be initiated only when the advance payment also is made instead of just placing the taxi order. Then, the new task *tSendAdvPayForTaxi* is added to the process instance *pdGold037*. The task triggers event *eTowAdvancePaid* as the post-condition so that this event can be used as an additional event in the pre-condition of the existing task *tProvideTaxi*. In order to initiate the newly added *tSendAdvPayForTaxi*, the event *eTaxiReqd* has been added as its pre-condition. The change is shown in Figure 8.6.

8.4.3 Controlled adaptations

Serendip allows both *ad hoc* and evolutionary adaptations as shown in previous sub-sections. However, RoSAS requires that the adaptations be carried out without violating the integrity of the composition. The impact of an adaptation needs to be analysed and potentially harmful adaptations need to be controlled. In the following discussion, we provide two scenarios (Scenarios 843.1 and 843.2) from the case study to show how the Serendip approach identifies the impacts and controls the changes.

Scenario 843.1 (*allowed change*): Let us revisit the adaptation mentioned in Scenario 842.2. In this adaptation the organiser attempts to realise an unforeseen requirement that is specific to a particular process instance by deviating it from the original process description. Suppose that there is a behaviour constraint *bTaxiProviding_c1* defined in the behaviour unit *bTaxiProviding* as shown in Listing 8.16. The constraint specifies that if a taxi order is placed, then it should be followed by a payment to the taxi. Would the adaptation mentioned in Scenario 842.2 violate this constraint?

Analysis: The constraint requires that if the *eTaxiOrderPlaced* event has triggered, then it should be followed by an *eTaxiPaid* event. As shown in Figure 8.6, every possible path of the modified process instance leads from *eTaxiOrderPlaced* to *eTaxiPaid* event. Therefore, this modification is a valid one and is allowed under the given constraints. Hence, the process validation mechanism (Section 6.4) will return a result of *true*, confirming no constraint violation.

Scenario 843.2 (*problematic change*): When a taxi service is declined or rejected by the motorist after a request has been made (e.g. the motorist finds his/her own transport), a compensation (instead of the full fair) needs to be paid to the taxi. This requirement needs to be captured in the taxi-providing behaviour. If the taxi service is provided, then the full fair needs to be paid. If the taxi is rejected, then compensation needs to be paid. The case officer needs to handle these two payments separately.

Analysis: In order to handle this new requirement, an evolutionary adaptation is carried out on the behaviour unit *bTaxiProviding* by adding a new task *tPayCompensation*. Moreover, it is required to change the post-conditions of task *tProvideTaxi* to a new event pattern (*eTaxiProvided* ∧ *eTaxiRejected*).[5] The deviation is visualised in Figure 8.7A. As shown, a new branch has been created from

```
Behaviour bTaxiProviding{
    // ...... Task descriptions
    Constraint bTaxiProviding_c1:"( eTaxiOrderPlaced>0)->(eTaxiPaid>0)";
}
```

Listing 8.16 A behaviour constraint of bTaxiProviding.

___

[5]∧ = XOR.

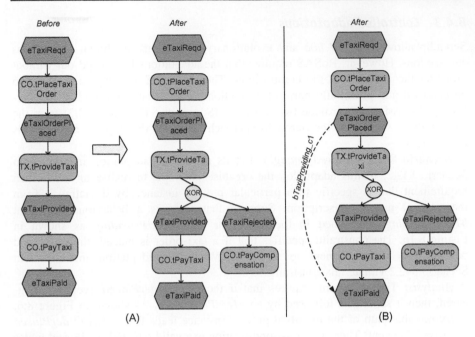

Figure 8.7 The deviation due to introduction of new task.

the original flow to handle the exceptional (taxi-rejected) situation. However, this has violated the constraint *bTaxiProviding_c1*, given in Listing 8.16. That is, there is a possibility that *eTaxiPaid* would not be triggered after the event *eTaxiOrderPlaced* when the taxi-rejected path is taken. The dependency constraint between the two events is shown in Figure 8.7B. Therefore, the adaptation engine rejects this change, prompting the organiser to find an alternative solution. Moreover, this adverse impact of the adaptation can be identified by the process validation mechanism. This adaptation affects both gold and platinum members, as both the *pdGold* and *pdPlat* process definitions refer to the behaviour unit *bTaxiProviding*.

Alternative solutions: The modification suggested for Scenario 843.2 is flawed due to a violation of constraint as detected by the validation module of the framework. However, there can be many alternative solutions that are valid.

One of the solutions is to trigger the event *eTaxiPaid* when the task *tPayCompensation* is completed, as shown in Figure 8.8A. This would satisfy the constraint *bTaxiProviding_c1*. However, this may compromise the understanding of the event *eTaxiPaid* as it now stands for both payments made for regular fees and compensations.

Another solution is to modify the constraint as shown in Figure 8.8B. In place of the event *eTaxiOrderPlaced*, the event *eTaxiProvided* can be used in the constraint, i.e. the expression of the constraint would look like '$(eTaxiOrderProvided > 0)->(eTaxiPaid > 0)$'. This means that the actual payment

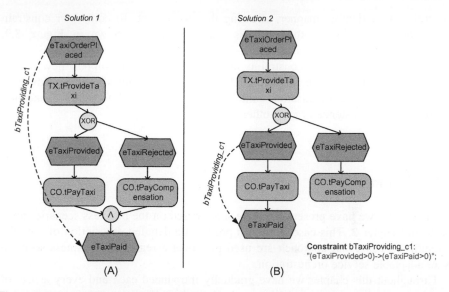

Figure 8.8 Alternative and valid solutions.

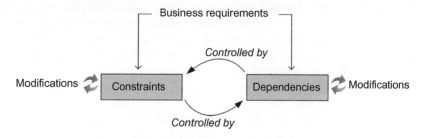

Figure 8.9 Changes to constraints and dependencies are controlled by each other.

needs to be carried out only if the taxi service is provided. In this solution, the organiser in fact modifies the constraint to allow the aforementioned change. Again, such a change in constraint is also subject to a validation against the existing dependencies.

In general, there is not a fixed solution for a particular adaptation requirement. A number of alternative solutions may exist, which the organiser as the decision-making entity can choose from depending on the business requirements. As shown, both the dependencies and the constraints can be changed. Both types of changes are 'controlled' as follows:

- The changes to dependencies are controlled by or checked against the existing constraints.
- The changes to the constraints are controlled by and checked against the existing dependencies.

The control does not originate from the rigidity of the language, but it is due to business requirements as specified by the constraints and dependencies. The Serendip language allows the specification of both the dependencies and constraints in a flexible manner, allowing the two aspects to control or constrain each other depending on the business requirements, as shown in Figure 8.9. The dependencies might need to be modified to suit the new business constraints. However, existing business constraints may also be relaxed to support new dependency modifications such as inclusion/deletion/property changes of tasks. However, for a given time, the organisation contains dependencies and constraints that only complement the existence of each other.

8.5 Summary

In this chapter we have presented a *case study* based on the business scenario introduced in Chapter 2. This case study has provided a detailed description of how the Serendip concepts and approach are used to model a real-world business scenario as an adaptable service orchestration.

Throughout this chapter we have gradually introduced each and every aspect of the service orchestration modelling and adaptation. Firstly, we have provided a broader view of how the RoSAS business model is envisioned as an organisation. We have identified the different roles of the organisation and the relationships between these roles, forming the organisation structure for the service orchestration or composition. Secondly, using the defined structure as the basis, we have defined the business processes of the RoSAS organisation. We have shown how the tasks are defined, how behaviour units capture the dependencies among these tasks and how the process definitions are formulated by re-using behaviour units to achieve different objectives. Thirdly, we have shown how the messages of the composition are interpreted and transformed. All these discussions are supported with a set of general guidelines and representative examples from the case study that follows these guidelines.

Based on these modelling aspects of the case study system, several scenarios from the case study have been presented to demonstrate the different adaptation capabilities of the Serendip approach and framework. These scenarios include both *operation-based* adaptations and *batch-mode* adaptations. Moreover, they also cover both evolutionary and *ad hoc* change requirements. Finally, scenarios have also been introduced to show how the adaptations are controlled by the business constraints.

Evaluation

9

In this chapter we evaluate the Serendip process support. To evaluate the benefits and the viability of the proposed Serendip process modelling approach, three types of evaluations have been performed.

Firstly, we systematically evaluated the flexibility of our approach. To evaluate the amount of flexibility, we used the *change patterns* introduced by Weber et al. [84]. These change patterns have been used in the past to evaluate a number of academic approaches and commercial products. A detailed description of such an evaluation conducted by the authors is available elsewhere [85]. A further extended version of these patterns are available in Weber et al. [324]. For each change pattern, we specify whether the Serendip supports the pattern. If supported, we present how the pattern is supported. The details about this evaluation are available in Section 9.1.

Secondly, we evaluated the runtime performance overhead of the newly introduced Serendip runtime. The Serendip runtime is specifically designed to support runtime adaptations to satisfy a set of design expectations as described in Section 5.1.1. The process enactment, representation and message mediation are designed to support the possible changes, both evolutionary and *ad hoc*. Therefore, evaluating the impact of such a design on process execution compared to a static service orchestration runtime is required. We used Apache ODE as the static service orchestration runtime for the comparison. The details about the experimentation set-up and the results are available in Section 9.2.

Thirdly, we assessed the Serendip approach against key requirements of a service orchestration, presented in Chapter 2. We used these key requirements to evaluate the existing approaches in Chapter 3. In this evaluation, we provide the features of the Serendip approach that provide improved support for these key requirements. The limitations of the existing framework are also highlighted. The details about this comparative assessment are available in Section 9.3.

9.1 Support for change patterns

Weber et al. [84] proposed a set of change patterns that should be supported by a process-aware information system (PAIS) [283]. These patterns and features have been used to evaluate a number of approaches in the past [146, 167, 325, 326]. The complete set of patterns can be found with more details elsewhere [85].

The authors separated these 17 patterns into two groups, *adaptation patterns* and *patterns for pre-defined changes*. The *adaptation patterns* allow modification of a process schema or a process instance using high-level change operations. These adaptations are not needed to be pre-defined and can be applied both to process definitions as well as to process instances. For example, an adaptation might allow a process instance to deviate by introducing a new task/activity. In contrast, the *patterns for pre-defined changes* allow an engineer to predict and define regions in the process schema where potential changes may be introduced during the runtime. For example, a placeholder in a process is filled by a selected process fragment during the runtime with the available knowledge.

Apart from these 17 patterns, the author also proposed six *change support features*. These change support features in a PAIS make these patterns useful in practice [84]. For example, the ability to provide *ad hoc* changes and ability to support schema evolution are example change support features.

In this section we evaluate the Serendip approach based on these *adaptation patterns* (Section 9.1.1), *patterns for pre-defined changes* (Section 9.1.2) and *change support features* (Section 9.1.3). To avoid a prolonged discussion and repetition of original article, we refrain from detailed analysis of these patterns. Rather, we explain the amount of support for each and every pattern/feature from the Serendip point of view. For a detailed explanation and examples of these change patterns/features, please refer Ref. [85]. Nevertheless, in the upcoming discussion, each pattern/feature is briefly described and explained. To make the clarification regarding *how* Serendip supports these patterns/ features consistent with the original publication, we use the same examples from the original publication [85]. Furthermore, there can be multiple possible solutions from the Serendip point of view to support these patterns. However, the intension of this discussion is to evaluate the ability of Serendip to support the presented patterns. Hence, we do not provide all the possible solutions, but rather just one solution. Finally, a summary of the analysis is available in Section 9.1.4.

9.1.1   Adaptation patterns

This section evaluates the support from the Serendip framework for *adaptation patterns* [85]. All the adaptation patterns need to be supported in the process schema level as well as in the process instance level. Each subsection provides a *description* of the pattern and *how* the pattern is supported. Note that the patterns shown and the solutions provided are for generic cases, but they can be applied to domain-specific scenarios as well.

Note that the following notations have been used throughout the explanation:

- X.pre means the value of pre-condition (event pattern) of task X.
- X.post means the value of post-condition (event pattern) of task X.
- EP1 = EP2 means the value of EP2 is assigned to value of EP1. Here, both EP1 and EP2 are event patterns.
- '*' => AND join/split, '|' => OR join/split, '⊗' => XOR join/split.

Moreover, the following rules are used:

- if X and Y are tasks, $\bowtie \in \{*, |, \otimes\}$ and $X_\emptyset$ = null-pre/post condition of X[1]
  - $X_\emptyset \bowtie X.pre = X.pre$
  - $X_\emptyset \bowtie X.post = X.post$
- if X and Y are tasks, $\bowtie \in \{*, |, \otimes\}$
  - $X.pre \bowtie Y.pre = Y.pre \bowtie X.pre$

9.1.1.1 AP1: insert process fragment

Description: A process fragment is inserted into a process schema. There are three types of insertions, i.e. (i) serial insert, (ii) parallel insert and (iii) conditional insert, as shown in Figure 9.1.

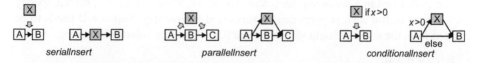

serialInsert   *parallelInsert*   *conditionalInsert*

Figure 9.1 AP1: insert process fragment.

How (Serial Insert): The requirement here is that X should be always executed after A. B should be always executed after X. Then,

- X.pre = A.post
- B.pre = X.post

How (Parallel Insert): The requirement here is that both X and B need to executed after A. C needs to be executed after both X and B. This pattern needs to be supported by modifying the pre-conditions and post-conditions of existing tasks A and C as follows. The properties of B are not needed to be changed.

- X.pre = A.post
- C.pre = B.post * X.post

How (Conditional Insert): This pattern needs to be supported by inserting a dynamic rule that will be evaluated upon the completion of task A. Then, the post-condition of A needs to be modified to trigger either B.pre or X.pre.

- Add rule R1, which will be evaluated when task A completes.
- A.post = B.pre $\otimes$ X.pre (A triggers either B.pre or X.pre. via rule R1).

9.1.1.2 AP2: delete process fragment

Description: A process fragment is deleted from a process schema (Figure 9.2).

---

[1]$X_\emptyset$ means that task X does not have pre-condition, or X does not have a post-condition.

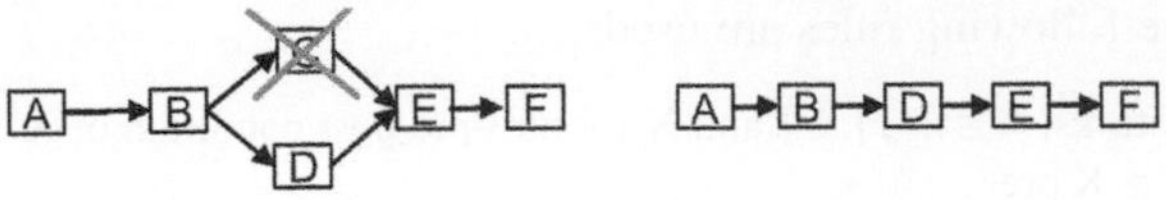

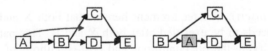

Figure 9.2 AP2: delete process fragment.

How: In order to support this pattern, the post-conditions of B and pre-conditions of E need to be modified as follows. Then, C needs to be deleted.

- B.post = D.pre.
- E.pre = D.post.
- Delete C.

Additional Note: This deletion is carried out in a parallel segment. Instead, a deletion can be performed in a serial segment, also. However, Weber et al. [85] do not specify such a pattern. But such patterns can be supported in Serendip. Suppose D needs to be deleted from the solution (right side of Figure 9.3). Then, the solution would be,

- E.pre = B.post.
- Delete D.

9.1.1.3   AP3: move process fragment

Description: A process fragment is moved from its current position in the process schema to another position.

Figure 9.3 AP3: move process fragment.

How: The requirement here is that D needs to be executed after A. Both A and C need to be executed after B. To support this pattern, the pre-conditions of D are changed with the value of A.post. Then, the task B needs to trigger the conditions to execute both A and C. Therefore, the post-conditions of B should be an AND combination of pre-conditions of A and C. Finally, the pre-conditions of B are set to be the initial condition, which could be a post-condition of a task that is not shown in the graph.

- D.pre = A.post.
- A.pre = B.post.
- B.pre = < init > (initial conditions, which is not shown in the graph).

9.1.1.4   AP4: replace process fragment

Description: A process fragment is replaced by another process fragment (Figure 9.4).

Figure 9.4 AP4: replace process fragment.

How: Here, C is replaced by X. To support this pattern, simply assign the pre-condition and post-condition of C to the new X.

- X.pre = C.pre.
- X.post = C.post.

9.1.1.5 AP5: swap process fragment

Description: Two existing process fragments are swapped (Figure 9.5).

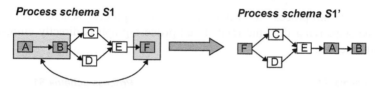

Figure 9.5 AP5: swap process fragment.

How: Swap the pre-conditions and post-conditions of the swapping fragments. To facilitate the swapping, temporary variable *var1* is used to back-up F.post as shown in the following steps.

- var1 = F.post.
- F.post = C.pre * D.pre.
- F.pre = A.pre.
- A.pre = E.post.
- B.post = var1.

9.1.1.6 AP6: extract sub-process

Description: Extract a process fragment from the given process schema and replace it with a corresponding sub-process.

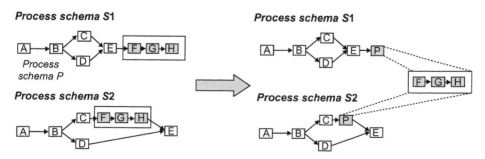

Figure 9.6 AP6: extract sub-process.

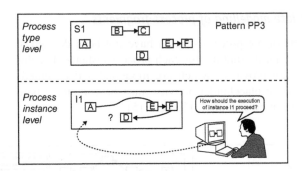

Figure 9.16 PP3: late composition of process fragments.

How: Supporting this pattern is straightforward in Serendip due to the declarative nature of behaviour modelling and the light-weight aspect of process definitions. A Serendip process definition is a collection of references to existing behaviour units. Behaviour units can be declaratively specified in the organisation. During runtime, new process definitions can be defined by referring to these behaviour units (composing behaviours). Please refer to Sections 4.2.1 and 4.2.2 for more details.

9.1.2.4 PP4: multi-instance activity

Description: This pattern allows the creation of multi-instances of a respective activity during runtime (Figure 9.17).

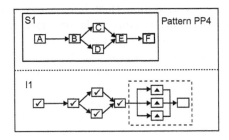

Figure 9.17 PP4: multi-instance activity.

How: The solutions to support this pattern can be divided into two categories: multiple activity instances executed sequentially and multiple activity instances executed concurrently.

a. In the case of sequential multi-instance activity, a Serendip task can be carried out multiple times provided that the pre-conditions for that task are triggered multiple times. For example, if task F needs to be carried out multiple times, then the pre-conditions of F, i.e. F.pre, need to be triggered multiple times. This can be done by a rule ($r1$) that inspects completion of F. For a given example [85], the rule $r1$ can trigger F.pre if one or more parcels remain for scan. Knowing the number or repetitions at the design time is not required.

b. In the case of concurrent multi-instance activity, it should be possible to let multiple instances of the same activity to be performed concurrently. However, to perform multiple activities concurrently, there should be multiple executing entities. In a real-world scenario, this is equivalent to hiring new labourers to speed the completion of construction. In Serendip, a role can be bound by a single player (executing entity) for a given time. As such, there is a requirement to dynamically add new roles $(R_1 \ldots R_n)$ to concurrently perform the same task (F). Dynamically adding new roles and tasks is supported by the Serendip runtime. Albeit appearing in different roles, these tasks $(R_1.F \ldots R_n.F)$ serve the same purpose. Moreover, these tasks subscribe to the same event pattern via a new behaviour unit, so that all the tasks become do-able at the same time and consequently are performed concurrently. The organiser can determine the number of role instances that need to be created based on runtime knowledge.

For both solutions, the number of repetitions or the concurrent executions (via $R_1 \ldots R_n$) do not need to be known *a priori*.

9.1.3 Change support features

This section evaluates how Serendip framework facilitates the *change support features* [85].

9.1.3.1 F1: schema evolution, version control and instance migration

Description: Schema evolution, version control for process specifications, should be supported. In addition, controlled migration might be required.

Note: Although, Weber has categorised these features into a single feature, we do not consider them as a single feature. Instead, for clarity, we tackle these three features individually. The next three paragraphs will provide the details on how Serendip supports *schema evaluation*, *version control* and *instance migration*.

How (a. Schema Evolution): Serendip allows carrying out adaptations on process definitions and behaviour definitions during the runtime. These changes are carried out on the models maintained in the MPF (see *Model Provider Factory* in Section 5.1). Process instances are enacted based on the currently available model of the process definition (and behaviours) as maintained by the MPF. By allowing changes to these models in MPF, Serendip framework supports the schema evolution. When a model corresponding to *pdGold* definition is changed (e.g. to alter the condition of termination (CoT)), an instance enacted after committing the change would use the new CoT. When a schema is evolved, running instances of old schema remain in the system (Option F1.2 of fig 19 [85]) unless individually aborted or migrated.

How (b. Version Control): The version control can be supported by duplicating a process definition and applying necessary changes to create a newer version without overriding. Both the new version and the old versions can co-exist and continue to instantiate process instances. Users may develop their own naming conventions to name the process definitions to identify the different versions, e.g.

pdGoldv1 or *pdGoldv2* (Option F1.3 of fig 19 [85]). Serendip allows both options, i.e. schema evolution and version control, without explicit support for instance migration.

How (c. Instance Migration): The framework does not explicitly support instance migration yet. That means, when a process instance is enacted, the process instance maintains its own runtime models. A change in the original process definition does not affect the runtime models maintained at the process instance at all. Newly enacted process instances will behave according to the new definition/schema, whereas already enacted process instances behave according to the schema at the time of enactment. Nonetheless, the individual process instances can be changed to reflect the changes of the original schema. This should be carried out case-by-case as the progress made by each process instance can be different to each other. Such realisation of adaptation should be carried out by considering the current state of the process instance (refer to Section 6.4 for state checks). It should be noted that the script-based adaptations make it easy to perform adaptations on multiple instances. The same adaptation script can be used repeatedly on different process instance scopes (see also support for *F6: Change Re-use*). For future work, such features can be used to automate the instance migration. We refer to previous work [327] for further details on process instance migration.

9.1.3.2   F2: support for ad hoc changes

Description: To deal with exceptions, PAIS must support changes at the process instance level.

How: Serendip supports *ad hoc* changes. Individual process instances can be changed to support the unexpected changes. For example, new tasks can be added and existing tasks can be deleted or modified. Please refer to Chapter 6, which extensively discusses the support for *ad hoc* modifications in Serendip.

9.1.3.3   F3: correctness of change

Description: The application of change patterns must not lead to runtime errors.

How: Changes to process definitions and instances are associated with an automated change validation process (Section 5.6). Such a change validation process ensures that the new schema or instance is sound and does not violate the business constraints. The soundness is ensured via the rules specified elsewhere [246]. The constraint violation is identified via the two-tier constraint validation feature introduced in Section 4.2.3. Moreover, for process instance–level changes, a state-check is carried out to ensure that the process instance is in a correct state to realise the change (Section 6.4). For example, a change of a property of a completed task is not allowed. These changes are carried out via the organiser interface. If the change is not successful, then the reply contains the reason for being unsuccessful as well.

9.1.3.4   F4: traceability and analysis

Description: All changes are logged so that they can be traced and analysed.
   How: Supporting this feature is out of the scope of this book.

9.1.3.5   F5: access control for changes

Description: Change at the specification and instance levels must be restricted to authorised users.
   How: Supporting this feature is out of the scope of this book.

9.1.3.6   F6: change re-use

Description: In the context of *ad hoc* changes, 'similar' deviations (i.e. combination of one or more adaptation patterns) can occur more than once.
   How: Serendip support batch-mode adaptations via adaptation scripts (Section 6.3). A script allows performing several adaptations in a single transaction. The same adaptation script can be re-used to apply adaptations on multiple instances via operation *scheduleScript ()*. This operation makes it possible for the same script to be executed upon multiple *process instances* and upon multiple *conditions*.

For example, suppose a script (*script1*) is defined to change a process instance *pdGold011*, then the same script can be re-used to adapt another process instance *pdGold012*.

- *scheduleScript ("script1.sas", "EventPattern", "**pdGold011**: eTowFailed");*
- *scheduleScript ("script1.sas", "EventPattern", "**pdGold012**: eTowFailed");*

As another example, the same script (*script1*) can be executed due to two events (*eTowFailed, eTowCancelled*) of the same process instance (*pdGold011*).

- *scheduleScript ("script1.sas", "EventPattern", "pdGold011: **eTowFailed**");*
- *scheduleScript ("script1.sas", "EventPattern", "pdGold011: **eTowCancelled**");*

9.1.4   Results and analysis

This evaluation shows that Serendip supports all 13 adaptation patterns and four patterns for pre-defined changes. However, the evaluation also acknowledges there is a lack of support for certain *change support features*, i.e. controlled migration (F1.c), traceability and analysis (F4) and access control for changes (F5). As mentioned, such support is beyond the scope of this book. For example, controlling the access for changes is handled in a separate security layer of the role-oriented adaptive design (ROAD) deployment infrastructure. Traceability and analysis needed to be handled not only in process-level changes but also in the complete composite level. Controlled migration needs to be handled at the management level (organiser), which involves a decision-making process. As such, the fundamental change

Table 9.1 Evaluation summary — the support for change patterns

AP1	AP2	AP3	AP4	AP5	AP6	AP7	AP8	AP9	AP10	AP11	AP12	AP13
✓	✓	✓	✓	✓	✓	✓	✓	✓	✓	✓	✓	✓
PP1	PP2	PP3	PP4									
✓	✓	✓	✓									
F1.a	F1.b	F1.c	F2	F3	F4	F5	F6					
✓	✓	✗	✓	✓	✗	✗	✓					
✓	Support	✗	No support									

operations and mechanisms can be used to facilitate such a controlled process migration.

One of the main characteristics of Serendip language that facilitated supporting the patterns is the loosely coupled and declarative nature of task descriptions (Section 4.2.1). This allows performing changes by simply modifying the properties of a task. Moreover, the behaviour-based process modelling (Section 4.2.2) improved the ability to easily introduce/remove/replace process fragments. The design of the Serendip runtime also aids in facilitating these patterns. For example, the event cloud allows new tasks (e.g. to support AP1) to dynamically subscribe to or publish events, and the support for dynamic business rules helps to dynamically change the conditions that will determine the cause of progression of the process instance (e.g. to support AP13). Table 9.1 has summarised the results of this evaluation.

9.2   Runtime performance overhead

As shown, the framework is implemented to provide the required runtime adaptability for service orchestration. The design and implementation of *a service orchestration runtime* that anticipate dynamic changes can compromise the performance. The performance of such a runtime can be inferior compared with the performance of another runtime (orchestration engine) that is designed and implemented to statically load and execute the orchestration descriptors. Such a *cost of performance* can arise due to the introduced dynamic rule evaluations, dynamic message routing, dynamic data transformations and event processing capabilities described in revised chapters of this book. To evaluate the *cost* of providing such adaptability in the performance of the service orchestration, we set up an in-lab experiment. In this experiment, we compared the performance of WS-BPEL descriptor deployed in Apache ODE orchestration engine [265] against Serendip descriptor deployed in the Serendip orchestration framework. The next sections provide details of the experiment followed by the observed results and an analysis.

9.2.1   Experimentation set-up

We designed a test scenario based on the case study presented here. The scenario requires serving a client request with the involvement of two partner services, i.e. a case officer service and tow truck service. In order to serve the client request, a service composition has to invoke these partner services. The service composition accepts a client request, which is a complaint about a car breakdown, and then invokes the partner services. Upon completion, the result is sent back in response to client's request. All the partner services are automated and do not require any human involvement. An overview is given in Figure 9.18. For this experiment we implemented two service composites.

1. *Composite 1 (Comp1)* is implemented using WS-BPEL and is deployed in Apache ODE orchestration engine.
2. *Composite 2 (Comp2)* is implemented using Serendip language and is deployed in the Serendip orchestration engine.

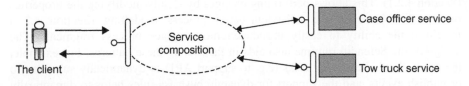

Figure 9.18 Performance overhead evaluation – experiment set-up.

The experiment intends to compare the average time taken (Δt) to serve the requests by *Comp1* and *Comp2*. Say that the average time taken by Comp1 is Δt_1 and the average time taken by Comp2 is Δt_2. The *percentage performance lost* (PPL) will be calculated by the following formula.

$$\text{PPL} = \frac{\Delta t_2 - \Delta t_1}{\Delta t_1} \times 100\% \tag{9.1}$$

We selected WS-BPEL as the supplementary orchestration language because it is the *de facto* standard for orchestrating Web services. We chose Apache ODE (v 1.3.5) to run the BPEL scripts due to its stability, performance, wide usage and free license. Moreover, Apache ODE can be easily integrated with Apache Tomcat, which is the same servlet container used by Serendip implementation as well. In this sense, both *Comp1* and *Comp2* use Apache Tomcat as the servlet container to accept SOAP messages over HTTP.

The experiment[2] was run in a controlled environment, where all the partner services and the two composites are located in the same machine and in the same server. We did not use external Web services to avoid the impacts such as inconsistent network delays and possible network failures on the overall execution and, therefore, the results. Moreover, both composites invoke the same partner service implementations. The test was run on a 2.52-GHz Intel Core i-5 with 4 GB RAM. The operating system was 32-bit Windows 7 Home Premium. The servlet container was Apache Tomcat 7.0.8.

9.2.2 Results and analysis

First, we evaluated the average time taken for Comp1 (BPEL + ODE) to serve requests. The average time was calculated based on 100 requests/responses. Then, similarly, the average time taken by the Comp2 (Serendip) was also calculated based on 100 request/responses. Figure 9.19 plots the time taken to serve 100 requests. The results are shown in Table 9.2. According to the results, the average time taken by Comp1 (Δt_1) is 210.28 ms, whereas the average time taken by

---

[2]The source files are available at http://www.ict.swin.edu.au/personal/mkapuruge/files/perfEval.zip.

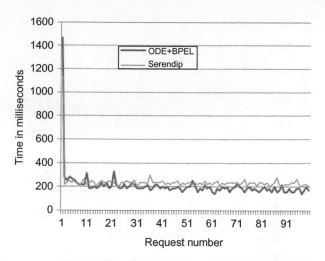

Figure 9.19 Performance comparison.

Comp2 (Δt_2) is 239.77 ms. This means the Comp2 is a little slower than the Comp1 serving the requests ($\Delta t_1 < \Delta t_2$), which is expected.

Table 9.2 Results of runtime performance overhead evaluation

Parameter	Response times (Δt)	
	Comp1 (ODE + BPEL)	**Comp2 (Serendip)**
Average	$\Delta t_1 = 210.28$	$\Delta t_2 = 239.77$
Maximum	1466	1139
Minimum	140	202

$$\therefore \text{PPL} = \frac{\Delta t_2 - \Delta t_1}{\Delta t_1} \times 100\% = \mathbf{14.02\%}$$

Figure 9.19 also shows that to serve the first request, both Comp1 and Comp2 take a significant amount of time. Later, both serve requests quickly. This behaviour is due to the additional initialisations that are carried out within the composite at the first request. This performance hit for both composites can be neglected in practical scenarios because initialisation is just a one-time activity. For clarity, Figure 9.20 shows the response time without the first request.

Note that these results were taken from a controlled environment where network delays were avoided. All the partner services, composites and clients reside on the same machine. In a real-world service orchestration environment, network delays also add to the response times (Δt_1 and Δt_2). Consequently, the PPL can be insignificant compared to the network delays.

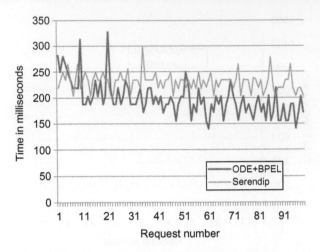

Figure 9.20 Performance comparison — neglecting the first request.

9.3   Comparative assessment

In Chapter 2 we discussed a set of key requirements that should be fulfiled by a service orchestration approach. Then, in Chapter 3, we analysed a number of existing approaches and how those approaches have addressed these key requirements. In this section we evaluate how the Serendip service orchestration approach fulfils these key requirements.

9.3.1   Flexible processes

Flexibility to change defined business processes is paramount to provide adaptive service orchestration support. We already provided an exhaustive evaluation of the amount of process flexibility exhibited by the Serendip framework based on the set of *change patterns* proposed by Weber et al. [84, 85] in Section 9.1.

In Serendip approach, the flexibility of adapting service orchestration has been achieved in two dimensions.

1. *The language and meta-model* (Chapter 4).
2. *The runtime design* (Chapters 5 and 6).

As shown in Section 4.2.1, in Serendip language, the task dependencies are not tightly coupled. Instead, the task dependencies are specified in a loosely coupled manner via *events (or event patterns)*. As shown in Section 4.2.1, this improves the flexibility of modifying the processes by easily adding/removing tasks and modifying dependencies of existing tasks. This flexibility is achieved both in the process definition level as well as in the process instance level to support both evolutionary and *ad hoc* changes that a service orchestration can be subjected to.

In addition, the Serendip meta-model de-couple the structure of the organisation from the processes. Again, the *events* are used to serve this purpose. Processes do not directly depend on the defined interactions. Rather, processes use the events, which are the outcomes of event interpretations (Section 4.6). With the advantage of de-coupling the processes from structure, many processes can be defined over the same structure and continuously optimised (Figure 9.21).

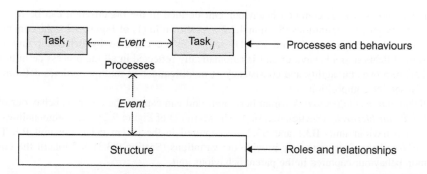

Figure 9.21 Two-dimensional de-coupling via events.

Such process flexibility is well supported by the design of the Serendip runtime as well. The Serendip runtime allows enacting such a declarative business processes via an event-driven enactment engine. As shown in Section 5.2, the task coordination is performed via the *publish—subscribe* mechanism, whereby the subscribers of specific event patterns are notified when the events are published in an event cloud. This de-couples the publishers and subscribers of a composite. Most importantly, from the flexibility point of view, this allows late modifications to task dependencies to deviate the running process instances, as illustrated in Figure 9.22.

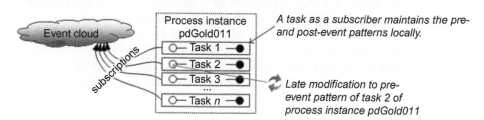

Figure 9.22 Late modifications to tasks of a process instance.

In addition, the Serendip runtime is an extension of the ROAD framework. The ROAD runtime provides adaptability to a composite structure. The roles and the contracts can be added, removed or modified. Moreover, the service end points or the player bindings can be altered during the runtime. This provides the required flexibility for a service orchestration to change the structural aspects as well.

9.3.2 Capturing commonalities

Capturing commonalities is essential to avoid the redundancy and improve the maintainability in software systems. Redundancy in service orchestration descriptions not only can make the modifications inefficient but also can make them error prone and inconsistent. This requirement has been addressed by two features of Serendip process modelling as follows:

1. *Behaviour re-use*: A common behaviour unit defined in the organisation can be re-used by many process definitions (Section 4.2.2). As shown in (1) of Figure 9.23, the commonalities of both process definitions PD1 and PD2 are captured by behaviour unit B2. A modification to a behaviour unit is automatically reflected in all the process definitions. This improves the agility and consistency of modifications of multiple process definitions of a service composition.
2. *Behaviour specialisation*: A parent behaviour unit can capture the common behaviour of a *behaviour hierarchy* (Section 4.2.4). As shown in (2) of Figure 9.23, the commonalities of both behaviour units B3.1 and B3.2 are captured in the parent behaviour unit B3. The *children* behaviour units only provide the variations (Section 9.3.3) and inherit the common behaviour captured in the parent behaviour unit.

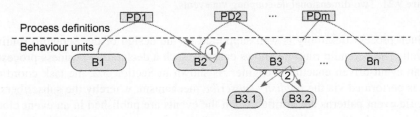

Figure 9.23 Capturing commonalities in a behaviour hierarchy.

The ability of capturing commonalities is important for developing SaaS applications [47]. The tenants of a SaaS application have common interests, and providing separate isolated process definitions can cause maintainability issues. Instead, a SaaS vendor's best interest is to increase the re-use of the application and thereby exploit the economies of scale [89, 92]. Contemporary service orchestration approaches need to improve the ability of capturing commonalities if a service orchestration truly needs to be used in a multi-tenanted SaaS applications.

9.3.3 Allowing variations

While the support for *behaviour specialisation* allows capturing commonalities, it also allows specifying the variations in organisational behaviour. An existing behaviour unit can be specialised to provide a varied behaviour. The benefit of using behaviour specialisation is that it allows *specifying variations without accounting for unnecessary redundancy*. As mentioned, only the additional or the varied part of behaviour is specified in the *specialised* or the *child* behaviour unit. The commonalities are still captured in the higher level of behaviour hierarchy.

Allowing such variations in service orchestration is important for multi-tenanted SaaS application development [47]. A SaaS application needs to serve multiple tenants or multiple groups of tenants via the same application instance (service composite) [89]. These tenants or tenant groups may have common business requirements, but there can be slight variations in the manner the processes should be implemented.

These variations can be unforeseen and appear when the business evolves as well. The Serendip orchestration framework allows specialising the existing behaviour units during the runtime. The SaaS vendor can dynamically switch from the parent behaviour unit to the new specialised behaviour unit at runtime to provide such unforeseen variations (Section 4.2.4).

This advantage of behaviour specialisation can be highlighted in contrast to other techniques such as aspect orientation [181, 190], variability descriptors [42], variability points [67] and templates [328]. In all these techniques, they assume there is a *fixed* and *volatile* part that could be pre-identified. For example, the aspects/rules viewed via point-cuts in the AO4BPEL [190] represent the volatile part, whereas the abstract process that defines the point-cuts represents the fixed part. Similarly [42], the variability points represent the volatile part, whereas the provided template represents the fixed part. However, with behaviour specialisation there is no such fixed part that restricts the amount of variability that can be shown during the runtime. The properties of the behaviour unit can be specialised to allow variations to facilitate unforeseen variations without requiring arrangements of volatile parts.

9.3.4 Controlled changes

The concept of two-tier constraints has been presented in Section 4.4. The primary objective of having a two-tier constraint concept is to control the changes to organisational behaviour. The constraints are specified at the behaviour level and at the process level. The behaviour level constraints specified in behaviour units ensure the changes to organisational behaviour do not violate collaboration objectives. However, the process-level constraints specified in process definitions ensure the objectives/goals of a business process are safeguarded amidst modifications to the collaborations. The validation is performed by formally mapping the organisational behaviours to the Petri-Net model (Section 5.6). Then, the Petri-Net model is validated via the integrated Romeo model checker [258].

Due to the two-tier constraints and the modularity provided via the behaviour modelling, only the relevant *minimal set of constraints* is used to validate a modification. The relevancy is captured by the interconnectedness of process definitions and the behaviour units (Section 4.2.3). This is an improvement in contrast to the global constraint specification practice. The use of two-tier constraints provides better modularity to specify business constraints. In addition, it helps to avoid the unnecessary restrictions on runtime changes, because, $CS_{msc} \subseteq CS_{global}$.

The approach also gives special attention to multi-tenanted environments where multiple tenants are served with a single application instance [47, 89]. Tenants tend to request customisation to their packages or business processes as if the tenant is the sole user of the system [45]. Facilitating the changed requirements of a particular tenant needs to be controlled so that the requirements expected by other tenants are not compromised. If possible, the changes should be accommodated. Again, this requirement is facilitated by the two-tier constraint specification mechanism. The interconnectedness of behaviour units and tenants processes would determine the possibility of allowing the changes to the single application instance.

9.3.5   Predictable change impacts

A service composition is a collaborative environment where a number of partner services are collectively used to achieve a business objective. In multi-tenant environments, the multiple processes need to be defined to suit different users/tenants upon the same service composition [47, 89, 92]. The changes carried out to facilitate a change of a tenant or underlying collaboration have an impact on other users/tenants and underlying service providers. In addition, the adaptations on an adaptive service orchestration can be frequent. Manually testing and verifying those adaptations and analysing the impact can be difficult and perhaps impossible in practice.

The work of this book has automated such impact analysis and predicts the possible impacts on collaborations and user/tenant goals. Such predictability is achieved due to two factors.

1. *Formal Validation*: A formal validation that is carried out prior to the change realisation (Section 6.3).
2. *Explicit Process—Behaviour Linkage*: The linkage among defined process definitions and the behaviour units are explicit (Section 4.2.3).

The formal validation based on Petri-Nets helps to automate the validation process. This allows identifying whether the change is valid prior to when the change is realised in the orchestration. Importantly, identifying the potentially affecting process definitions or behaviours is possible due to the explicit representation of *process—behaviour linkage* that is used by the formal validation mechanism. The impact upon tenants, due to a proposed modification in an underlying collaboration, is identified via the *linkage* between the process serving the tenant/customer and behaviour unit representing the collaboration. The same is true for the reverse also, because the impact upon underlying collaborations, due to a change proposed from a tenant's point of view, is possible due to the explicit representation of *process—behaviour linkage*.

9.3.6   Managing the complexity

The complexity of a service orchestration may reflect the complexity of the underlying business. A business with complex business processes may lead to a complex service orchestration. For example, for a service orchestration that supports business processes in a *multi-tenanted environment*, the complexity can be relatively high, primarily because a single application instance needs to be used to serve multiple tenants. In addition, the support for *adaptability* can also increase the complexity due to numerous runtime changes that are not expected during the design time. An adaptive architecture that leads to increasingly complex service orchestration systems can gradually become unusable. Therefore, the architecture or the design of the service orchestration needs to give special attention to managing the complexity.

A service orchestration designed as per Serendip architecture manages the complexity in two different conducts.

1. By applying ROAD concepts to adaptive service orchestrations (see 1.1−1.4).
2. By applying the concepts introduced as part of process support (see 2.1−2.4).

Serendip concepts are grounded upon ROAD. ROAD provides several concepts regarding how to manage the complexity of a composite application [79]. Hence, Serendip also benefits from ROAD concepts that help managing the complexity. There are four main concepts of ROAD that are being used to reduce the complexity of a Serendip orchestration.

1.1 *Separation of Management and Functional System*: ROAD separates the management system from the functional system (Section 6.2.1). The controller is always external to the composite that is being controlled. A composite only specifies how the functional system is designed, separating out the complexity of the controlling entity. Mapping this to Serendip, the core orchestration is kept simple and independent from the adaptation logic, which specifies how the orchestration should be adapted. In addition, the runtime also reflect this separation via a clear separation of functional system (enactment engine, MPF) from the management system (adaptation engine, organiser role, validation module).

1.2 *Indirection among Changing Entities*: Provides freedom to function irrespective of changes to other entities. ROAD views a software system as entities that are connected via adaptive connectors. In the service orchestration domain, this means that the individual services are not connected directly, but rather via the adaptive contracts providing the required indirection. The adaptability is seen as a property of the relationship (contracts) rather than roles itself. This advantage of ROAD is naturally reflected in Serendip service orchestration as well (Section 4.1.1). The individual partner services and their dependencies are not captured directly into a process flow. Rather, the actual services that perform tasks are represented by roles and their interactions are captured by contracts.

1.3 *Support for Heterogeneity in Task Execution*: ROAD provides platform-independent mechanisms for interactions among heterogeneous entities that reside in a distributed environment. Player implementation is independent of that of the composite. Adopting this concept, a task defined in a Serendip core orchestration does not specify how the player should perform the task. Serendip processes are grounded upon abstract structure formed by contracts and roles, rather than being directly ground upon possibly heterogeneous individual services. This design provides a cleaner separation for addressing process-level concerns without concerning about the *heterogeneity* of underlying services.

1.4 *Recursive Composition*: ROAD allows the deconstructing of a larger service composition into a manageable number of smaller composites [79]. All the composites are mutually opaque and do not attempt to micro-manage each other. Instead, each composite is self-managed with its own management system. In this sense, a larger service orchestration can be deconstructed into a number of relatively smaller orchestrations (Section 4.3.3). Each composite can consist of its own structure and processes without requiring defining a larger single-service orchestration.

Apart from reusing ROAD concepts and applying those concepts in a service orchestration environment, Serendip also introduces four novel concepts to manage the complexity in an adaptive service orchestration.

2.1 *Modular Behaviour*: According to Parnas [329], 'the effectiveness of modularisation is dependent upon a criteria that divides a complete system into several modules'. The modularity provided by the behaviour-based process modelling helps to divide a complete service orchestration into several modular behaviour units. Relevant tasks and constraints upon them can be brought together and defined as a single behaviour unit (Section 4.2.2). The existence of a behaviour unit is independent of the processes being used. A complete service orchestration to serve a consumer demand is built by assembling these modularised behaviour units.

2.2 *Avoiding Unnecessary Redundancy*: The reusability of the common organisational behaviours helps to avoid the unnecessary redundancy. The unnecessary redundancy increases the complexity of managing the composite. The modifications need to be carried out repetitively in multiple locations of separate processes. With behaviour-based process modelling, the commonalities are captured in reusable behaviour units. This avoids the requirement of changing multiple process definitions. Instead, a common behaviour unit is modified. Subsequently, the change is reflected in all the process views automatically (Section 4.2.2).

2.3 *Separation of Control-Flow and Data-Flow Concerns*: Serendip isolates the control-flow and data-flow concerns (Section 4.1.2). The control-flow concerns are handled in the behaviour layer of the architecture, whereas the data-flow concerns are handled in the contractual interactions layer as shown in Figure 4.6. The process layer is driven by the events triggered in the interaction layer. The task dependencies in behaviour units are specified as patterns of events. This allows changing the interactions with minimal effect on process layer and vice versa.

2.4 *Separation of Internal and External Interactions*: The membranous design (Section 4.2.5) isolates the internal interaction from the external interactions. This separation allows both internal and external interactions to evolve independently. For example, when a player (service) is swapped with another or when an existing player changes its interface, the external interaction tends to change. This can be facilitated by adapting the transformation (Section 5.4.1) without requiring any modifications to internal interactions (unless there is a requirement for new source of data, which is a separate issue). The same isolation is applicable for the reverse direction also. This means the internal interactions may change over time due to contractual changes. However, the transformation can be adapted without requiring any modifications to external interactions.

9.3.7   Summary of comparison

Table 9.3 presents a summary of this analysis. Table 9.4 compares Serendip with other approaches in terms of the given criteria.

Table 9.3 **Serendip features to satisfy key requirements – a summary**

Key requirement	Features of Serendip that satisfy
Flexibility	• Language and meta-model promotes loose-coupling • Event-driven publish−subscribe mechanism
Capturing commonalities	• Behaviour re-use • Behaviour specialisation
Allowing variations	• Behaviour specialisation
Controlled changes	• Two-tier constraints
Predictable change impacts	• Formal validation • Explicit process−behaviour linkage
Managing the complexity	• Separation of management and functional system • Indirection among changing entities • The support for heterogeneity • Recursive composition • Modular behaviours • Avoiding unnecessary redundancy • Separation of control-flow and data-flow concerns • Separation of internal and external interactions

9.4   Summary

In this chapter we evaluated the Serendip approach for modelling and enacting service orchestrations on three different fronts.

Firstly, the adaptability of the approach has been systematically evaluated against the change patterns and change support features introduced by Weber et al. [84, 85]. The results of this evaluation showed that Serendip supports all 13 *adaptation patterns* and four *patterns for pre-defined changes*. However, Serendip falls short in supporting three of six *change support features*.

Secondly, the runtime performance overhead due to the support for adaptability was evaluated by performing an in-lab experiment. The experiment compared Serendip runtime against Apache ODE runtime, which executes static processes. The experiment showed that there is a performance overhead. However, the performance overhead is negligible when compared to the benefits of adaptability that Serendip runtime offers. We expect to further increase the performance by improving the implementation of Serendip runtime.

Table 9.4 Results of the comparative assessment

Approach	Improved flexibility	Capturing commonalities	Allowing variations	Controlled changes	Predictable change impacts	Managing complexity
RobustBPEL2 [223]	+	-	-	-	-	-
TRAP–BPEL [140]	+	-	?	-	-	-
RobustBPEL2 [65]	+	-	-	-	-	-
eFlow [156]	+	-	-	+	-	-
Canfora et al. [157]	+	-	?	-	-	-
WASA [159,160]	+	-	-	-	-	-
Chautauqua [163]	+	-	-	-	-	-
WIDE [164,165]	+	-	-	-	-	-
ADEPTflex [167]	+	-	-	+	-	-
Fang et al. [57]	+	-	-	-	-	-
SML4BPEL [170]	+	-	-	-	-	-
Yonglin et al. [141]	+	-	-	-	-	-
Rosenberg [179]	+	?	-	-	-	-
Graml et al. [181]	+	?	+	-	-	-
rBPMN [184]	+	?	?	+	-	-
AO4BPEL [68]	+	?	?	?	-	+
MoDAR [149]	+	?	?	?	-	+
Courbis [191]	+	-	?	?	-	-
VicDAME [192]	+	-	-	?	-	?

Approach						
AdaptiveBPEL [194]	~	−	~	−	−	+
VxBPEL [67]	+	−	~	~	~	+
Karastoyanova et al. [66]	+	−	−	~	~	+
Padus [193]	+	−	−	~	~	+
Geebelen [203]	−	−	−	~	~	+
Lazovic and Ludwig [205]	−	~	~	~	~	+
Mietzner [42]	−	−	−	~	~	+
PAWS [209]	−	−	−	−	−	+
Discorso [210]	−	−	−	−	−	+
Zan et al. [211]	~	~	~	+	+	+
Mangan and Sadiq [213]	~	~	+	−	−	+
Rychkova et al. [215]	−	~	+	−	−	+
DecSerFlow[71]	−	−	+	~	~	+
Condec [73]	−	−	+	~	~	+
Guenther [69]	−	−	+	−	−	+
Serendip	+	+	+	+	+	+

+ explicitly supported, ~ supported to a certain extent, − not supported.

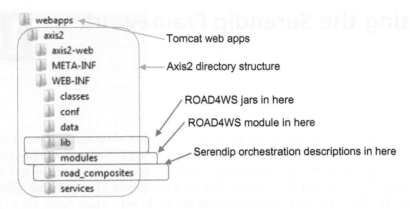

Figure 10.1 ROAD4WS installed in Apache Axis2.

10.2 Install ROAD4WS platform

Download and extract the ROAD4WS archive from the following location. For convenience, this pack is bundled with ROADfactory 2.0.jar, which contains the Serendip orchestration runtime.

> https://github.com/road-framework/ROAD4WS/wiki/Download

Follow these installation steps:

1. Set environment variable AXIS2_HOME to the WEB-INF directory,
   e.g. AXIS2_HOME=C:\software\apache-tomcat-6.0.18\webapps\axis2\WEB-INF
2. Set the environment variable TOMCAT_HOME to the Tomcat installation,
   e.g. TOMCAT_HOME=C:\software\apache-tomcat-6.0.18\
3. Add the following line to the %AXIS2_HOME%/conf/axis2.xml under the root node,
   i.e. <axisConfig>
   <deployer extension=".xml" directory="road_composites" class="au.swin.ict.research.cs3.road.road4ws.core.deployer.DefaultROADDeployer"/>
4. Run install.bat to install the required libraries in Axis2.

A successful installation should result in the following directory structure in Figure 10.1.

10.3 Deploy Serendip orchestration descriptions

For demonstration purposes, we use the RoSAS example scenario. A simplified sample can be downloaded from the following location.

> https://github.com/road-framework/ROADFactory/tree/master/sample/Scenario6

Follow the steps here to install it in ROAD4WS:

1. Copy the Serendip orchestration descriptor file, i.e. RoSAS.xml, to the AXIS2_HOME\road_composites directory. This XML file along with related message transformations and rule

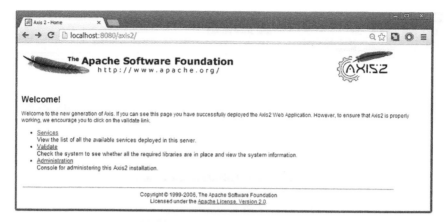

Figure 10.2 Axis2 Home Page.

files are generated by the Serendip modelling tool (Section 7.3.1) for the Serendip description of the RoSAS organisation presented in Appendix B. The complete case study has been presented in Chapter 8.

2. Copy the data directory, which contains both rule files (*.drl) and transformation files (*.xslt) to TOMCAT_HOME/bin/

   NOTE: Here we use the default location, but you may copy the data directory to any location and specify the path in the Serendip orchestration descriptor in the value of the dataDir attribute of SMC element: <tns:SMC dataDir="path/to/data/files">

3. Start TOMCAT via TOMCAT_HOME/bin/startup.bat

   Open the Web browser and open the Axis2 home page as shown in Figure 10.2 to verify the installation, e.g. http://localhost:8080/axis2/ (here we assume the port number is 8080).

4. Click on services to see the deployed services.

10.4   Send Web service requests to the deployed composite

There are many ways to send a request to the composite. Writing a Web service client program using, e.g. Axis2 client API,[1] will provide more control over the SOAP message construction. Another quick and easy way is to use a tool such as the SOAP UI or Eclipse Web Service Explorer. In this section we explain how SOAP UI[2] is used to test the deployed service composition.

1. Start the SOAP UI tool and select menu File > New SOAP Project.
2. Name the new project. Then, enter the URL for the WSDL of the service to be invoked. Note that for our example, a motorist sends the request (complain/request assistance). Therefore, the

---

[1]http://axis.apache.org/axis2/java/core/docs/dii.html.
[2]http://www.soapui.org/.

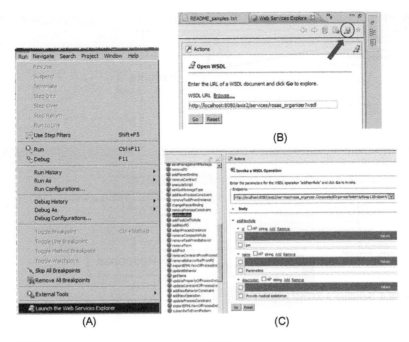

Figure 10.5 Invoking organiser operations via Web services.

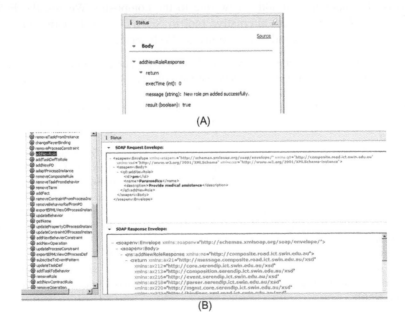

Figure 10.6 Viewing invocation results.

10.6 Summary

In this chapter we have provided a tutorial on how to deploy, enact and manage Serendip composites. We have used Apache Tomcat as the servlet container and used ROAD4WS, which is an Apache Axis2 extension, as the platform to deploy the Serendip composites.

Although there are detailed descriptions throughout the book on how to deploy, enact and manage the Serendip composites, this chapter serves as a concise summary for a software engineer to refer to and follow. In addition, detailed descriptions on how to download the related software and how to configure them are also provided.

Conclusion 11

In this book we have presented an approach for realising adaptive service orchestration systems. The approach adopts an *organisation-centric* viewpoint of a service orchestration in contrast to the *process-centric* viewpoint. A service orchestration is modelled as an adaptive organisation that facilitates the changes in both the processes and partner services. The motivation for this new perspective stems from the need to address the limitations of existing approaches as well as the new challenges faced by the design of service orchestration systems in terms of adaptability. The outcome of this study is a novel approach to the design and enactment of adaptive service orchestrations.

In this chapter, we first highlight the important *contributions* this book makes to the field of adaptive service orchestration, and then discuss some related *topics for future investigation*.

11.1 Contributions

The existing norm of using process-based or workflow-based wiring of services to define a service orchestration has major limitations in achieving adaptability for two reasons. Firstly, processes or workflows define a '*way*' of achieving a business goal and are short lived compared to its business goal. A service composition defined with such a process-centric viewpoint is bound to fail when the '*way*' is no longer valid or efficient and there is an '*alternative/better way*' to achieve the business goal. Secondly, there are many '*simultaneous ways*' to provide services using the same composition of services. Due to these two reasons, it should be possible to define many processes as well as change them accordingly in a service composition. It follows that, rather than a process, the business goals should be represented in the centre of a service orchestration.

In addition, the existing norm is to ground a service orchestration upon a concrete set of services. The orchestration logic is defined to support interactions of currently bound concrete services and there is no sufficient abstraction to explicitly represent the service relationships. However, a service orchestration is usually operated in a distributed and volatile environment where participating services can appear and disappear. Grounding a service orchestration directly upon such volatile services makes the core service orchestration inherently brittle in the long run. It follows that, rather than defining a service orchestration based on a concrete set of services, it should be possible to define a service orchestration upon an abstract structure that captures the relationships among services.

In the *Serendip approach* of this book, we have consequently proposed to have an organisational structure that captures the service relationships among collaborators to provide an extra layer of abstraction between the processes and the underlying services. This relationship-based organisational layer provides the necessary stability for defining and evolving business processes over a volatile base of partner services. In fact, different partner services can be bound, swapped and unbound to the organisation as the base of partner services and as the organisational goals change. Furthermore, different processes can be defined on top of the same organisation of services for customers or customer groups that have similar and yet different requirements, achieving the managed sharing of partner services in an effective manner.

We have proposed *a new meta-model and a language* for defining service orchestrations according to the organisation-based approach in Serendip. The meta-model is a further extension of the role-oriented adaptive design (ROAD) meta-model. ROAD provides the capability of modelling an adaptive software system as having an organisation structure with the key concepts of roles, contracts and players (services) [81]. In Serendip, we extend ROAD to achieve adaptable process support with a number of further key concepts or constructs, including tasks, behaviour units and process definitions. These new concepts are naturally based on or relate to the ROAD concepts, and together they form the basis for defining adaptable service orchestrations. Serendip uses a declarative, event-driven language to specify the dependencies among tasks and define organisational behaviours and processes in a loosely coupled manner. This provides the greater flexibility required in modifying Serendip processes and realising both evolutionary and *ad hoc* change requirements. We have analysed the amount of flexibility offered by Serendip in terms of the evaluation criteria proposed by Weber et al. [84].

The Serendip language has provided explicit support for capturing commonalities and allowing variations in business processes. In doing so, special attention has been paid to avoid the unnecessary redundancy in process definitions and to achieve better maintainability. This has been achieved by *behaviour-based process modelling* and *behaviour specialisation*. Variations of the same behaviour unit can co-exist within an organisation, having hierarchies of behaviours. Process definitions refer to and re-use these behaviour units to capture the commonalities while achieving variations. Such capabilities are beneficial when different business processes are defined over the same set of resources/services. In online marketplaces, it is necessary to quickly respond to the diverse requirements of service consumers. Especially in the software as a service environment, the same application instance and its underlying partner services/resources can be re-used to cater for the requirements of tenants, who have similar or common and yet different requirements.

A service orchestration is an IT realisation of a business. The business goals expected by the service aggregator as well as its collaborators need to be duly represented in the design of the service orchestration. Without such a representation, it is difficult to assess the impact of proposed changes to processes and thereby control them. Uncontrolled changes on a service orchestration can easily damage the objectives of its underlying business. Therefore, for a given process change, it should be possible to identify a *safe boundary* in which the change can be realised without any impact to goals of the aggregator as well as collaborators. However, this boundary need not be unnecessarily restrictive such that even the possible changes are prevented, hindering the business opportunities. In Serendip, we use the modularity provided by the process definitions and behaviour units to identify the *minimal set of constraints* that form the safe boundary for a modification.

A novel runtime environment for Serendip has been developed to meet the runtime adaptability requirements. Instead of executing statically loaded process definitions, the runtime is designed to support changes to both process definitions and running process instances. The runtime adaptability has been achieved by adopting a number of key concepts, including event cloud, publish–subscribe-driven process progression and dynamic workflow construction. Furthermore, the Serendip runtime uses clear separation of concerns in its design, including a membranous design to separate the internal and external data flows, business rules integration to separate message interpretation and the control flow and the *Organiser* concept to separate the functional and management concerns.

The Serendip *adaptation management system* provides a design and associated mechanisms to systematically manage the runtime adaptation of service orchestrations. Both evolutionary and *ad hoc* adaptations can be carried out during the runtime without requiring a system restart. To ensure the atomicity, consistency, isolation and durability properties when carrying out multiple adaptation actions, batch-mode adaptation has been introduced. A scripting language has been defined and an interpreter has been implemented as part of the adaptation management framework to ensure the transactional properties of batch-mode adaptations. Furthermore, to ensure the goals of the consumers, the aggregator and collaborators are protected during adaptation, a validation mechanism based on the aforementioned *minimal set of constraints concept* has been introduced to check the validity of the changes before the adaptations are applied to the service orchestration.

The capabilities of Axis2 [298, 299] have been extended in ROAD4WS, providing the *deployment environment* for Serendip. The design of ROAD4WS [261] allows users to deploy an adaptive service orchestration and enact adaptive business processes using the Serendip runtime. The Serendip runtime works together with the Axis2 runtime to allow message mediation based on enacted processes. This has been done by extending the Axis2 modular architecture without requiring any modifications to the Axis2 code base. Such a design ensures that this work is not locked into a particular version of Axis2. Moreover, the work can be integrated with the Axis2 runtime in production environments without any interruptions.

Overall, Serendip addresses the key requirements of a novel service orchestration system, i.e. *increased flexibility, capturing commonalities, allowing variations, controlled changes, automated impact analysis capabilities* and *managing complexity*. In this book we have presented how these key requirements are addressed in terms of three essential aspects of an adaptable service orchestration, i.e. *flexible modelling*, an *adapt-ready enactment* and an *adaptation management mechanism*.

11.2 Future work

Much work can be done to further enhance the Serendip framework. The following is a list of possible topics for future investigation.

- *Organiser Player*: To provide the self-adaptiveness for a service orchestration, it is necessary that the organiser player entity is modelled as an automated software system that makes decisions on *how to adapt*. An organiser player with such decision-making capabilities integrated with the framework would close the feedback loop, which is necessary in self-adaptive software design [260]. For example, heuristic, control-theoretic or rule-based strategies could be explored to make such decisions in an automated manner with no or minimal requirements for human involvement. We note that such self-adaptive systems with automatic decision-making capabilities are an active area of research in their own right and may be possible only for some selected well-understood application situations.

- *Process Instance Migration*: The current adaptation management design does not explicitly support automated process instance migration. Upon an evolutionary change, only consequent new process instances behave according to the changed process definition by default. There is no automated mass migration of existing instances to the new definition. However, the existing process instances can be migrated (or adapted) case-by-case via adaptation scripts. As future work, such mass process instance migration strategies can be investigated and automated to further enhance the capability of the framework.

- *Impact Analysis of Structural Changes*: Currently, the impact analysis capability of the validation module, which is based on a Petri-Net tool, is limited to process-level changes as the focus of this book. However, this needs to be further extended to analyse the impact of structural changes (roles/contracts) on the orchestration. Serendip uses ROAD to perform the structural changes of a service orchestration, but ROAD does not have such impact analysis capability for structural changes at present. A formal validation mechanism needs to be built by further extending the Serendip validation module to address this requirement.

- *Traceability and Analysis*: Currently, the framework provides an Apache Log4j[1]-based logging mechanism to create execution logs. However, this is not adequate for more sophisticated traceability and analysis of change operations [85]. These logs need to be annotated with more semantics such as reasons and context of change [330]. The framework could be further improved by integrating such logging and by changing the mining mechanism to enable more sophisticated traceability and analysis [284, 331] of Serendip processes.

- *Access Control*: In Serendip, only the organiser is authorised to perform adaptations. Therefore, the access control needs to be embodied in the design of the organiser player. As such, different levels and granularities of access to change operations can be made. From the implementation point of view, the Apache Rampart [323] module could be easily integrated with the framework for this purpose due to the use of WS-*compliant standards and Apache Axis2 in the current implementation.

- *Improvement for Tool Support*: The Serendip Modelling Tool (Section 7.3.1) supports the development of Serendip models and automatically generates the ROAD descriptors (in XML) and other related artefacts. This helps software engineers to quickly define Serendip processes. However, this tool could be further enhanced by integrating with the

---

[1]http://logging.apache.org/log4j/.

ROADdesigner,[2] which is a graphical modelling tool for the ROAD framework still under construction. The Serendip monitoring and adaptation tools also help to manage a service orchestration at runtime. However, this support can be further enhanced to provide better usability for software engineers. For example, the current composite monitoring capabilities are limited to local monitoring (or a limited support for remote monitoring via the available operations – see Appendix C – exposed as Web service operations). This could be further improved by allowing a remotely located human organiser to monitor the composite via the ROADdesigner and thereby make decisions to adapt the composite in a comprehensive manner.

- *Other Messaging Protocols*: At present, the Serendip framework implementation is limited to SOAP-based [22, 262] message exchanges with the players. However, the Serendip core is implemented independent of a specific message exchange protocol. This has been done with the intention of using the framework over an array of technologies such as *RESTful Services* [263, 300, 301], *XML/RPC* [264] and *Mobile Web services* [302]. Introducing such capabilities into the framework is also valuable.

---

[2]http://www.swinburne.edu.au/ict/research/cs3/road/roaddesigner.htm.

Bibliography

[1] M. Weske, Business Process Management: Concepts, Languages, Architectures, second ed., Springer, Vol XVI, p. 404 < http://www.amazon.com/Business-Process-Management-Languages-Architectures/dp/3642286151 > , 2012.

[2] M.P. Papazoglou, W.-J. Heuvel, Service oriented architectures: approaches, technologies and research issues, VLDB J. 16 (2007) 389−415.

[3] G.K. Behara, BPM and SOA: A Strategic Alliance − BPTrends, 2006.

[4] F. Cummins, BPM meets SOA, in: J.V. Brocke, M. Rosemann (Eds.), Handbook on Business Process Management, Springer, Berlin/Heidelberg, 2010, pp. 461−479.

[5] A. Barros, M. Dumas, The rise of web service ecosystems, IEEE Comput. Soc. 8 (2006) 31−37.

[6] J. Sinur, J.B. Hill, Magic Quadrant for Business Process Management Suites, Gartner Research, 2010.

[7] W.M.P. van der Aalst, A.H.M. ter Hofstede, M. Weske, Business process management: a survey, in: W.M.P. van der Aalst et al. (Eds.), Proceedings of the First International Conference on Business Process Management, LNCS, 2003, pp. 1−12.

[8] B. Curtis, M.I. Kellner, J. Over, Process modeling, Commun. ACM 35 (1992) 75−90.

[9] M. Hammer, J. Champy, Reengineering the Corporation, Harper Business, New York, NY, 1993.

[10] D. Simchi-Levi, P. Kaminsky, E. Simchi-Levi, Designing and Managing the Supply Chain: Concepts, Strategies, and Case Studies, McGraw-Hill/Irwin, 2003.

[11] M. Havey, Essential Business Process Modeling, O'Reilly, 2005.

[12] M. Klein, C. Dellarocas, Designing robust business processes, in: Organizing Business Knowledge: The MIT Process Handbook, MIT Press, Cambridge, MA, 2003, pp. 434−438.

[13] OMG, Business Process Modeling Notation (BPMN) Specification 1.1. <www.omg.org/spec/BPMN/1.1>, 2006.

[14] I.B.M. Odeh, S. Green, J. Sa, Modelling Processes Using RAD and UML Activity Diagrams: An Exploratory Study.

[15] S.A. White, Introduction to BPMN, IBM, 2004.

[16] S.A. White, Process Modeling Notations and Workflow Patterns, BPTrends, March, 2004.

[17] A.-W. Scheer, Business Process Engineering: Reference Models for Industrial Enterprises, Springer-Verlag New York, Inc., Secaucus, NJ, 1994.

[18] T. Andrews et al., Business Process Execution Language for Web Services, Version 1.1, 2003, BEA, IBM, Microsoft, SAP, AG, Siebel Systems.

[19] XLANG Overview. <http://xml.coverpages.org/xlang.html>, 2001.

[20] I. Foster, Z. Yong, I. Raicu, S. Lu, Cloud computing and grid computing 360-degree compared, in: Proceedings of the Grid Computing Environments Workshop, 2008, pp. 1−10.

[21] D. Peleg, Distributed Computing: A Locality-Sensitive Approach, Society for Industrial and Applied Mathematics, 2000.

[22] S. Weerawarana, F. Curbera, F. Leymann, T. Storey, D.F. Ferguson, Web Services Platform Architecture: SOAP, WSDL, WS-Policy, WS-Addressing, WS-BPEL, WS-Reliable Messaging and More, Prentice Hall PTR, 2005.

[62] G. Regev, P. Soffer, R. Schmidt, Taxonomy of Flexibility in Business Processes, 2006.

[63] H. Schonenberg, R. Mans, N. Russell, N. Mulyar, W.M.P. van der Aalst, Process flexibility: a survey of contemporary approaches, in: Advances in Enterprise Engineering, 2008, pp. 16–30.

[64] M.H. Schonenberg, R.S. Mans, N. Russell, N.A. Mulyar, W.M.P. van der Aalst, Towards a taxonomy of process flexibility (extended version). BPM Center Report BPM-07-11, 2007.

[65] O. Ezenwoye, S.M. Sadjadi, RobustBPEL2: transparent autonomization in business processes through dynamic proxies, in: Proceedings of the International Symposium on Autonomous Decentralized Systems (ISADS), 2007, pp. 17–24.

[66] D. Karastoyanova, F. Leymann, BPEL'n'Aspects: adapting service orchestration logic, in: Proceedings of the IEEE International Conference on Web Services, 2009, pp. 222–229.

[67] K. Michiel, S. Chang-ai, S. Marco, A. Paris, VxBPEL: supporting variability for web services in BPEL, Inf. Softw. Technol. 51 (2009) 258–269.

[68] A. Charfi, Aspect-Oriented Workflow Languages: AO4BPEL and Applications, PhD Thesis, Darmstadt University of Technology, Darmstadt, Germany, 2007.

[69] C.W. Guenther, M. Reichert, W.M.P. van der Aalst, Supporting flexible processes with adaptive workflow and case handling, in: Proceedings of the IEEE 17th Workshop on Enabling Technologies: Infrastructure for Collaborative Enterprises, 2008, pp. 229–234.

[70] W.M.P. van der Aalst, M. Weske, D. Grünbauer, Case handling: a new paradigm for business process support, Data Knowl. Eng. 53 (2005) 129–162.

[71] W.M.P. van der Aalst, M. Pesic, DecSerFlow: Towards a truly declarative service flow language, in: Web Services and Formal Methods, 2006, pp. 1–23.

[72] J. Wainer, F. de Lima Bezerra, Constraint-based flexible workflows, Groupware: Design, Implementation, and Use, vol. 2806, Springer, Berlin/Heidelberg, 2003, pp. 151–158.

[73] M. Pesic, W.M.P. van der Aalst, A declarative approach for flexible business processes management, in: Business Process Management Workshops, 2006, pp. 169–180.

[74] G. Kiczales, E. Hilsdale, Aspect-oriented programming, SIGSOFT Softw. Eng. Notes 26 (2001) 313.

[75] K. Czarnecki, Generative Programming: Principles and Techniques of Software Engineering Based on Automated Configuration and Fragment-Based Component Models, Technical University of Ilmenau, 1998.

[76] G. Regev, I. Bider, A. Wegmann, Defining business process flexibility with the help of invariants, Softw. Process Improv. Pract. 12 (2007) 65–79.

[77] M. Kapuruge, J. Han, A. Colman, Controlled flexibility in business processes defined for service compositions, in: Proceedings of the Services Computing (SCC), Washington, DC, 2011, pp. 346–353.

[78] M. Kapuruge, J. Han, A. Colman, Support for business process flexibility in service compositions: an evaluative survey, in: Proceedings of the Australian Software Engineering Conference – ASWEC. IEEE Computer Society, Auckland, NZ, 2010, pp. 97–106.

[79] J. Han, A. Colman, The four major challenges of engineering adaptive software architectures, in: Proceedings of the 31st Annual International Conference on Computer Software and Applications, 2007, pp. 565–572.

[80] C. Baier, J.-P. Katoen, Principles of Model Checking, MIT Press, 2008.

[81] A. Colman, Role-Oriented Adaptive Design, PhD Thesis, Swinburne University of Technology, Melbourne, 2007.

[82] A. Colman, Exogenous management in autonomic service compositions, in: Third International Conference on Autonomic and Autonomous Systems, 2007, pp. 19−25.

[83] A. Colman, J. Han, Roles, players and adaptable organizations, Appl. Ontol. 2 (2007) 105−126.

[84] B. Weber, S. Rinderle, M. Reichert, Change patterns and change support features in process-aware information systems, in: Advanced Information Systems Engineering, 2007, pp. 574−588.

[85] B. Weber, S.B. Rinderle, M. Reichert, Identifying and evaluating change patterns and change support features in process-aware information systems. Technical Report No. TR-CTIT-07-22, University of Twente, The Netherlands, 2007.

[86] L. Chen, X. Lu, Achieving business agility by integrating SOA and BPM technology, in: Proceedings of the International Forum on Information Technology and Applications, 2009, pp. 334−337.

[87] L. Hyun Jung, C. Si Won, K. Soo Dong, Technical challenges and solution space for developing SaaS and mash-up cloud services, in: Proceedings of the IEEE International Conference on e-Business Engineering, 2009, pp. 359−364.

[88] A. Azeez, S. Perera, D. Gamage, R. Linton, P. Siriwardana, D. Leelaratne, et al., Multi-tenant SOA middleware for cloud computing, in: Proceedings of the IEEE Third International Conference on Cloud Computing, 2010, pp. 458−465.

[89] G. Chang Jie, S. Wei, H. Ying, W. Zhi Hu, G. Bo, A Framework for native multi-tenancy application development and management, in: Proceedings of the Enterprise Computing, CEC/EEE, 2007, pp. 551−558.

[90] Architecture strategies for catching the long tail, MSDN Library. <http://msdn.micro-soft.com/en-us/library/aa479069.aspx>, 2006.

[91] H. Kitagawa, Y. Ishikawa, Q. Li, C. Watanabe, S. Kang, J. Myung, et al., A general maturity model and reference architecture for SaaS service, in: Proceedings of the Database Systems for Advanced Applications, 2010, pp. 337−346.

[92] R. Mietzner, F. Leymann, M.P. Papazoglou, Defining composite configurable SaaS application packages using SCA, variability descriptors and multi-tenancy patterns, in: Proceedings of the Internet and Web Applications and Services (ICIW), 2008, pp. 156−161.

[93] J. Jeston, J. Nelis, Business Process Management: Practical Guidelines to Successful Implementations, Butterworth−Heinemann, 2008.

[94] J.F. Chang, Business Process Management Systems: Strategy and Implementation, Auerbach Publications, 2006.

[95] R.K.L. Ko, A computer scientist's introductory guide to business process management (BPM), Crossroads 15 (2009) 11−18.

[96] R. Milner, A Calculus of Communicating Systems, Springer-Verlag, 1980.

[97] R. Milner, Communicating and Mobile Systems: The π-Calculus, Cambridge University Press, 1999.

[98] C.A. Petri, Kommunikation mit Automaten, Technische Hochschule, Darmstadt, 1962.

[99] T. Murata, Petri nets: properties, analysis and applications, Proc. IEEE 77 (1989) 541−580.

[100] H. Smith, P. Fingar, Business Process Management: The Third Wave, Meghan-Kiffer Press, 2006.

[101] H. Reijers, S. van Wijk, B. Mutschler, M. Leurs, in: R. Hull, et al. (Eds.), BPM in practice: who is doing what? Business process management, vol. 6336, Springer, Berlin/Heidelberg, 2010, pp. 45−60.

[102] R. Ko, S. Lee, E. Lee, Business process management (BPM) standards: a survey, Bus. Process Manage. J. 15 (2009) 744−791.

[103] W.M.P. van der Aalst, A.H.M. ter Hofstede, YAWL: yet another workflow language, Inf. Syst. 30 (2005) 245−275.

[104] T. Andrews, F. Curbera, H. Dholakia, Y. Goland, Y. Klein, F. Leymann, et al., Business Process Execution Language for Web Services version 1.1, BEA Systems, International Business Machines Corporation, Microsoft Corporation, SAP AG, Siebel Systems 2003.

[105] W.M.P. Van der Aalst, Patterns and XPDL: A Critical Evaluation of the XML Process Definition Language, Department of Technology Management Eindhoven University of Technology, The Netherlands, 2003.

[106] H. Weigand, W. van den Heuvel, M. Hiel, Rule-Based Service Composition and Service-Oriented Business Rule Management, INFOLAB, Tilburg University, Warandelaan 2, The Netherlands, 2009.

[107] P. Baptiste, C.L. Pape, W. Nuijten, Constraint-Based Scheduling: Applying Constraint Programming to Scheduling Problems, Kluwer Academic, 2001.

[108] I. Rychkova, G. Regev, A. Wegmann, High-level design and analysis of business processes the advantages of declarative specifications, in: Proceedings of the Second International Conference on Research Challenges in Information Science, 2008, pp. 99−110.

[109] OMG, Object Constraint Language, Version 2.2, ed, 2010.

[110] M. Pesic, M. Schonenberg, N. Sidorova, W.M.P. van der Aalst, Constraint-based workflow models: change made easy, in: Proceedings of the On the Move to Meaningful Internet Systems, 2007, pp. 77−94.

[111] R. Lu, S. Sadiq, V. Padmanabhan, G. Governatori, Using a temporal constraint network for business process execution, in: Proceedings of the 17th Australasian Database Conference, Hobart, Australia, 2006, pp. 157−166

[112] R. Hull, Artifact-Centric Business Process Models: Brief Survey of Research Results and Challenges, in: On the Move to Meaningful Internet Systems: OTM 2008, 2008, pp. 1152−1163.

[113] A. Nigam, N.S. Caswell, Business artifacts: an approach to operational specification, IBM Syst. J. 42 (2003) 428−445.

[114] Pallas Athena: Case Handling with FLOWer: Beyond workflow. <http://www.pallas-athena.com/>, 2002.

[115] I. Vanderfeesten, H.A. Reijers, W.M.P. van der Aalst, Case Handling Systems as Product Based Workflow Design Support, in: Enterprise Information Systems, 2009, pp. 187−198.

[116] A.W. Swan, The gantt chart as an aid to progress control, The Institution of Production Engineers, 21 (1942) 402−414.

[117] G. Di Battista, E. Pietrosanti, R. Tamassia, I.G. Tollis, Automatic layout of PERT diagrams with X-PERT, in: Proceedings of IEEE Workshop on Visual Languages, 1989, pp. 171−176.

[118] N.L. Wu, J.A. Wu, Introduction to Management Science: A Contemporary Approach, Rand McNally College Pub. Co., 1980.

[119] A. Caetano, M. Zacarias, A. Rito Silva, J. Tribolet, A role-based framework for business process modeling, in: Proceedings of the 38th Annual Hawaii International Conference on System Sciences, 2005, pp. 13−19.

[120] P. Balabko, A. Wegmann, A. Ruppen, N. Clément, The value of roles in modeling business processes, in: Proceedings of the CAiSE Workshops, Riga, Latvia, 2004, pp. 207−214.

[121] M.A. Ould, Business Processes: Modelling and Analysis for Re-Engineering and Improvement, John Wiley & Sons, 1995.

[122] T. Reenskaug, Working with Objects: The OOram Software Engineering Method: Manning, Prentice Hall, 1995.

[123] I. Vanderfeesten, H. Reijers, W.M.P. van der Aalst, Product based workflow support: dynamic workflow execution, in: Advanced Information Systems Engineering, 2008, pp. 571−574.

[124] B. Singh, G. Rein, Role Interaction Nets (RINs): A process Description Formalism, MCC. Austin, TX, USA,Technical Report CT-083-92, 1992.

[125] L. Fischer, BPM & Workflow Handbook: Future Strategies, 2007.

[126] L. Yang, H. Enzhao, C. Xudong, Architecture of information system combining SOA and BPM, in: Proceedings of the International Conference on Information Management, Innovation Management and Industrial Engineering, 2008, pp. 42−45.

[127] M. Fiammante, Dynamic SOA and BPM: Best Practices for Business Process Management and SOA Agility, IBM Press/Pearson, 2010.

[128] D. Krafzig, K. Banke, D. Slama, Enterprise Soa: Service-Oriented Architecture Best Practices, Prentice Hall Professional Technical Reference, 2005.

[129] A. Guceglioglu, O. Demirors, in: W. van der Aalst, et al. (Eds.), Using Software Quality Characteristics to Measure Business Process QualityBusiness Process Management, vol. 3649, Springer, Berlin/Heidelberg, 2005, pp. 374−379.

[130] I. Vanderfeesten, H.A. Reijers, W.M.P. van der Aalst, Evaluating workflow process designs using cohesion and coupling metrics, Comput. Ind. 59 (2008) 420−437.

[131] W. Van Der Aalst, K. Van Hee, M. Hee, R. De Vries, J. Rigter, E. Verbeek, et al., Workflow Management: Models, Methods, and Systems, 2002.

[132] W. Van Der Aalst, Don't go with the flow: Web services composition standards exposed, 2003.

[133] IBM WebSphere MQ Workflow. <http://www-01.ibm.com/software/integration/wmqwf>.

[134] A. Arkin, S. Askary, S. Fordin, Web Service Choreography Interface (WSCI) 1.0. Technical report <http://www.w3.org/TR/wsci/>, 2002.

[135] ebXML Business Process Specification Schema 6 Version 1.01, 2001.

[136] W.M.P. van der Aalst, M. Dumas, A.H.M. ter Hofstede, N. Russell, H.M.W. Verbeek, P. Wohed, Life After BPEL? in: Formal Techniques for Computer Systems and Business Processes, 2005, pp. 35−50.

[137] T. Andrews, F. Curbera, H. Dholakia, Y. Goland, Y. Klein, F. Leymann, et al., Web Services Business Process Execution Language Version 2.0, OASIS 2007.

[138] I. Rychkova, A. Wegmann, Refinement Propagation. Towards Automated Construction of Visual Specifications, 2007.

[139] Y. Wu, P. Doshi, Making BPEL Flexible − Adapting in the Context of Coordination Constraints Using WS-BPEL, IEEE International Conference on Services Computing, vol. 1, 2008, pp. 423−430.

[140] O. Ezenwoye, S.M. Sadjadi, TRAP/BPEL: a framework for dynamic adaptation of composite services, in: Proceedings of the WEBIST, Barcelona, Spain, 2007, pp. 1−10.

[141] X. Yonglin, W. Jun, Context-driven business process adaptation for *ad hoc* changes, in: Proceedings of the IEEE International Conference on e-Business Engineering, 2008, pp. 53−60.

[142] G. Regev, A. Wegmann, Why do we need business process support? Balancing specialization and generalization with BPS systems, in: Proceedings of the Fourth BPMDS Workshop on Requirements Engineering for Business Process Support, 2003.

[143] M.J. Adams, A.H.M. ter Hofstede, D. Edmond, W.M.P. van der Aalst, Worklets: a service-oriented implementation of dynamic flexibility in workflows, On the Move to Meaningful Internet Systems 2006: CoopIS, DOA, GADA, and ODBASE, 2006, pp. 291–308.

[144] K. Knoll, S.L. Jarvenpaa, Information technology alignment or "fit"; in highly turbulent environments: the concept of flexibility, in: Proceedings of the Computer Personnel Research Conference on Reinventing IS: Managing Information Technology in changing Organizations, Alexandria, VA, 1994, pp. 1–14.

[145] S.W. Sadiq, W. Sadiq, M.E. Orlowska, Pockets of flexibility in workflow specification, Proceedings of the 20th International Conference on Conceptual Modeling, 2001, pp. 513–526.

[146] M.J. Adams, Facilitating Dynamic Flexibility and Exception Handling for Workflows, PhD Thesis, Faculty of Information Technology, QUT, Brisbane, 2007.

[147] N. Mulyar, M. Pesic, Declarative and Procedural Approaches for Modelling Clinical Guidelines: Addressing Flexibility Issues, Informal Proceedings of ProHealth '07, Brisbane, Australia, 2007.

[148] P. Soffer, On the notion of flexibility in business processes, in: Proceedings of the Workshop on Business Process Modeling, Design and Support (BPMDS05), 2005, pp. 35–42.

[149] J. Yu, Q. Sheng, J. Swee, Model-driven development of adaptive service-based systems with aspects and rules, in: Proceedings of the Web Information System Engineering (WISE), 2010, pp. 548–563.

[150] M. Pesic, Constraint-Based Workflow Management Systems: Shifting Control to User, Eindhoven University of Technology, Eindhoven, The Netherlands, 2008.

[151] S.A. Gurguis, A. Zeid, Towards autonomic web services: achieving self-healing using web services, SIGSOFT Softw. Eng. Notes 30 (2005) 1–5.

[152] O. Ezenwoye, S.M. Sadjadi, Enabling robustness in existing BPEL processes, in: Proceedings of the Eighth International Conference on Enterprise Information Systems (ICEIS), 2006, pp. 95–102.

[153] M. Blow, Y. Goland, M. Kloppmann, F. Leymann, G. Pfau, D. Roller, et al., BPELJ: BPEL for Java, Joint Whitepaper 1–24, 2004.

[154] S.M. Sadjadi, P.K. McKinley, Using transparent shaping and web services to support self-management of composite systems, in: Proceedings of the Second International Conference on Automatic Computing, 2005, pp. 76–87.

[155] S.M. Sadjadi, P.K. McKinley, B.H.C. Cheng, Transparent shaping of existing software to support pervasive and autonomic computing, SIGSOFT Softw. Eng. Notes 30 (2005) 1–7.

[156] F. Casati, S. Ilnicki, L. Jin, V. Krishnamoorthy, M.-C. Shan, Adaptive and dynamic service composition in eFlow, in: Advanced Information Systems Engineering, 2000, pp. 13–31.

[157] G. Canfora, M.D. Penta, R. Esposito, M.L. Villani, A framework for QoS-aware binding and re-binding of composite web services, J. Syst. Softw. 81 (2008) 1754–1769.

[158] J. Cardoso, J.A. Miller, A. Sheth, J. Arnold, Quality of service for workflows and web service processes, J. Web Semant. 1 (2004) 281–308.

[159] M. Weske, Flexible modeling and execution of workflow activities, in: Proceedings of the 31st Hawaii International Conference on System Sciences, vol. 7, 1998, pp. 713–722.

[160] C. Medeiros, G. Vossen, M. Weske, WASA: a workflow-based architecture to support scientific database applications, in: N. Revell, A. Tjoa (Eds.), Database and Expert Systems Applications, vol. 978, Springer, Berlin/Heidelberg, 1995, pp. 574–583.

[161] G. Vossen, M. Weske, The WASA approach to work-flow management for scientific applications, in: Workflow Management Systems and Interoperability, NATO ASI Workshop. vol. 164, Computer and Systems Sciences, Berlin: Springer 1997, pp. 145−164.

[162] M. Weske, G. Vossen, C.B. Medeiros, Scientific Workflow Management: WASA Architecture and Applications. Technical Report 03/96-I, Universität Münster, 1996.

[163] C. Ellis, C. Maltzahn, The Chautauqua workflow system, in: Proceedings of the 30th Hawaii International Conference on System Sciences, vol. 4, 1997, pp. 427−436.

[164] F. Casati, S. Ceri, B. Pernici, G. Pozzi, Workflow evolution, Data Knowl. Eng. 24 (1998) 211−238.

[165] F. Casati, P. Grefen, B. Pernici, G. Pozzi, G. Sánchez, B. Pernici, WIDE Workflow Model and Architecture, Technical Report, University of Milano, Italy, 1996.

[166] C.A. Ellis, G.J. Nutt, Office information systems and computer science, ACM Comput. Surv. 12 (1980) 27−60.

[167] M. Reichert, P. Dadam, ADEPTflex − supporting dynamic changes of workflows without losing control, J. Intell. Inf. Syst. 10 (1998) 93−129.

[168] M. Reichert, C. Hensinger, P. Dadam, Supporting adaptive workflows in advanced application environments, in: Proceedings of the EDBT Workshop on Workflow Management Systems, 1998, pp. 100−109.

[169] P. Dadam, M.U. Reichert, S.B. Rinderle, M. Jurisch, H. Acker, K. Göser, et al., ADEPT2 − next generation process management technology, in: Proceedings of the Fourth Heidelberg Innovation Forum, Heidelberg, Germany, 2007.

[170] Y. Sanghyun, R. Yo-han, S. In-Chul, J. Joo Hyuk, K. Myoung Ho, K. Hak Soo, et al., Rule-based dynamic business process modification and adaptation, in: Proceedings of the International Conference on Information Networking, 2008, pp. 1−5.

[171] R.G. Ross, Principles of the Business Rule Approach, Addison-Wesley, 2003.

[172] T. Morgan, Business Rules and Information Systems: Aligning IT with Business Goals, Addison-Wesley, 2002.

[173] D. Hay, K.A. Healy, GUIDE Business Rules Project, Final Report − Revision 1.2, GUIDE International Corporation, Chicago, IL, 1997.

[174] JESS: The Java Expert System Shell. <http://www.jessrules.com/>.

[175] JRules. <http://www-01.ibm.com/software/integration/business-rule-management/jrules/>.

[176] P. Browne, JBoss Drools Business Rules, Packt Publishing, 2009.

[177] L. Chen, M. Li, J. Cao, ECA rule-based workflow modeling and implementation for service composition, IEICE − Trans. Inf. Syst. E89-D (2006) 624−630.

[178] K. Geminiuc, A Services-Oriented Approach to Business Rules Development, 2007.

[179] F. Rosenberg, S. Dustdar, Business rules integration in BPEL − a service-oriented approach, in: Proceedings of the International Conference on E-Commerce Technology, 2005, pp. 476−479.

[180] F. Rosenberg, S. Dustdar, Design and implementation of a service-oriented business rules broker, in: Proceedings of the Seventh IEEE International Conference on E-Commerce Technology Workshops, 2005, pp. 55−63.

[181] T. Graml, R. Bracht, M. Spies, Patterns of business rules to enable agile business processes, in: Proceedings of the IEEE International Conference on Enterprise Distributed Object Computing (EDOC), 2008, pp. 385−402.

[182] W3C, XSL transformations (XSLT) version 2.0. W3C working draft, 2003.

[183] M. Kay, XPath 2.0 Programmer's Reference (Programmer to Programmer): Wrox, 2004.

[268] R. von Ammon, T. Ertlmaier, O. Etzion, A. Kofman, T. Paulus, Integrating Complex Events for Collaborating and Dynamically Changing Business Processes, Event Processing Technical Society, 2009.

[269] G.J. Nalepa, M.A. Mach, Business rules design method for business process management, in: Proceedings of the International Multiconference on Computer Science and Information Technology, 2009, pp. 165−170.

[270] P. Jackson, Introduction to Expert Systems, Addison-Wesley, 1999.

[271] B. Orriens, J. Yang, M. Papazoglou, A rule driven approach for developing adaptive service oriented business collaboration, in: Proceedings of the International Conference on Service-Oriented Computing, 2005, pp. 61−72.

[272] D. Richards, Two decades of ripple down rules research, Knowl. Eng. Rev. 24 (2009) 159−184.

[273] Defining Business Rules∼What Are They Really?. <http://www.businessrulesgroup.org/first_paper/br01c0.htm>, March 2012.

[274] S. Kabicher, S. Rinderle-Ma, in: H. Mouratidis, C. Rolland (Eds.), Human-Centered Process Engineering Based on Content Analysis and Process View Aggregation Advanced Information Systems Engineering, vol. 6741, Springer, Berlin/Heidelberg, 2011, pp. 467−481.

[275] A.-W. Scheer, Architecture of integrated information systems (ARIS), in: Proceedings of the JSPE/IFIP TC5/WG5.3 Workshop on the Design of Information Infrastructure Systems for Manufacturing, 1993, pp. 85−99.

[276] G. Keller, T. Teufel, SAP R/3 Process-Oriented Implementation: Iterative Process Prototyping, Addison Wesley Longman, 1998.

[277] P.S. Santos Jr., J.P.A. Almeida, G. Guizzardi, An ontology-based semantic foundation for ARIS EPCs, in: Proceedings of the ACM Symposium on Applied Computing, Sierre, Switzerland, 2010, pp. 124−130.

[278] ProM framework. <http://prom.win.tue.nl/tools/prom/>, 2009.

[279] P. Barborka, L. Helm, G. Köldorfer, J. Mendling, G. Neumann, Integration of EPC-related tools with ProM, in: Proceedings of the Fifth GI Workshop on Event-Driven Process Chains, 2006, pp. 105−120.

[280] B.F. van Dongen, W.M.P. van der Aalst, H.M.W. Verbeek, Verification of EPCs: using reduction rules and Petri nets, in: Advanced Information Systems Engineering, 2005, pp. 372−386.

[281] V.T. Nunes, C.M.L. Werner, F.M. Santoro, Dynamic process adaptation: a context-aware approach, in: Proceedings of the 15th International Conference on Computer Supported Cooperative Work in Design (CSCWD), 2011, pp. 97−104.

[282] M. Dumas, W. van der Aalst, A.H. ter Hofstede, Process Aware Information Systems: Bridging People and Software Through Process Technology, Wiley-Interscience, 2005.

[283] C. Günther, S. Rinderle, M. Reichert, W. van der Aalst, Change mining in adaptive process management systems, in: On the Move to Meaningful Internet Systems 2006: CoopIS, DOA, GADA, and ODBASE, 2006, pp. 309−326.

[284] R. Lu, S. Sadiq, G. Governatori, X. Yang, Defining adaptation constraints for business process variants, in: Business Information Systems, 2009, pp. 145−156.

[285] B. Weber, Beyond rigidity − dynamic process lifecycle support: a survey on dynamic changes in process-aware information systems, Comput. Sci. 23 (2009) 47−65.

[286] L. Chen, M. Reichert, A. Wombacher, Mining process variants: goals and issues, in: Proceedings of the IEEE International Conference on Services Computing, 2008, pp. 573−576.

[287] J. King, A. Colman, A multi faceted management interface for Web services, Australian Software Engineering Conference, IEEE Computer Society, vol. 0, 2009, pp. 191–199.

[288] T. Haerder, A. Reuter, Principles of transaction-oriented database recovery, ACM Comput. Surv. 15 (1983) 287–317.

[289] K. Lee, R. Sakellariou, N.W. Paton, A.A.A. Fernandes, Workflow adaptation as an autonomic computing problem, in: Proceedings of the Second Workshop on Workflows in Support of Large-Scale Science, Monterey, CA, 2007, pp. 29–34.

[290] S. Fritsch, A. Senart, D.C. Schmidt, S. Clarke, Scheduling time-bounded dynamic software adaptation, in: Proceedings of the International Workshop on Software Engineering for Adaptive and Self-managing Systems, Leipzig, Germany, 2008, pp. 89–96.

[291] P.K. McKinley, S.M. Sadjadi, E.P. Kasten, B.H.C. Cheng, Composing adaptive software, Computer 37 (2004) 56–64.

[292] G. Gardey, O.H. Roux, O.F. Roux, State space computation and analysis of time Petri nets, Theory Pract. Log. Program. 6 (2006) 301–320.

[293] D. Lime, O.H. Roux, Model checking of time Petri nets using the state class timed automaton, Discrete Event Dyn. Syst. 16 (2006) 179–205.

[294] J. Dehnert, P. Rittgen, Relaxed soundness of business processes, in: Proceedings of the Advanced Information Systems Engineering, 2001, pp. 157–170.

[295] D. Giannakopoulou, K. Havelund, Automata-based verification of temporal properties on running programs, in: Proceedings of the 16th IEEE International Conference on Automated Software Engineering, 2001.

[296] Apache Axis2 – Next Generation Web Services. <http://ws.apache.org/axis2/>, 2012.

[297] S. Perera, C. Herath, J. Ekanayake, E. Chinthaka, A. Ranabahu, D. Jayasinghe, et al., Axis2, diddleware for next generation web services, in: Proceedings of the International Conference on Web Services, 2006, pp. 833–840.

[298] D. Jayasinghe, Quickstart Apache Axis2, Packt Publishing, 2008.

[299] R.T. Fielding, Architectural Styles and the Design of Network-Based Software Architectures, University of California, Irvine, CA, 2000.

[300] S. Kumaran, R. Liu, P. Dhoolia, T. Heath, P. Nandi, F. Pinel, A RESTful architecture for service-oriented business process execution, in: Proceedings of the IEEE International Conference on e-Business Engineering, 2008.

[301] S.N. Srirama, M. Jarke, W. Prinz, Mobile web services mediation framework, in: Proceedings of the Second Workshop on Middleware for Service Oriented Computing: held at the ACM/IFIP/USENIX International Middleware Conference, Newport Beach, CA, 2007, pp. 6–11.

[302] Drools: Business Logic integration Platform. <http://www.jboss.org/drools/>.

[303] L. Haifeng, H.A. Jacobsen, Modeling uncertainties in publish/subscribe systems, in: Proceedings of the 20th International Conference on Data Engineering, 2004, pp. 510–521.

[304] I. Burcea, H.A. Jacobsen, E. de Lara, V. Muthusamy, M. Petrovic, Disconnected operation in publish/subscribe middleware, in: Proceedings of the IEEE International Conference on Mobile Data Management, 2004, pp. 39–50.

[305] ANTLR parser generator v3, <http://www.antlr.org/>, 2011.

[306] R. Wiener, L.J. Pinson, Fundamentals of OOP and Data Structures in Java, Cambridge University Press, 2000.

[307] Drools Expert. <http://www.jboss.org/drools/drools-expert>.

[308] Sun Developer Network, Java Specification Requests – Java Rule Engine API – JSR 94, 2004.

[309] C. Forgy, Rete: a fast algorithm for the many pattern/many object pattern match problem, 1990, pp. 324–341.

[310] R.J. Schalkoff, Intelligent Systems: Principles, Paradigms, and Pragmatics, Jones & Bartlett Publishers, 2009.

[311] L. Amador, Drools Developer's Cookbook, Packt Publishing, 2012.

[312] XSLT Tutorial – W3Schools. <http://www.w3schools.com/xsl/>.

[313] M. Kay, XSLT 2.0 Programmer's Reference (Programmer to Programmer): Wrox, 2004.

[314] D. Brownell, Sax2, O'Reilly, 2002.

[315] World-Wide-Web-Consortium, XML Path Language (XPath), ed, 1999.

[316] Sun Developer Network, JSR 222 Java Specification Requests – Java Architecture for XML Binding (JAXB) 2.0, 2006.

[317] XML Schema. <http://www.w3.org/XML/Schema>, 2001.

[318] ROADdesigner. <http://www.swinburne.edu.au/ict/success/research-projects-and-grants/role-oriented-adaptive-design/implementations/road-designer.html>.

[319] Eclipse GMF. <www.eclipse.org/gmf/>.

[320] D. Parsons, Dynamic Web Application Development Using XML and Java, Cengage Learning, 2008.

[321] B. McLaughlin, J. Edelson, Java and XML, O'Reilly, 2007.

[322] Apache Rampart – An Implementation WS-Security specifications. <http://axis.apache.org/axis2/java/rampart/>.

[323] D. Steinberg, F. Budinsky, E. Merks, M. Paternostro, EMF: Eclipse Modeling Framework, Pearson Education, 2008.

[324] B. Weber, M. Reichert, S. Rinderle-Ma, Change patterns and change support features – enhancing flexibility in process-aware information systems, Data Knowl. Eng. 66 (3) (2008) 438–466.

[325] M. Weske, Formal foundation and conceptual design of dynamic adaptations in a workflow management system, in: Proceedings of the 34th Annual Hawaii International Conference on System Sciences, 2001, pp. 10–20.

[326] B. Weber, W. Wild, R. Breu, CBRFlow: enabling adaptive workflow management through conversational case-based reasoning, in: P. Funk, P.A. González Calero (Eds.), Advances in Case-Based Reasoning, vol. 3155, Springer, Berlin/Heidelberg, 2004, pp. 89–101.

[327] M. Kradolfer, A. Geppert, Dynamic workflow schema evolution based on workflow type versioning and workflow migration, in: Proceedings of the Fourth IECIS International Conference on Cooperative Information Systems, 1999.

[328] K. Rajaram, C. Babu, Template based SOA framework for dynamic and adaptive composition of web services, in: Proceedings of the International Conference on Networking and Information Technology (ICNIT), 2010, pp. 49–53.

[329] D.L. Parnas, On the criteria to be used in decomposing systems into modules, Commun. ACM, 15, 1972.

[330] S. Rinderle, B. Weber, M. Reichert, W. Wild, Integrating process learning and process evolution – a semantics based approach, in: Proceedings of the Third International Conference on Business Process Management, 2005, pp. 252–267.

[331] W. van der Aalst, T. Weijters, L. Maruster, Workflow mining: discovering process models from event logs, IEEE Trans. Knowl. Data Eng. 16 (2004) 1128–1142.

Appendix A: SerendipLang Grammar

Presented here is the grammar for the Serendip Language (SerendipLang). The grammar is presented in an EBNF dialect used by XTEXT framework. For more information about the XTEXT EBNF dialect, please refer to XTEXT documentation (Listing A.1).[1]

```
grammar org.serendip.SerendipLang with org.eclipse.xtext.common.Terminals

generate serendipLang "http://www.serendip.org/SerendipLang"

Script:
    (imports+=Import)*
    ('Organization' orgName=ID ';')
    (processDefs+=PdDef)*
    (btDefs+=Behavior)*
    (roleDefs+=Role)*
    (contracts+=Contract)*
    (playerBindings+=PlayerBinding)*
    (organizerBinding=OrganizerBinding)?;

Import:
    'import' qlfdName=path 'as' name=ID ';';

PdDef:
    'ProcessDefinition' name=ID '{'
    cos=Cos
    cot=Cot
    brefs+=BehaviorRef+
    cons+=Cons*
    '}';

Behavior:
    (abstract='abstract')? 'Behavior' name=ID ('extends' superType=[Behavior])? '{'
    tasks+=TaskRef+
    cons+=Cons*
    '}';

TaskRef:
    'TaskRef' role=[Role] '.' name=ID '{'
    'InitOn' eppre=Eppre ';'
    ('Triggers' eppost=Eppost ';')?
    ('PerfProp' 'type' ppType=("time" | "cost") pp=ppVal ';')?
    '}';

TaskDef:
    'Task' name=ID '{'
    ('UsingMsgs' srcMsgs=Msgs ';')?
    ('ResultingMsgs' resultMsgs=Msgs ';')?
    ('DeliveryType' deliveryType=("push" | "pull") ';')?
    '}';

Msgs:
    msgs+=Msg (',' msgs+=Msg)*;
```

Listing A.1 Grammar of SerendipLang.

---

[1]http://www.eclipse.org/Xtext/documentation/.

```
Msg:
    (contractPart=[Contract]) '.' (termPart=ID) '.' (direction=("Req" | "Res")) ;

Eppre:
    value=STRING;

Eppost:
    value=STRING;

ppVal:
    value=INT ID;

Cot:
    'CoT' value=STRING ';';

Cos:
    'CoS' value=STRING ';';

Cons:
    'Constraint' name=ID ':' expression=STRING ';';

BehaviorRef:
    'BehaviorRef' parentBT=[Behavior] ';';

Role:
    'Role' name=ID ('is a' descr=STRING)? ('playedBy' playedBy=[PlayerBinding])? '{'
    taskDefs+=TaskDef*
    '}';

Contract:
    'Contract' name=ID '{'
    'A is' roleA=[Role] ',' 'B is' roleB=[Role] ':'
    (facts+=FactType)*
    terms+=ITerm*
    ('RuleFile' ruleFileName=STRING ';')?
    '}';

ITerm:
    'ITerm' name=ID
    '(' params+=ParamType (',' params+=ParamType)* ')'
    ('withResponse' '(' returnParam=(ParamType) ')')?
    'from' direction=("AtoB" | "BtoA") ';';

FactType:
    'Fact' name=ID '(' attribs+=FactAttrib (',' attribs+=FactAttrib)* ')' ';';

FactAttrib:
    type=ID ':' name=ID;

ParamType:
    paramType=ID ':' paramName=ID;

PlayerBinding:
    'PlayerBinding' name=ID player=STRING 'is a' role=[Role] ';';

OrganizerBinding:
    'OrganizerBinding' name=ID player=STRING 'is the Organizer' ';';

path:
    pathValue=ID ('.' ID)*;
```

Listing A.1 (*Continued*)

Appendix B: RoSAS Description

This appendix contains the Serendip descriptor files used for the case study (Listing B.1). A high-level overview of RoSAS organisation structure and the processes are given in Figure B.1. Due to space limitations, we do not include all the Drools rule files (6) and XSLT transformation files (37) used. However, a sample Drools rule file and an XSLT transformation file are given in Listings B.2 and B.3, respectively, and were used to describe the case study previously. The generated deployable XML descriptor is given in Listing B.4. All the related files for the RoSAS scenario are available to download from: http://www.ict.swin.edu.au/personal/mkapuruge/files/RoSAS_Scenario6.zip.

```
Organization RoSAS;
/*Process Definitions*/
ProcessDefinition pdSilv   {
    CoS "eComplainRcvdSilv";
    CoT "(eMMNotifDone * eTTPaid * eGRPaid) ^ eExceptionHandled";
    BehaviorRef bComplaining;
    BehaviorRef bTowing;
    BehaviorRef bRepairing;
    BehaviorRef bHandleAnyException;
    Constraint pdSilv_c1: "(eComplainRcvdSilv>0)->(eMMNotifDone>0)";
}

ProcessDefinition pdGold   {
    CoS "eComplainRcvdGold";
    CoT "(eMMNotifDone * eTTPaid * eGRPaid * eTaxiPaid) ^ eExceptionHandled";
    BehaviorRef bComplainingGold;
    BehaviorRef bTowing;
    BehaviorRef bRepairing;
    BehaviorRef bTaxiProviding;
    BehaviorRef bHandleAnyException;
    Constraint pdGold_c1:"(eComplainRcvdGold>0)->(eMMNotifDone>0)";
}

ProcessDefinition pdPlat {
    CoS "eComplainRcvdPlat";
    CoT "(eMMNotifDone * eTTPaid * eGRPaid * eTaxiPaid * eHotelPaid) ^
eExceptionHandled";
    BehaviorRef bComplainingPlat;
    BehaviorRef bTowingAlt2;
    BehaviorRef bRepairing;
    BehaviorRef bTaxiProviding;
    BehaviorRef bAccommodationProviding;
    BehaviorRef bHandleAnyException;
    Constraint pdPlat_c1:"(eComplainRcvdPlat>0)->(eMMNotifDone>0)";
}
/*Behavior Definitions*/
Behavior bComplaining {
  TaskRef CO.tAnalyze {
     InitOn "eComplainRcvdSilv";
     Triggers "eTowReqd * eRepairReqd";
  }
```

Listing B.1 RoSAS orchestration description in SerendipLang.

```
        TaskRef CO.tNotify {
            InitOn "eMMNotif";
            Triggers "eMMNotifDone";
        }
    }
    Behavior bComplainingGold extends bComplaining{
        TaskRef CO.tAnalyze {
            InitOn "eComplainRcvdGold";
            Triggers "eTowReqd * eRepairReqd * eTaxiReqd";
        }
    }
    Behavior bComplainingPlat extends bComplaining{
        TaskRef CO.tAnalyze {
            InitOn "eComplainRcvdPlat";
            Triggers "eTowReqd * eRepairReqd * eTaxiReqd * eAccommoReqd";
        }
    }
    Behavior bRepairing{
        TaskRef GR.tAcceptRepairOrder {
            InitOn "eRepairReqd";
            Triggers "eDestinationKnown";
        }
        TaskRef GR.tDoRepair {
            InitOn "eTowSuccess";
            Triggers "eRepairSuccess ^ eRepairFailed";
        }
        TaskRef CO.tPayGR {
            InitOn "eRepairSuccess";
            Triggers "eGRPaid * eMMNotif";
        }
        Constraint bRepairing_c1:"(eRepairSuccess>0)->(eGRPaid>0)";
    }
    Behavior bTowing{
        TaskRef TT.tTow {
            InitOn "eTowReqd * eDestinationKnown";
            Triggers "eTowSuccess ^ eTowFailed";
        }
        TaskRef CO.tPayTT {
            InitOn "eTowSuccess";
            Triggers "eTTPaid";
        }
        Constraint bTowing_c1:"(eTowSuccess>0)->(eTTPaid>0)";
    }
    Behavior bTowingAlt extends bTowing {
        TaskRef CO.tAlertTowDone {
            InitOn "eTowSuccess";
            Triggers "eMemberTowAlerted";
        }
    }
    Behavior bTowingAlt2 extends bTowing {
        TaskRef TT.tTow {
            InitOn "eTowReqd * eDestinationKnown * eTaxiProvided";
        }
    }
    Behavior bTaxiProviding{
        TaskRef CO.tPlaceTaxiOrder {
            InitOn "eTaxiReqd";
            Triggers "eTaxiOrderPlaced";
        }
        TaskRef TX.tProvideTaxi {
            InitOn "eTaxiOrderPlaced";
            Triggers "eTaxiProvided";
        }
```

Listing B.1 (*Continued*)

```
      TaskRef CO.tPayTaxi {
         InitOn "eTaxiProvided";
         Triggers "eTaxiPaid";
      }
      Constraint bTaxiProviding_c1:"(eTaxiReqd>0)->(eTaxiPaid>0)";
      Constraint bTaxiProviding_c2:"(eTaxiOrderPlaced>0)->(eTaxiProvided>0)";
   Behavior bAccommodationProviding{
      TaskRef CO.tBookHotel {
         InitOn "eAccommoReqd";
         Triggers "eAccommoReqested";
      }
      TaskRef HT.tConfirmBooking {
         InitOn "eAccommoReqested";
         Triggers "eAccommoBookingConfirmed";
      }
      TaskRef CO.tPayHotel{
         InitOn "eAccommoBookingConfirmed";
         Triggers "eHotelPaid";
      }
   }
   Behavior bHandleAnyException{
      TaskRef CO.tHandleException {
         InitOn "eTowFailed ^ eRepairFailed";
         Triggers "eExceptionHandled";
      }
   }
/*Role Definitions*/
Role CO is a 'CaseOfficer' playedBy copb{
   Task tNotify{
      ResultingMsgs CO_MM.complain.Res;
   }
   Task tAnalyze{
      UsingMsgs  CO_MM.complain.Req;
      ResultingMsgs CO_TT.orderTow.Req,  CO_GR.orderRepair.Req, CO_TX.orderTaxi.Req,
CO_HT.orderHotel.Req;
   }
   Task  tPayGR  {
      UsingMsgs  CO_GR.orderRepair.Res;
      ResultingMsgs CO_GR.payRepair.Req, CO_MM.complain.Res;
   }
   Task  tPayTT
 {
      UsingMsgs CO_TT.orderTow.Res;
      ResultingMsgs CO_TT.payTow.Req;
   }
   Task  tPlaceTaxiOrder {
      ResultingMsgs CO_TX.orderTaxi.Req;
   }
   Task tPayTaxi {
      UsingMsgs CO_TX.orderTaxi.Res;
      ResultingMsgs CO_TX.payTaxi.Req;
   }
   Task tBookHotel{
      ResultingMsgs CO_HT.orderHotel.Req;
   }
   Task tPayHotel{
      UsingMsgs CO_HT.orderHotel.Res;
      ResultingMsgs CO_HT.payHotel.Req;
   }
   Task tHandleException{
      ResultingMsgs CO_MM.complain.Res;
   }
}
```

Listing B.1 (*Continued*)

```
Role GR is a 'Garage' playedBy  grpb {
   Task tAcceptRepairOrder{
      UsingMsgs CO_GR.orderRepair.Req;
      ResultingMsgs CO_TT.sendGRLocation.Req;
      DeliveryType pull ;
   }
   Task  tDoRepair {
      UsingMsgs  GR_TT.sendGRLocation.Res;
      ResultingMsgs CO_GR.orderRepair.Res;
   }
   Task  tAcceptPayment {
      UsingMsgs  CO_GR.payRepair.Req;
   }
}
Role TT is a 'TowTruck' playedBy ttpb{
   Task  tTow  {
      UsingMsgs CO_TT.orderTow.Req , GR_TT.sendGRLocation.Req;
      ResultingMsgs CO_TT.orderTow.Res,  GR_TT.sendGRLocation.Res;
   }
   Task  tAcceptPayment {
      UsingMsgs  CO_TT.payTow.Req;
   }
}
Role TX is a 'Taxi' playedBy txpb{

   Task  tProvideTaxi {
      UsingMsgs CO_TX.orderTaxi.Req;
      ResultingMsgs CO_TX.orderTaxi.Res;
   }
   Task  tAcceptPayment {
      UsingMsgs  CO_TX.payTaxi.Req;
   }
}
Role HT is a 'Hotel' playedBy htpb{
   Task  tConfirmBooking {
      UsingMsgs CO_HT.orderHotel.Req;
      ResultingMsgs CO_HT.orderHotel.Res;
   }
   Task  tAcceptPayment {
      UsingMsgs  CO_HT.payHotel.Req;
   }
}
Role MM is a 'Member'{
}
/*Contract Definitions*/
Contract  CO_MM{
   A is CO, B is MM ;
   ITerm complain (String:memId, String:complainDetails ) withResponse (String:response)
from BtoA;
}
Contract CO_TT{
   A is CO, B is TT;
   Fact TowCounter(int:counter) ;
   Fact ContractState(String:state);
   ITerm orderTow  (String:pickupInfo) withResponse (String:ackTowing) from AtoB;
   ITerm payTow (String:paymentInfo) from AtoB;
   RuleFile "CO_TT.drl";
}
Contract CO_GR{
   A is CO, B is GR;
   Fact ContractState(String:state);
   ITerm orderRepair (String:repairInfo)  withResponse (String:ackRepairing)  from AtoB;
   ITerm payRepair (String:paymentInfo)  from AtoB;
   RuleFile "CO_GR.drl";
}
```

Listing B.1 (*Continued*)

```
Contract  CO_TX{
   A is CO, B is TX;
   Fact ContractState(String:state);
   ITerm orderTaxi (String:taxiInfo)  withResponse (String:ackTaxiAccept)  from AtoB;
   ITerm payTaxi (String:paymentInfo)  from AtoB;
   RuleFile "CO_TX.drl";
}
Contract GR_TT{
   A is GR, B is TT;
   Fact ContractState(String:state);
   ITerm sendGRLocation (String:addressOfGarage) withResponse (String:ack) from AtoB ;
   RuleFile "GR_TT.drl";
}
Contract CO_HT{
   A is CO, B is HT ;
   Fact ContractState(String:state);
   ITerm orderHotel (String:guestName  ) withResponse (String:response) from AtoB;
   ITerm payHotel (String:paymentInfo  )  from AtoB;
   RuleFile "CO_HT.drl";
}
/*Player Binding Definitions*/
PlayerBinding copb "http://127.0.0.1:8080/axis2/services/S6COService" is a CO ;
PlayerBinding ttpb "http://136.186.7.228:8080/axis2/services/S6TTService" is a TT ;
PlayerBinding grpb "http://136.186.7.228:8080/axis2/services/S6GRService" is a GR ;
PlayerBinding txpb "http://136.186.7.228:8080/axis2/services/S6TXService" is a TX ;
PlayerBinding htpb "http://136.186.7.228:8080/axis2/services/S6HTService" is a HT ;
OrganizerBinding org "http://127.0.0.1:8080/axis2/services/rosas_organizer" is the
Organizer ;
```

Listing B.1 (*Continued*)

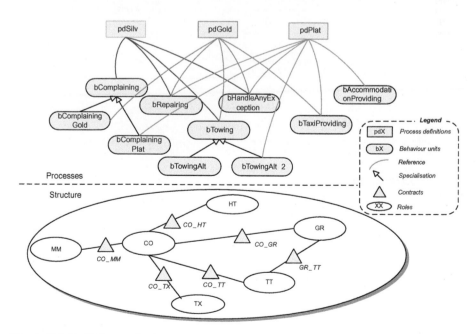

Figure B.1 RoSAS organisation — an overview.

```
/**Generated by Serendip**/
import au.edu.swin.ict.road.composite.rules.events.contract.MessageRecievedEvent;
import au.edu.swin.ict.road.composite.rules.events.contract.ObligationComplianceEvent;
import au.edu.swin.ict.road.composite.rules.events.contract.TermExecutedEvent;
import au.edu.swin.ict.road.composite.contract.Contract;
import au.edu.swin.ict.road.composite.message.MessageWrapper;
import au.edu.swin.ict.road.regulator.FactObject;
import au.edu.swin.ict.road.regulator.FactTupleSpace;
import au.edu.swin.ict.road.regulator.FactTupleSpaceRow;
import java.util.List;
import au.edu.swin.ict.serendip.rosas.util.DroolsUtil;

/** Global variables **/
global Contract contract;
global FactTupleSpace fts;

/** Interaction message **/
declare MessageRecievedEvent
  @role(event)
end
/* Fact to keep the state of the contract */
declare ContractState
   state : String
end
/*Fact to keep the number of tow requests*/
declare TowCounter
   count : int
end
/** 1. The rule to evaluate the interaction orderTow on the request path **/
rule "orderTowRequestRule"
    when
      $msg : MessageRecieved(operationName == "orderTow", response == false)
    then
      $msg.triggerEvent("eTowReqd");
end

/** 2. The rules to evaluate the interaction orderTow on the response path. In here we
have two rules to check if evaluation of message is successful or not. Here, DroolsUtil
is a Java class implemented to evaluate the message **/
rule "orderTowResponseRule Valid"
    when
      $msg : MessageRecieved(operationName  == "orderTow" , response == true)
      eval(true==DroolsUtil.evaluate($msg))
    then
     //Everything is fine, trigger success event
     $msg.triggerEvent("eTowSuccess");
end
rule "orderTowResponseRule Invalid"
    when
      $msg : MessageRecieved(operationName == "orderTow" , response == true)
      eval(false==DroolsUtil.evaluate($msg))
    then
     //Something is wrong, trigger the failure event
     $msg.triggerEvent("eTowFailed");
end
/** 3. The rule to evaluate the interaction payTow on the request path **/
rule "payTowRequestRule"
    when
      $msg : MessageRecieved(operationName == "payTow", response == false)
    then
      $msg.triggerEvent("eTTPaid");
end
```

Listing B.2 Sample Drools rule file for CO_TT.drl.

```
/** 4. The rule to pay Bonus **/
rule "Pay some bonus"
  when
      $msg : MessageRecievedEvent(operationName == "orderTow", response ==true)
      $tc: TowCounter( count > 20)
  then
      $msg.triggerEvent("eTowBonusAllowed");
      $tc.setCount(0);
end
/** 4. The rule to increment the tow counter **/
rule "IncrementTowCount"
  when
      $msg : MessageRecievedEvent(operationName == "orderTow", response ==false)
      $tc: TowCounter( count < 20)
  then
      $tc.setCount($tc.getCount()+ 1); //Increment
end
```

Listing B.2 (*Continued*)

```
<?xml version="1.0" encoding="UTF-8"?>
<xsl:stylesheet version="2.0"
   xmlns:xsl=http://www.w3.org/1999/XSL/Transform
   xmlns:soapenv="http://schemas.xmlsoap.org/soap/envelope/"
   xmlns:q0="http://ws.apache.org/axis2">
   <xsl:output method="xml" indent="yes" />
   <xsl:param name="CO_MM.complain.Req" />
   <xsl:template match="/">
      <soapenv:Envelope xmlns:soapenv="http://schemas.xmlsoap.org/soap/envelope/">
         <soapenv:Body>
            <q0:analyze xmlns:q0="http://ws.apache.org/axis2">
               <memId>
                  <xsl:value-of
select="$CO_MM.complain.Req/soapenv:Envelope/soapenv:Body/q0:complain/args0" />
               </memId>
               <complainDetails>
                  <xsl:value-of
select="$CO_MM.complain.Req/soapenv:Envelope/soapenv:Body/q0:complain/args1" />
               </complainDetails>
            </q0:analyze>
         </soapenv:Body>
      </soapenv:Envelope>
   </xsl:template>
</xsl:stylesheet>
```

Listing B.3 Sample XSLT file to generate the CO.tAnalyze.Req.

```xml
                    enabled="true" soft="false" />
            <tns1:Constraint Id="bTaxiProviding_c2"
                Expression="(eTaxiOrderPlaced>0)->(eTaxiProvided>0)" enabled="true"
                soft="false" />
        </tns1:Constraints>
    </tns1:BehaviorTerm>
    <tns1:BehaviorTerm id="bAccommodationProviding"
        isAbstract="false">
        <tns1:TaskRefs>
            <tns1:TaskRef Id="CO.tBookHotel" preEP="eAccommoReqd"
                postEP="eAccommoReqested" />
            <tns1:TaskRef Id="HT.tConfirmBooking" preEP="eAccommoReqested"
                postEP="eAccommoBookingConfirmed" />
            <tns1:TaskRef Id="CO.tPayHotel" preEP="eAccommoBookingConfirmed"
                postEP="eHotelPaid" />
        </tns1:TaskRefs>
        <tns1:Constraints>
        </tns1:Constraints>
    </tns1:BehaviorTerm>
    <tns1:BehaviorTerm id="bHandleAnyException"
        isAbstract="false">
        <tns1:TaskRefs>
            <tns1:TaskRef Id="CO.tHandleException" preEP="eTowFailed ^ eRepairFailed"
                postEP="eExceptionHandled" />
        </tns1:TaskRefs>
        <tns1:Constraints>
        </tns1:Constraints>
    </tns1:BehaviorTerm>
    <tns1:BehaviorTerm id="bTowingAlt" extends="bTowing"
        isAbstract="false">
        <tns1:TaskRefs>
            <tns1:TaskRef Id="CO.tAlertTowDone" preEP="eTowSuccess"
                postEP="eMemberTowAlerted" />
        </tns1:TaskRefs>
        <tns1:Constraints>
        </tns1:Constraints>
    </tns1:BehaviorTerm>
    <tns1:BehaviorTerm id="bTowingAlt2" extends="bTowing"
        isAbstract="false">
        <tns1:TaskRefs>
            <tns1:TaskRef Id="TT.tTow"
                preEP="eTowReqd * eDestinationKnown * eTaxiProvided" postEP="" />
        </tns1:TaskRefs>
        <tns1:Constraints>
        </tns1:Constraints>
    </tns1:BehaviorTerm>
</BehaviorTerms>
<!--Contract Definitions will be listed below -->
<Contracts>
    <Contract id="CO_MM" type="permissive" ruleFile="CO_MM.drl">
        <Abstract>false</Abstract>
        <State>Incipient</State>
        <LinkedFacts>
        </LinkedFacts>
        <Terms>
            <Term id="complain" name="complain">
                <Operation name="complain">
                    <Parameters>
                        <Parameter>
                            <Type>String</Type>
                            <Name>memId</Name>
                        </Parameter>
                        <Parameter>
                            <Type>String</Type>
                            <Name>complainDetails</Name>
                        </Parameter>
                    </Parameters>
```

Listing B.4 (Continued)

```xml
                    <Return>String</Return>
                </Operation>
                <Direction>BtoA</Direction>
                <Description>Term for complain</Description>
            </Term>
        </Terms>
        <RoleAID>CO</RoleAID>
        <RoleBID>MM</RoleBID>
        <Description>This is the contract btwn the CO and MM
        </Description>
    </Contract>
    <Contract id="CO_TT" type="permissive" ruleFile="CO_TT.drl">
        <Abstract>false</Abstract>
        <State>Incipient</State>
        <LinkedFacts>
            <Fact name="TowCounter" />
            <Fact name="ContractState" />
        </LinkedFacts>
        <Terms>
            <Term id="orderTow" name="orderTow">
                <Operation name="orderTow">
                    <Parameters>
                        <Parameter>
                            <Type>String</Type>
                            <Name>pickupInfo</Name>
                        </Parameter>
                    </Parameters>
                    <Return>String</Return>
                </Operation>
                <Direction>AtoB</Direction>
                <Description>Term for orderTow</Description>
            </Term>
            <Term id="payTow" name="payTow">
                <Operation name="payTow">
                    <Parameters>
                        <Parameter>
                            <Type>String</Type>
                            <Name>paymentInfo</Name>
                        </Parameter>
                    </Parameters>
                    <Return>void</Return>
                </Operation>
                <Direction>AtoB</Direction>
                <Description>Term for payTow</Description>
            </Term>
        </Terms>
        <RoleAID>CO</RoleAID>
        <RoleBID>TT</RoleBID>
        <Description>This is the contract btwn the CO and TT
        </Description>
    </Contract>
    <Contract id="CO_GR" type="permissive" ruleFile="CO_GR.drl">
        <Abstract>false</Abstract>
        <State>Incipient</State>
        <LinkedFacts>
            <Fact name="ContractState" />
        </LinkedFacts>
        <Terms>
            <Term id="orderRepair" name="orderRepair">
                <Operation name="orderRepair">
                    <Parameters>
                        <Parameter>
                            <Type>String</Type>
                            <Name>repairInfo</Name>
                        </Parameter>
                    </Parameters>
```

Listing B.4 (*Continued*)

```xml
            <tns1:In isResponse="true">
            </tns1:In>
            <tns1:ResultMsgs>
                <tns1:ResultMsg contractId="CO_MM" termId="complain"
                    isResponse="true" transformation="CO_tHandleException_CO_MM_complain_Res.xsl" />
            </tns1:ResultMsgs>
        </tns1:Task>
    </Tasks>
    <Description>This is a CaseOfficer role</Description>
</Role>
<Role id="GR" name="GR">
    <Tasks>
        <tns1:Task id="tAcceptRepairOrder" isMsgDriven="false">
            <tns1:Out deliveryType="pull">
                <tns1:Operation name="tAcceptRepairOrder">
                    <Return>Return</Return>
                </tns1:Operation>
            </tns1:Out>
            <tns1:In isResponse="true">
            </tns1:In>
        <tns1:SrcMsgs transformation="GR_tAcceptRepairOrder.xsl">
            <tns1:SrcMsg contractId="CO_GR" termId="orderRepair"
                isResponse="false" />
        </tns1:SrcMsgs>
        <tns1:ResultMsgs>
            <tns1:ResultMsg contractId="CO_TT" termId="sendGRLocation"
                isResponse="false"
                transformation="GR_tAcceptRepairOrder_CO_TT_sendGRLocation_Req.xsl" />
        </tns1:ResultMsgs>
</tns1:Task>
<tns1:Task id="tDoRepair" isMsgDriven="false">
    <tns1:Out deliveryType="push">
        <tns1:Operation name="tDoRepair">
            <Return>Return</Return>
        </tns1:Operation>
    </tns1:Out>
    <tns1:In isResponse="true">
    </tns1:In>
    <tns1:SrcMsgs transformation="GR_tDoRepair.xsl">
        <tns1:SrcMsg contractId="GR_TT" termId="sendGRLocation"
            isResponse="true" />
    </tns1:SrcMsgs>
    <tns1:ResultMsgs>
        <tns1:ResultMsg contractId="CO_GR" termId="orderRepair"
            isResponse="true" transformation="GR_tDoRepair_CO_GR_orderRepair_Res.xsl" />
    </tns1:ResultMsgs>
</tns1:Task>
<tns1:Task id="tAcceptPayment" isMsgDriven="false">
    <tns1:Out deliveryType="push">
        <tns1:Operation name="tAcceptPayment">
            <Return>Return</Return>
        </tns1:Operation>
    </tns1:Out>
    <tns1:In isResponse="true">
    </tns1:In>
    <tns1:SrcMsgs transformation="GR_tAcceptPayment.xsl">
        <tns1:SrcMsg contractId="CO_GR" termId="payRepair"
            isResponse="false" />
    </tns1:SrcMsgs>
    </tns1:Task>
    </Tasks>
    <Description>This is a Garage role</Description>
</Role>
<Role id="TT" name="TT">
    <Tasks>
```

Listing B.4 (*Continued*)

```
        <tns1:Task id="tTow" isMsgDriven="false">
          <tns1:Out deliveryType="push">
            <tns1:Operation name="tTow">
              <Return>Return</Return>
            </tns1:Operation>
          </tns1:Out>
          <tns1:In isResponse="true">
          </tns1:In>
          <tns1:SrcMsgs transformation="TT_tTow.xsl">
            <tns1:SrcMsg contractId="CO_TT" termId="orderTow"
              isResponse="false" />
            <tns1:SrcMsg contractId="GR_TT" termId="sendGRLocation"
              isResponse="false" />
          </tns1:SrcMsgs>
          <tns1:ResultMsgs>
            <tns1:ResultMsg contractId="CO_TT" termId="orderTow"
              isResponse="true" transformation="TT_tTow_CO_TT_orderTow_Res.xsl" />
            <tns1:ResultMsg contractId="GR_TT" termId="sendGRLocation"
              isResponse="true" transformation="TT_tTow_GR_TT_sendGRLocation_Res.xsl" />
          </tns1:ResultMsgs>
        </tns1:Task>
        <tns1:Task id="tAcceptPayment" isMsgDriven="false">
          <tns1:Out deliveryType="push">
            <tns1:Operation name="tAcceptPayment">
              <Return>Return</Return>
            </tns1:Operation>
          </tns1:Out>
          <tns1:In isResponse="true">
          </tns1:In>
          <tns1:SrcMsgs transformation="TT_tAcceptPayment.xsl">
            <tns1:SrcMsg contractId="CO_TT" termId="payTow"
              isResponse="false" />
          </tns1:SrcMsgs>
        </tns1:Task>
    </Tasks>
    <Description>This is a TowTruck role</Description>
</Role>
<Role id="TX" name="TX">
    <Tasks>
        <tns1:Task id="tProvideTaxi" isMsgDriven="false">
          <tns1:Out deliveryType="push">
            <tns1:Operation name="tProvideTaxi">
              <Return>Return</Return>
            </tns1:Operation>
          </tns1:Out>
          <tns1:In isResponse="true">
          </tns1:In>
          <tns1:SrcMsgs transformation="TX_tProvideTaxi.xsl">
            <tns1:SrcMsg contractId="CO_TX" termId="orderTaxi"
              isResponse="false" />
          </tns1:SrcMsgs>
          <tns1:ResultMsgs>
            <tns1:ResultMsg contractId="CO_TX" termId="orderTaxi"
              isResponse="true" transformation="TX_tProvideTaxi_CO_TX_orderTaxi_Res.xsl" />
          </tns1:ResultMsgs>
        </tns1:Task>
        <tns1:Task id="tAcceptPayment" isMsgDriven="false">
          <tns1:Out deliveryType="push">
            <tns1:Operation name="tAcceptPayment">
              <Return>Return</Return>
            </tns1:Operation>
          </tns1:Out>
          <tns1:In isResponse="true">
          </tns1:In>
          <tns1:SrcMsgs transformation="TX_tAcceptPayment.xsl">
            <tns1:SrcMsg contractId="CO_TX" termId="payTaxi"
```

Listing B.4 (*Continued*)

```
                        isResponse="false" />
            </tns1:SrcMsgs>
        </tns1:Task>
    </Tasks>
    <Description>This is a Taxi role</Description>
</Role>
<Role id="HT" name="HT">
    <Tasks>
        <tns1:Task id="tConfirmBooking" isMsgDriven="false">
            <tns1:Out deliveryType="push">
                <tns1:Operation name="tConfirmBooking">
                    <Return>Return</Return>
                </tns1:Operation>
            </tns1:Out>
            <tns1:In isResponse="true">
            </tns1:In>
            <tns1:SrcMsgs transformation="HT_tConfirmBooking.xsl">
                <tns1:SrcMsg contractId="CO_HT" termId="orderHotel"
                    isResponse="false" />
            </tns1:SrcMsgs>
            <tns1:ResultMsgs>
                <tns1:ResultMsg contractId="CO_HT" termId="orderHotel"
                            isResponse="true"
        transformation="HT_tConfirmBooking_CO_HT_orderHotel_Res.xsl" />
                </tns1:ResultMsgs>
            </tns1:Task>
            <tns1:Task id="tAcceptPayment" isMsgDriven="false">
                <tns1:Out deliveryType="push">
                    <tns1:Operation name="tAcceptPayment">
                        <Return>Return</Return>
                    </tns1:Operation>
                </tns1:Out>
                <tns1:In isResponse="true">
                </tns1:In>
                <tns1:SrcMsgs transformation="HT_tAcceptPayment.xsl">
                    <tns1:SrcMsg contractId="CO_HT" termId="payHotel"
                        isResponse="false" />
                </tns1:SrcMsgs>
            </tns1:Task>
        </Tasks>
        <Description>This is a Hotel role</Description>
    </Role>
    <Role id="MM" name="MM">
        <Tasks>
        </Tasks>
        <Description>This is a Member role</Description>
    </Role>
</Roles>
<!--Player bindings will be listed below -->
<PlayerBindings>
    <PlayerBinding id="copb_binding">
        <Endpoint>http://127.0.0.1:8080/axis2/services/S6COService</Endpoint>
        <Roles>
            <RoleID>CO</RoleID>
        </Roles>
        <Description>This is the binding for CO</Description>
    </PlayerBinding>
    <PlayerBinding id="ttpb_binding">
        <Endpoint>http://136.186.7.228:8080/axis2/services/S6TTService</Endpoint>
        <Roles>
            <RoleID>TT</RoleID>
        </Roles>
        <Description>This is the binding for TT</Description>
    </PlayerBinding>
    <PlayerBinding id="grpb_binding">
        <Endpoint>http://136.186.7.228:8080/axis2/services/S6GRService</Endpoint>
        <Roles>
```

Listing B.4 (*Continued*)

```
            <RoleID>GR</RoleID>
        </Roles>
        <Description>This is the binding for GR</Description>
    </PlayerBinding>
    <PlayerBinding id="txpb_binding">
        <Endpoint>http://136.186.7.228:8080/axis2/services/S6TXService</Endpoint>
        <Roles>
            <RoleID>TX</RoleID>
        </Roles>
        <Description>This is the binding for TX</Description>
    </PlayerBinding>
    <PlayerBinding id="htpb_binding">
        <Endpoint>http://136.186.7.228:8080/axis2/services/S6HTService</Endpoint>
        <Roles>
            <RoleID>HT</RoleID>
        </Roles>

    </tns:SMC>

        <Description>This is the binding for HT</Description>
    </PlayerBinding>
</PlayerBindings>
<OrganiserBinding>http://127.0.0.1:8080/axis2/services/rosas_organizer</OrganiserBinding>
<Description>This is the descriptor for the organisation RoSAS,
Generated by Serendip Modelling Tool </Description>
```

Listing B.4 (*Continued*)

Appendix C: Organiser Operations

The operations exposed in the organiser interface allow an organiser player to monitor, adapt and regulate the service orchestration. These operations are exposed as WSDL operations in a Web service environment. This interface could be accessed by URL: http://[host]:[port]/axis2/services/[CompositeName]_Organizer?wsdl.

Each of the operations results in a result message, which captures result of the operation. For example, if an adaptation is carried out via an operation, the success/failure of adaptation and the possible reasons it failed are captured in these operations. If the operation is a monitoring operation, then the result message contains the observed input.

We categorise the operations into several sets (as captured by Tables C.1−C.5) depending on their purpose, as shown in Figure C.1.

Table C.1 presents the operations for batch-mode adaptations that can be commonly used to perform both structural and process (definition as well as instance level) adaptations. Table C.2 presents the operations for process instance−level adaptations. The operations for process definition−level adaptations are presented in Table C.3. The structure of the orchestration can be adapted via the operations presented in Table C.4. Finally, the monitoring operations are presented in Table C.5.

We follow a CRUD (create, read, update and delete) style API to define the operations. For the currently supported operations, we use prefixes add, read, update and remove to make clear what the operation is.

All the parameter values are string values. The following acronyms (alphabetically ordered) are used in naming parameters of operations. We list them in order to avoid a repetitive explanation. Operation-specific parameters are described in corresponding operations.

- bId = Behaviour Unit Identifier
- cExpression = A Constraint Expression
- cId = Constraint Identifier
- cos = Condition of Start
- cot = Condition of Termination
- ctId = Contract Identifier
- descr = A Description
- eId = Event Identifier
- extend = The Extends Property
- factId = A Fact Identifier
- name = A Name
- obligRole = Obligated Role
- pbId = Player Binding Identifier
- pdId = Process Definition Identifier
- pId = Process Instance Identifier

Table C.1 Operations commonly used for instance- and definition-level adaptations

Operation	Description
executeScript (scriptFileName)	Executes an adaptation script immediately. A script (written in a @scriptFileName, e.g. script.sas) allows performing number of adaptations in a single transaction. A script is written using Serendip Adaptation Script Language (Appendix D). The script need to be in the file system of the server, e.g. send via FTP.
scheduleScript (scriptFileName, conditionType, conditionValue)	Schedules and adaptation script (see command executeScript). The @conditionType is either an *EventPattern* or *Clock*. The condition value specified the value in which the adaptation should trigger. If the condition is an EventPattern, the condition value is used to specify a specific pattern of events. When the condition type is Clock, the adaptation is started based on a specific time of system clock. EventPattern - > <pId>: < event_pattern > Clock - > yyyy.MM.dd.HH.mm.ss.Z
applyPatch (patchFileName)	Applies a patch file (*xml) to add new entities, e.g. roles, contracts to a running composite. The patch file is same as a ROAD deployable descriptor file, yet only specifies additional entities that need to be added. The adaptation engine will read the descriptions and adds the entities to the running composite. No name conflicts are allowed with existing entities. This command is useful in situations where adding complex entities such as roles and contracts become tedious with individual operations.

- postEP = Post-Event Pattern
- pp = Performance Property
- preEP = Pre-Event Pattern
- prop = A Property
- rid = Role Identifier
- ruleFile = Rule File Name
- ruleId = A Rule Identifier
- status = A Status
- tId = Task Identifier
- tmid = An Interaction Term Identifier
- val = A Value of a Property

Table C.2 Operations for process instance—level adaptations

Operation	Description
updateStateOfProcessInst (pId, state)	Updates the current status of a process instance. @status = (pause/aborted/active)
addTaskToProcessInst (pId, bId, tId, preEP, postEP, obligRole, pp)	Adds a new task to a process instance.
removeTaskFromProcessInst (pId, tId)	Deletes a task from a process instance.
updateTaskOfProcessInst (pId, tId, prop, val)	Updates a property such as pre-event pattern of a task of a process instance. Here, @prop=(preEP/postEP/pp/obligRole).
addConstraintToProcessInst (pId, cId, cExpression)	Adds a new process instance—level constraint.
removeContraintFromProcessInst (pId, cId)	Deletes a constraint of a process instance.
updateContraintOfProcessInst (pId, cId, cExpression)	Updates a constraint of a process instance.
updateProcessInst (pId, prop, val)	Updates a property such as CoT of a process instance. Here, @prop = (CoS). *Updating CoS is not applicable for a process instance.
addEventToProcessInst (pId, eId, expire)	Forcefully adds a new event to Event Cloud. Can be used to support *ad hoc* adaptations.
removeEventFromProcessInst (pId, eId)	Forcefully removes an existing event from Event Cloud. Can be used to support *ad hoc* adaptations.
updateEventOfProcessInst (pId, prop, val)	Forcefully update an event in Event Cloud to a specific instance. Here, @prop = (Expire). *Updating other properties is not permitted.

Table C.3 Operations for process definition—level adaptations

Operation	Description
addProcessDef (pdId, cos, cot)	Adds a new process definition to the organisation.
removeProcessDef (pdId)	Removes an existing process definition from the organisation.
updateProcessDef (pdId, prop, val)	Updates a process definition. Here, @prop= (CoT/CoS).
addBehaviorRefToProcessDef (pdId, bId)	Adds a new behaviour reference to a process definition.
removeBehaviorRefFromProcessDef (pdId, bId)	Removes an existing behaviour reference form the process definition.
addConstraintToProcessDef (pdId, cId, cExpression, enabled)	Adds a new process-level constraint to a process definition.

(Continued)

Table C.5 Operations for monitoring

Operation	Description
readPropertyOfProcessInst(pId, tId, prop)	To retrieve the current value of a property of a process instance. prop=(CoS/CoT)
readPropertyOfTaskOfProcessInst(pId, tId, prop)	To retrieve the current value of a property of a task as specified in parameter. prop = (PreEP/PostEP/PP/role)
readPropertyOfConstraintOfProcessInstanc (pId, cId)	To retrieve the current expression value of a constraint.
getCurrentStatusOfProcessInst(pId)	To retrieve the current status of a process instance.
getCurrentStatusOfTaskOfProcessInst (pId, tId)	To retrieve the current status of a task of a process instance.
takeSnapShot()	Takes a snapshot of the current composite.
getNextManagementMessage()	Pulls the next management message from the composite.
subscribeToEventPattern (eventPattern)	Subscribe to interested patterns of events. Here, eventPattern is a pattern of events.

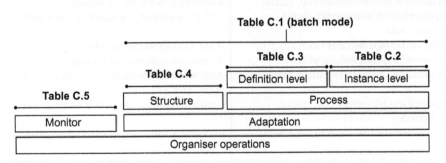

Figure C.1 A summary of available organiser operations.

Appendix D: Adaptation Scripting Language

The adaptation scripting language is used to perform batch-mode adaptations in the Serendip orchestration framework. The grammar of the scripting language is given here. The grammar is described in XTEXT format, which is an EBNF dialect. For more information about the XTEXT EBNF dialect, please refer to XTEXT documentation (Listing D.1).[1]

The *commandName* is the same as atomic operations listed in Appendix C. The property keys are same as the property names of those operations. The property order does not matter, e.g. to execute the command, removeTaskFromProcessInst (pId, tId) using script language, **removeTaskFromProcessInst pId**=pgGold037 **tId**=tPlaceTaxiOrder.

```
grammar org.serendip.adaptScripting.AdaptScripting with org.eclipse.xtext.common.Terminals

generate adaptScripting "http://www.serendip.org/adaptScripting/AdaptScripting"

/* Script may contain multiple blocks*/
Script: (block+=Block)*;

/* A block (a Scope) may contain multiple commands*/
Block: (scope=Scope ':' scopeId=ScopeId) '{'
    commands+=Command*
  '}'
;
/* A command may contain multiple properties*/
Command: name=CommandName (properties+=Property)* ';';

/* Use EVOL for Phase 2 adaptations
 USE INST for Phase 3 adaptations*/
Scope: "EVOL" | "INST";

/* For Phase 3 adaptations, the ScopeId MUST be the process instance identifier*/
ScopeId:name=ID;

/* A property is a key value pair*/
Property:key=ID'=''value=STRING; //Allows freedom of having specific key value pairs

/* A command is an atomic operation */
CommandName: ID ;
```

Listing D.1 Grammar of adaptation scripting language.

---

[1]http://www.eclipse.org/Xtext/documentation/.

Appendix E: Schema Definitions

The schema definition of the deployable descriptor is given here. The schema definition is captured by the files *smc.xsd*, *serendip.xsd*, *contract.xsd*, *role.xsd*, *player.xsd*, *fact.xsd*, *term.xsd* and *monitor.xsd*. These files can be visualised and navigated via suitable software tool such as *Eclipse XSD Editor.*[1]

```
smc.xsd

<?xml version="1.0" encoding="UTF-8"?>
<xsd:schema xmlns:xsd="http://www.w3.org/2001/XMLSchema"
   targetNamespace="http://www.swin.edu.au/ict/road/smc"
xmlns:tns="http://www.swin.edu.au/ict/road/smc"
   xmlns:role="http://www.swin.edu.au/ict/road/role"
xmlns:contract="http://www.swin.edu.au/ict/road/contract"
   xmlns:player="http://www.swin.edu.au/ict/road/player"
xmlns:fact="http://www.swin.edu.au/ict/road/fact"
   xmlns:ser="http://www.ict.swin.edu.au/serendip/types"
elementFormDefault="unqualified" version="1.3"
   xmlns:Q1="http://www.ict.swin.edu.au/serendip/types">
   <!-- schema imports -->
   <xsd:import schemaLocation="serendip.xsd"
   namespace="http://www.ict.swin.edu.au/serendip/types"></xsd:import>
   <xsd:import namespace="http://www.swin.edu.au/ict/road/contract"
schemaLocation="contract.xsd" />
   <xsd:import namespace="http://www.swin.edu.au/ict/road/role"
   schemaLocation="role.xsd" />
   <xsd:import namespace="http://www.swin.edu.au/ict/road/player"
   schemaLocation="player.xsd" />
   <xsd:import namespace="http://www.ict.swin.edu.au/serendip/types"
   schemaLocation="serendip.xsd" />
   <xsd:import namespace="http://www.swin.edu.au/ict/road/fact"
   schemaLocation="fact.xsd" />
   <!-- ROAD 2.0 self-managed composite -->
   <xsd:element name="SMC">
      <xsd:complexType>
         <xsd:sequence>
            <xsd:element name="ProcessDefinitions" type="ser:ProcessDefinitionsType"
               maxOccurs="1" minOccurs="0">
            </xsd:element>
            <xsd:element name="BehaviorTerms" type="ser:BehaviorTermsType"
               maxOccurs="1" minOccurs="0">
            </xsd:element>
            <xsd:element name="Messages" type="ser:MessagesType"
               maxOccurs="1" minOccurs="0">
            </xsd:element>
            <xsd:element name="Events" type="ser:EventsType"
               maxOccurs="1" minOccurs="0">
            </xsd:element>
            <xsd:element name="Facts" minOccurs="0" maxOccurs="1">
               <xsd:complexType>
                  <xsd:sequence>
                     <xsd:element name="Fact" type="fact:FactType"
                        minOccurs="1" maxOccurs="unbounded" />
                  </xsd:sequence>
               </xsd:complexType>
            </xsd:element>
```

[1]http://wiki.eclipse.org/index.php/Introduction_to_the_XSD_Editor.

```xml
                  <xsd:element name="Roles" minOccurs="0" maxOccurs="1">
                     <xsd:complexType>
                        <xsd:sequence>
                           <xsd:element name="Role" type="role:RoleType"
                              minOccurs="0" maxOccurs="unbounded" />
                        </xsd:sequence>
                     </xsd:complexType>
                  </xsd:element>
                  <xsd:element name="Contracts" minOccurs="0" maxOccurs="1">
                     <xsd:complexType>
                        <xsd:sequence>
                           <xsd:element name="Contract" type="contract:ContractType"
                              minOccurs="0" maxOccurs="unbounded" />
                        </xsd:sequence>
                     </xsd:complexType>
                  </xsd:element>
                  <xsd:element name="PlayerBindings" minOccurs="0"
                     maxOccurs="1">
                     <xsd:complexType>
                        <xsd:sequence>
                           <xsd:element name="PlayerBinding" type="player:PlayerBindingType"
                              minOccurs="0" maxOccurs="unbounded" />
                        </xsd:sequence>
                     </xsd:complexType>
                  </xsd:element>
                  <xsd:element name="OrganiserBinding" type="xsd:string"
                     minOccurs="0" maxOccurs="1" />
                  <xsd:element name="Description" type="xsd:string"
                     minOccurs="0" maxOccurs="1" />
                  <xsd:element name="MessageAnalyzers" type="ser:MessageAnalyzersType"
                     maxOccurs="1" minOccurs="0"></xsd:element>
               </xsd:sequence>
               <!-- smc attributes -->
               <xsd:attribute name="name" type="xsd:string" use="required" />
               <xsd:attribute name="dataDir" type="xsd:string" use="required" />
               <xsd:attribute name="routingRuleFile" type="xsd:string" use="required" />
               <xsd:attribute name="compositeRuleFile" type="xsd:string" use="required" />
            </xsd:complexType>
         </xsd:element>
      </xsd:schema>


   serendip.xsd

<?xml version="1.0" encoding="UTF-8"?>
<xsd:schema targetNamespace="http://www.ict.swin.edu.au/serendip/types"
   elementFormDefault="qualified" xmlns:xsd="http://www.w3.org/2001/XMLSchema"
   xmlns:tns="http://www.ict.swin.edu.au/serendip/types"
   xmlns:ecore="http://www.eclipse.org/emf/2002/Ecore"
   xmlns:Q1="http://www.swin.edu.au/ict/road/term">
   <xsd:import schemaLocation="term.xsd"
namespace="http://www.swin.edu.au/ict/road/term"></xsd:import>
   <xsd:complexType name="BehaviorTermType">
      <xsd:sequence>
         <xsd:element name="TaskRefs" type="tns:TaskRefsType"
            maxOccurs="1" minOccurs="1"></xsd:element>
         <xsd:element name="Constraints" type="tns:ConstraintsType"
            maxOccurs="1" minOccurs="0">
         </xsd:element>
      </xsd:sequence>
      <xsd:attribute name="id" type="xsd:string" use="required"></xsd:attribute>
      <xsd:attribute name="extension" type="xsd:string" use="optional"></xsd:attribute>
      <xsd:attribute name="extends" type="xsd:string" use="optional"></xsd:attribute>
      <xsd:attribute name="isAbstract" type="xsd:boolean" use="optional"
         default="false"></xsd:attribute>
   </xsd:complexType>
   <xsd:complexType name="EventType">
```

```xml
            <xsd:attribute name="id" type="xsd:string" use="required"></xsd:attribute>
            <xsd:attribute name="isInit" type="xsd:boolean"></xsd:attribute>
            <xsd:attribute name="isError" type="xsd:boolean"></xsd:attribute>
            <xsd:attribute name="descr" type="xsd:string"></xsd:attribute>
    </xsd:complexType>
    <xsd:simpleType name="EventPatternType">
        <xsd:restriction base="xsd:string"></xsd:restriction>
    </xsd:simpleType>
    <xsd:complexType name="ProcessDefinitionType">
        <xsd:sequence>
            <xsd:element name="CoS" type="xsd:string" maxOccurs="1"
                minOccurs="1">
            </xsd:element>
            <xsd:element name="CoT" type="xsd:string" maxOccurs="1"
                minOccurs="1">
            </xsd:element>
            <xsd:element name="BehaviorTermRefs" type="tns:BehaviorTermRef"
                maxOccurs="1" minOccurs="1">
            </xsd:element>
            <xsd:element name="Constraints" type="tns:ConstraintsType"
                maxOccurs="1" minOccurs="0">
            </xsd:element>
        </xsd:sequence>
        <xsd:attribute name="id" type="xsd:string" use="required"></xsd:attribute>
        <xsd:attribute name="descr" type="xsd:string"
default="Description"></xsd:attribute>
    </xsd:complexType>
    <xsd:complexType name="TaskType">
        <xsd:sequence>
            <xsd:element name="Out" type="tns:OutMsgType" maxOccurs="1"
                minOccurs="0">
            </xsd:element>
            <xsd:element name="In" type="tns:InMsgType" maxOccurs="1"
                minOccurs="0">
            </xsd:element>
            <xsd:element name="SrcMsgs" type="tns:SrcMsgsType"
                maxOccurs="1" minOccurs="0">
            </xsd:element>
            <xsd:element name="ResultMsgs" type="tns:ResultMsgsType"
                maxOccurs="1" minOccurs="0">
            </xsd:element>
        </xsd:sequence>
        <xsd:attribute name="id" type="xsd:string"></xsd:attribute>
        <xsd:attribute name="msgAnalyser" type="xsd:string"></xsd:attribute>
        <xsd:attribute name="isMsgDriven" type="xsd:boolean"
            use="required"></xsd:attribute>
    </xsd:complexType>
    <xsd:complexType name="BehaviorTermRef">
        <xsd:sequence>
            <xsd:element name="BehavirTermId" type="xsd:string"
                maxOccurs="unbounded" minOccurs="0"></xsd:element>
        </xsd:sequence>
    </xsd:complexType>
    <xsd:complexType name="EventsType">
        <xsd:sequence>
            <xsd:element name="Event" type="tns:EventType" maxOccurs="unbounded"
                minOccurs="0">
            </xsd:element>
        </xsd:sequence>
    </xsd:complexType>
    <xsd:simpleType name="OutputEventType">
        <xsd:restriction base="xsd:string"></xsd:restriction>
    </xsd:simpleType>
    <xsd:complexType name="ConstraintsType">
        <xsd:sequence>
            <xsd:element name="Constraint" type="tns:ConstraintType"
                maxOccurs="unbounded" minOccurs="0">
```

```
            </xsd:element>
        </xsd:sequence>
    </xsd:complexType>
    <xsd:complexType name="MessageType">
        <xsd:attribute name="id" type="xsd:string"></xsd:attribute>
        <xsd:attribute name="interactionTerm" type="xsd:string"></xsd:attribute>
        <xsd:attribute name="type" type="xsd:string"></xsd:attribute>
        <xsd:attribute name="contract" type="xsd:string"></xsd:attribute>
    </xsd:complexType>
    <xsd:complexType name="MessagesType">
        <xsd:sequence>
            <xsd:element name="Message" type="tns:MessageType"
            maxOccurs="unbounded" minOccurs="0">
            </xsd:element>
        </xsd:sequence>
    </xsd:complexType>
    <xsd:complexType name="PerformancePropertyType">
        <xsd:sequence>
            <xsd:any></xsd:any>
        </xsd:sequence>
    </xsd:complexType>
    <xsd:complexType name="ApplicationPropertyType">
        <xsd:attribute name="key" type="xsd:string"></xsd:attribute>
        <xsd:attribute name="value" type="xsd:string"></xsd:attribute>
    </xsd:complexType>
    <xsd:complexType name="ConstraintType">
        <xsd:attribute name="Id" type="xsd:string"></xsd:attribute>
        <xsd:attribute name="Expression" type="xsd:string"></xsd:attribute>
        <xsd:attribute name="enabled" type="xsd:boolean"></xsd:attribute>
        <xsd:attribute name="language" type="xsd:string"></xsd:attribute>
        <xsd:attribute name="soft" type="xsd:boolean"></xsd:attribute>
    </xsd:complexType>
    <xsd:complexType name="BehaviorTermsType">
        <xsd:sequence>
            <xsd:element name="BehaviorTerm" type="tns:BehaviorTermType"
            maxOccurs="unbounded" minOccurs="1">
            </xsd:element>
        </xsd:sequence>
    </xsd:complexType>
    <xsd:complexType name="ProcessDefinitionsType">
        <xsd:sequence>
            <xsd:element name="ProcessDefinition" type="tns:ProcessDefinitionType"
            maxOccurs="unbounded" minOccurs="1"></xsd:element>
        </xsd:sequence>
    </xsd:complexType>
    <xsd:complexType name="TasksType">
        <xsd:sequence>
            <xsd:element name="Task" type="tns:TaskType" maxOccurs="unbounded"
            minOccurs="0"></xsd:element>
        </xsd:sequence>
    </xsd:complexType>
    <xsd:complexType name="TaskRefsType">
        <xsd:sequence>
            <xsd:element name="TaskRef" type="tns:TaskRefType"
            maxOccurs="unbounded" minOccurs="0"></xsd:element>
        </xsd:sequence>
    </xsd:complexType>
    <xsd:complexType name="TaskRefType">
        <xsd:attribute name="Id" type="xsd:string" use="required"></xsd:attribute>
        <xsd:attribute name="preEP" type="xsd:string"></xsd:attribute>
        <xsd:attribute name="postEP" type="xsd:string"></xsd:attribute>
        <xsd:attribute name="performanceVal" type="xsd:string"></xsd:attribute>
        <xsd:attribute name="type" type="xsd:string"></xsd:attribute>
    </xsd:complexType>
    <xsd:complexType name="OutMsgType">
        <xsd:sequence>
            <xsd:element name="Operation" type="Q1:OperationType"
```

```xml
                    maxOccurs="1" minOccurs="1">
          </xsd:element>
      </xsd:sequence>
      <xsd:attribute name="deliveryType" type="xsd:string"></xsd:attribute>
      <xsd:attribute name="isResponse" type="xsd:boolean" use="optional"
          default="false"></xsd:attribute>
  </xsd:complexType>
  <xsd:complexType name="InMsgType">
      <xsd:sequence>
          <xsd:element name="Operation" type="Q1:OperationType"
              maxOccurs="1" minOccurs="1">
          </xsd:element>
      </xsd:sequence>
      <xsd:attribute name="isResponse" type="xsd:boolean" use="optional"
          default="false"></xsd:attribute>
  </xsd:complexType>
  <xsd:complexType name="ResultMsgsType">
      <xsd:sequence>
          <xsd:element name="ResultMsg" type="tns:ResultMsgType"
              maxOccurs="unbounded" minOccurs="1"></xsd:element>
      </xsd:sequence>
  </xsd:complexType>
  <xsd:complexType name="ResultMsgType">
      <xsd:attribute name="contractId" type="xsd:string"></xsd:attribute>
      <xsd:attribute name="termId" type="xsd:string"></xsd:attribute>
      <xsd:attribute name="isResponse" type="xsd:boolean" use="optional"
          default="false"></xsd:attribute>
      <xsd:attribute name="transformation" type="xsd:string"></xsd:attribute>
  </xsd:complexType>
  <xsd:complexType name="MessageAnalyzerType">
      <xsd:attribute name="id" type="xsd:string" use="required"></xsd:attribute>
      <xsd:attribute name="class" type="xsd:string"></xsd:attribute>
  </xsd:complexType>
  <xsd:complexType name="Parameter">
      <xsd:sequence>
          <xsd:any></xsd:any>
      </xsd:sequence>
  </xsd:complexType>
  <xsd:complexType name="MessageAnalyzersType">
      <xsd:sequence>
          <xsd:element name="MessageAnalyzer" type="tns:MessageAnalyzerType"
              maxOccurs="unbounded" minOccurs="0">
          </xsd:element>
      </xsd:sequence>
  </xsd:complexType>
  <xsd:complexType name="SrcMsgsType">
      <xsd:sequence>
          <xsd:element name="SrcMsg" type="tns:SrcMsgType"
              maxOccurs="unbounded" minOccurs="1">
          </xsd:element>
      </xsd:sequence>
      <xsd:attribute name="transformation" type="xsd:string"></xsd:attribute>
  </xsd:complexType>
  <xsd:complexType name="SrcMsgType">
      <xsd:attribute name="contractId" type="xsd:string"></xsd:attribute>
      <xsd:attribute name="termId" type="xsd:string"></xsd:attribute>
      <xsd:attribute name="isResponse" type="xsd:boolean" use="optional"
          default="false"></xsd:attribute>
  </xsd:complexType>
</xsd:schema>

  contract.xsd

<?xml version="1.0" encoding="UTF-8"?>
<xsd:schema xmlns:xsd="http://www.w3.org/2001/XMLSchema"
```

```xml
    targetNamespace="http://www.swin.edu.au/ict/road/contract"
xmlns:tns="http://www.swin.edu.au/ict/road/contract"
    xmlns:term="http://www.swin.edu.au/ict/road/term"
xmlns:monitor="http://www.swin.edu.au/ict/road/monitor"
    xmlns:ser="http://www.ict.swin.edu.au/serendip/types"
    elementFormDefault="unqualified" version="1.4"
    xmlns:Q1="http://www.ict.swin.edu.au/serendip/types">
    <!-- schema imports -->
    <xsd:import schemaLocation="serendip.xsd"
        namespace="http://www.ict.swin.edu.au/serendip/types"></xsd:import>
    <xsd:import namespace="http://www.swin.edu.au/ict/road/term"
        schemaLocation="term.xsd" />
    <xsd:import namespace="http://www.swin.edu.au/ict/road/monitor"
        schemaLocation="monitor.xsd" />
    <xsd:import namespace="http://www.ict.swin.edu.au/serendip/types"
        schemaLocation="serendip.xsd" />
    <xsd:complexType name="ContractLinkedFactType">
        <xsd:attribute name="name" type="xsd:string" use="required" />
    </xsd:complexType>
    <!-- contract type -->
    <xsd:complexType name="ContractType">
        <xsd:sequence>
            <xsd:element name="Types" minOccurs="1" maxOccurs="1">
                <xsd:complexType>
                <xsd:sequence>
                    <xsd:any />
                </xsd:sequence>
                </xsd:complexType>
            </xsd:element>
            <xsd:element name="LinkedFacts" minOccurs="0" maxOccurs="1">
                <xsd:complexType>
                    <xsd:sequence>
                        <xsd:element name="Fact" type="tns:ContractLinkedFactType"
                            minOccurs="1" maxOccurs="unbounded" />
                    </xsd:sequence>
                </xsd:complexType>
            </xsd:element>
            <xsd:element name="Abstract" type="xsd:boolean"
                minOccurs="0" maxOccurs="1" />
            <xsd:element name="State" type="xsd:string" minOccurs="1"
                maxOccurs="1" />
            <xsd:element name="Terms" minOccurs="0" maxOccurs="1">
                <xsd:complexType>
                    <xsd:sequence>
                        <xsd:element name="Term" type="term:TermType"
                            minOccurs="0" maxOccurs="unbounded" />
                    </xsd:sequence>
                </xsd:complexType>
            </xsd:element>
            <xsd:element name="Monitors" minOccurs="0" maxOccurs="1">
                <xsd:complexType>
                    <xsd:sequence>
                        <xsd:element name="Monitor" type="monitor:MonitorRoleType"
                            minOccurs="0" maxOccurs="unbounded" />
                    </xsd:sequence>
                </xsd:complexType>
            </xsd:element>
            <xsd:element name="RoleAID" type="xsd:string" minOccurs="1"
                maxOccurs="1" />
            <xsd:element name="RoleBID" type="xsd:string" minOccurs="1"
                maxOccurs="1" />
            <xsd:element name="Description" type="xsd:string"
                minOccurs="0" maxOccurs="1" />
        </xsd:sequence>
        <!-- contract attributes -->
```

```xml
            <xsd:attribute name="id" type="xsd:string" use="required"    />
            <xsd:attribute name="name" type="xsd:string" />
            <xsd:attribute name="type" type="xsd:string" />    use="required" />
            <xsd:attribute name="ruleFile" type="xsd:string"
        </xsd:complexType>
    </xsd:schema>

    role.xsd

<?xml version="1.0" encoding="UTF-8"?>
<xsd:schema xmlns:xsd="http://www.w3.org/2001/XMLSchema"
    targetNamespace="http://www.swin.edu.au/ict/road/role"
xmlns:tns="http://www.swin.edu.au/ict/road/role"
    xmlns:player="http://www.swin.edu.au/ict/road/player"elementFormDefault="unqualified"
version="1.3"
    xmlns:Q1="http://www.ict.swin.edu.au/serendip/types">
    <!-- schema imports -->
    <xsd:import namespace="http://www.ict.swin.edu.au/serendip/types"
schemaLocation="serendip.xsd" />
    <xsd:import namespace="http://www.swin.edu.au/ict/road/contract"
schemaLocation="contract.xsd" />
    <xsd:complexType name="RoleLinkedFactType">
        <xsd:sequence>
            <xsd:element name="AcquisitionRegime">
                <xsd:complexType>
                    <xsd:attribute name="mode" use="required">
                        <xsd:simpleType>
                            <xsd:restriction base="xsd:string">
                                <xsd:enumeration value="Active" />
                                <xsd:enumeration value="Passive" />
                            </xsd:restriction>
                        </xsd:simpleType>
                    </xsd:attribute>
                    <xsd:attribute name="SyncInterval" type="xsd:int"
                        use="required" />
                </xsd:complexType>
            </xsd:element>
            <xsd:element name="ProvisionRegime">
                <xsd:complexType>
                    <xsd:attribute name="mode" use="required">
                        <xsd:simpleType>
                            <xsd:restriction base="xsd:string">
                                <xsd:enumeration value="Active" />
                                <xsd:enumeration value="Passive" />
                            </xsd:restriction>
                        </xsd:simpleType>
                    </xsd:attribute>
                    <xsd:attribute name="SyncInterval" type="xsd:int" use="required" />
                </xsd:complexType>
            </xsd:element>
            <xsd:element name="OnChange" type="xsd:boolean" />
        </xsd:sequence>
        <xsd:attribute name="name" type="xsd:string" use="required" />
        <xsd:attribute name="monitor" type="xsd:boolean" use="required" />
        <xsd:attribute name="provide" type="xsd:boolean" use="required" />
    </xsd:complexType>
    <!-- role type -->
    <xsd:complexType name="RoleType">
        <xsd:sequence>
            <xsd:element name="Description" type="xsd:string"
                minOccurs="0" maxOccurs="1" />
            <xsd:element name="LinkedFacts" minOccurs="0" maxOccurs="1">
                <xsd:complexType>
                    <xsd:sequence>
                        <xsd:element name="Fact" type="tns:RoleLinkedFactType"
                            minOccurs="1" maxOccurs="unbounded" />
```

```
                </xsd:sequence>
              </xsd:complexType>
          </xsd:element>
          <xsd:element name="ManagementResponsibilities" type="xsd:string"
              minOccurs="0" maxOccurs="1" />
          <xsd:element name="Tasks" type="Q1:TasksType" maxOccurs="1"
              minOccurs="0"></xsd:element>
        </xsd:sequence>
        <!-- role attributes -->
        <xsd:attribute name="id" type="xsd:string" use="required" />
        <xsd:attribute name="name" type="xsd:string" />
      </xsd:complexType>
    </xsd:schema>
```

player.xsd

```
<?xml version="1.0" encoding="UTF-8"?>
<xsd:schema xmlns:xsd="http://www.w3.org/2001/XMLSchema"
    targetNamespace="http://www.swin.edu.au/ict/road/player"
xmlns:tns="http://www.swin.edu.au/ict/road/player"
    elementFormDefault="unqualified" version="1.3">
    <!-- player type -->
    <xsd:complexType name="PlayerBindingType">
        <xsd:sequence>
            <xsd:choice>
                <xsd:element name="Endpoint" type="xsd:anyURI" />
                <xsd:element name="Implementation" type="xsd:string" />
            </xsd:choice>
            <xsd:element name="Roles" minOccurs="0" maxOccurs="1">
                <xsd:complexType>
                    <xsd:sequence>
                        <xsd:element name="RoleID" type="xsd:string"
                            minOccurs="1" maxOccurs="unbounded" />
                    </xsd:sequence>
                </xsd:complexType>
            </xsd:element>
            <xsd:element name="Description" type="xsd:string"
                minOccurs="0" maxOccurs="1" />
        </xsd:sequence>
        <!-- player attributes -->
        <xsd:attribute name="id" type="xsd:string" use="required" />
        <xsd:attribute name="name" type="xsd:string" />
    </xsd:complexType>
    </xsd:schema>
```

fact.xsd

```
<?xml version="1.0" encoding="UTF-8"?>
<xsd:schema xmlns:xsd="http://www.w3.org/2001/XMLSchema"
    targetNamespace="http://www.swin.edu.au/ict/road/fact"
xmlns:tns="http://www.swin.edu.au/ict/road/fact"
    elementFormDefault="unqualified" version="1.3">
    <!-- monitor type -->
    <xsd:complexType name="FactType">
        <xsd:sequence>
            <xsd:element name="Identifier" type="xsd:string"
                minOccurs="1" maxOccurs="1" />
            <xsd:element name="Attributes" minOccurs="1" maxOccurs="1">
                <xsd:complexType>
                    <xsd:sequence>
                        <xsd:element name="Attribute" type="xsd:string"
                            minOccurs="1" maxOccurs="unbounded" />
                    </xsd:sequence>
                </xsd:complexType>
            </xsd:element>
        </xsd:sequence>
```

```xml
        <!-- player attributes -->
        <xsd:attribute name="name" type="xsd:string" />
        <xsd:attribute name="source" type="xsd:string" />
    </xsd:complexType>
  </xsd:schema>


  term.xsd

<?xml version="1.0" encoding="UTF-8"?>
<xsd:schema xmlns:xsd="http://www.w3.org/2001/XMLSchema"
    targetNamespace="http://www.swin.edu.au/ict/road/term"
xmlns:tns="http://www.swin.edu.au/ict/road/term"
    elementFormDefault="unqualified" version="1.3">
    <!-- term type -->
    <xsd:complexType name="TermType">
        <xsd:sequence>
            <xsd:element name="Operation" type="tns:OperationType"  maxOccurs="1"
minOccurs="1" />
            <xsd:element name="Direction" type="tns:DirectionType"  minOccurs="1"
maxOccurs="1" />
            <xsd:element name="Description" type="xsd:string" minOccurs="0"
maxOccurs="1"/>
        </xsd:sequence>
        <!-- term attributes -->
        <xsd:attribute name="id" use="required" type="xsd:string" />
        <xsd:attribute name="name" type="xsd:string" />
        <xsd:attribute name="messageType" default="push" use="optional">
            <xsd:simpleType>
                <xsd:restriction base="xsd:string">
                    <xsd:enumeration value="push" />
                    <xsd:enumeration value="pull" />
                </xsd:restriction>
            </xsd:simpleType>
        </xsd:attribute>
        <xsd:attribute name="deonticType" default="permission"
            use="optional">
            <xsd:simpleType>
                <xsd:restriction base="xsd:string">
                    <xsd:enumeration value="permission" />
                    <xsd:enumeration value="obligation" />
                </xsd:restriction>
            </xsd:simpleType>
        </xsd:attribute>
    </xsd:complexType>
    <!-- Simple type for direction -->
    <xsd:simpleType name="DirectionType">
        <xsd:restriction base="xsd:string">
            <xsd:enumeration value="AtoB" />
            <xsd:enumeration value="BtoA" />
        </xsd:restriction>
    </xsd:simpleType>
    <xsd:complexType name="OperationType">
        <xsd:sequence>
            <xsd:element name="Parameters" type="tns:ParamsType"
                maxOccurs="1" minOccurs="0">
            </xsd:element>
            <xsd:element name="Return" type="xsd:string" maxOccurs="1"
                minOccurs="0">
            </xsd:element>
        </xsd:sequence>
        <xsd:attribute name="name" type="xsd:string" use="required" />
    </xsd:complexType>
    <xsd:complexType name="ParamsType">
        <xsd:sequence>
            <xsd:element name="Parameter" minOccurs="1" maxOccurs="unbounded">
```

```
        <xsd:complexType>
            <xsd:sequence>
                <xsd:element name="Type" type="xsd:string" maxOccurs="1"
                    minOccurs="1" />
                <xsd:element name="Name" type="xsd:string" maxOccurs="1"
                    minOccurs="1" />
            </xsd:sequence>
        </xsd:complexType>
    </xsd:element>
  </xsd:sequence>
 </xsd:complexType>
 </xsd:schema>
```

monitor.xsd

```
<?xml version="1.0" encoding="UTF-8"?>
<xsd:schema xmlns:xsd="http://www.w3.org/2001/XMLSchema"
    targetNamespace="http://www.swin.edu.au/ict/road/monitor"
    xmlns:tns="http://www.swin.edu.au/ict/road/monitor"
    elementFormDefault="unqualified"
    version="1.3">
  <!-- monitor type -->
  <xsd:complexType name="MonitorRoleType">
      <!-- player attributes -->
      <xsd:attribute name="id" type="xsd:string" use="required"/>
      <xsd:attribute name="name" type="xsd:string"/>
  </xsd:complexType>
</xsd:schema>
```

Printed and bound by CPI Group (UK) Ltd, Croydon, CR0 4YY

03/10/2024

01040427-0007